# Using Online
# Scientific & Engineering
# Databases

# Using Online Scientific & Engineering Databases

*Harley Bjelland*

Windcrest®/McGraw-Hill

FIRST EDITION
FIRST PRINTING

© 1992 by **Windcrest Books**, an imprint of TAB Books.
TAB Books is a division of McGraw-Hill, Inc.
The name "Windcrest" is a registered trademark of TAB Books.

**Library of Congress Cataloging-in-Publication Data**

Bjelland, Harley.
   Using online scientific & engineering databases / by Harley
Bjelland.
     p.   cm.
   Includes bibliographical references and index.
   ISBN 0-8306-3056-2 (paper)
   1. On-line data processing. 2. Science—Data bases.
3. Engineering—Data bases.  I. Title.  II. Title: Using online
scientific and engineering databases.
QA76.55.B54  1992
025.06'5—dc20               91-42778
                           CIP

TAB Books offers software for sale. For information and a catalog, please contact
TAB Software Department, Blue Ridge Summit, PA 17294-0850.

Acquisitions Editor: Roland S. Phelps
Book Editor: David M. McCandless
Director of Production: Katherine G. Brown
Book Design: Jaclyn J. Boone
Cover Design: Sandra Blair Design and Brent Blair Photography,
  Harrisburg, PA                             WR1

To my fellow engineers and scientists
who serve mankind in so many ways,
making this a better world for all to live in.
May their thirst for knowledge be heightened
and encouraged by this volume.

# Other books by Harley Bjelland

*How to Sell Your House Without a Broker,* Simon and Schuster

*How to Buy the Right Home,* Simon and Schuster

*Writing Better Technical Articles,* TAB Books

*The Write Stuff,* Career Press

*Business Writing—The Modular Way,* AMACOM Books

*Online Systems: Searching Medical Databases,*
Practice Management Information Corporation

# Notices

Each of the following products is a trademark, registered trademark, or service mark of the company listed after the product name(s):

| | |
|---|---|
| **APPLE FILE EXCHANGE** | Apple Computer Co. |
| **ARCNET** | Datapoint Corp. |
| **ABI/INFORM** | UMI/Data Courier |
| **Apple, Macintosh** | Apple Computer, Inc. |
| **AT&T,UNIX** | American Telephone and Telegraph Corp. |
| **Atari** | Atari Corp. |
| **Bitcom Deluxe** | BIT Software, Inc. |
| **BOYAN** | Boyan Communications |
| **BRS/SEARCH, BRS COLLEAGUE, BRS AFTER DARK** | BRS Information Technology |
| **CANVAS** | Deneba Software |
| **Commodore, Amiga** | Commodore Electronics, Ltd. |
| **CompuServe** | CompuServe, Inc. |
| **Crosstalk** | Digital Communications Associates, Inc. |
| **DEC, VAX, VT** | Digital Equipment Corp. |
| **DESK PAINT, DESK DRAW** | Zedcor Corp. |
| **DIALOG, KNOWLEDGE INDEX** | Dialog Information Services, Inc. |
| **DISCLOSURE II** | Disclosure |
| **DowQuest, News/Retrieval** | Dow Jones & Co., Inc. |
| **EAASY SABRE** | American Airlines |
| **EasyNet, IQUEST** | Telebase Systems, Inc. |
| **ETHERNET** | Xerox Corp. |
| **FLODRAW** | George Fruend |
| **GEnie** | General Electric Corp. |
| **Hayes, Smartcom, Smartmodem** | Hayes Microcomputer Products, Inc. |
| **Hercules** | Hercules Computer Technology |
| **IBM, AT, XT, PC** | International Business Machines Corp. |
| **Magazine Index, Magazine ASAP** | Information Access Corp. |
| **ITT** | International Telephone and Telegraph, Inc. |

| | |
|---|---|
| **Kermit** | Henson Associates, Inc. |
| **LEXIS, NEXIS** | Mead Data Central, Inc. |
| **MacLinkPlus** | DataVix |
| **MacDraw,** **MacWrite** | Claris Corp. |
| **MCI Mail** | MCI Communications Corp. |
| **Menuworks Advanced** | PC Dynamics |
| **Microcom,** **MNP** | Microcom, Inc. |
| **Microphone** | Software Ventures |
| **Microsoft,** **Microsoft Word,** **Microsoft Works,** **Windows** | Microsoft Corp. |
| **Mirror** | SoftKlone |
| **NewsNet** | NewsNet, Inc. |
| **NEXIS,** **LEXIS,** **MEDIX** | Mead Data Central, Inc. |
| **Novell** | Novell, Inc. |
| **Official Airline Guide** | Dun & Bradstreet |
| **Osborne** | Osborne Computers |
| **PC-Write,** **PC-Write Lite** | Quicksoft, Inc. |
| **Portal** | Portal Communications Co. |
| **Procomm Plus** | Datastorm Technologies, Inc. |
| **Prodigy** | Prodigy Services Corp. |
| **Q & A Write** | Symantec Corp. |
| **QModem** | The Forbin Project |
| **Resident Expert** | Parsons Technology Co. |
| **Sprintnet** | (formerly Telenet) GTE Telenet |
| **SuperPaint** | Silicon Beach Software |
| **TeleMate** | White River Software |
| **Teletype** | Teletype Corp. |
| **Telix** | Exis, Inc. |
| **Texas Instruments** | Texas Instruments, Inc. |
| **Token Ring** | IBM |
| **Tymnet, X.PC** | Tymnet, Inc. |
| **US Sprint** | US Sprint Communications Co. |
| **VU/TEXT** | Knight-Ridder |
| **Wang** | Wang Laboratories, Inc. |

| | |
|---|---|
| **White Knight, Red Ryder** | FreeSoft |
| **Word Perfect** | Word Perfect Corp. |
| **YModem** | Omen Technology |

# Permissions

Copyrighted material obtained in the sample online searches for this book has been obtained from the database vendors listed here:

| | |
|---|---|
| **AMERICA ONLINE** | America Online, Inc. |
| **BRS** | Bibliographic Retrieval Services |
| **COMPUSERVE** | CompuServe Information Services |
| **Compendex** | Engineering Information Inc. |
| **DATATIMES** | DataTimes Corp. |
| **DELPHI** | General Videotex Corp. |
| **DIALOG, KNOWLEDGE INDEX** | Dialog Information Services, Inc. |
| **NEWS RETRIEVAL, DOWQUEST** | Dow Jones & Co., Inc. |
| **EASYNET** | Telebase Systems, Inc. |
| **EPIC** | OCLC—Online Computer Library Center, Inc. |
| **GEnie** | Genie Electric Information Center, Inc. |
| **MCI MAIL** | MCI International, Inc. |
| **MEAD DATA CENTRAL** | Mead Data Central, Inc. |
| **NEWSNET** | NewsNet, Inc. |
| **ORBIT** | Orbit Search Service |
| **PORTAL** | Portal Communications |
| **Prodigy** | Prodigy Services |
| **STN** | STN International |
| **VU/TEXT** | VU/TEXT Information Services, Inc. |
| **WilsonLine** | H.W. Wilson |

# Contents

**3    Software**
## The intellect                                                29

## 4    The anatomy of databases                                45

## 5   Prepare before you go online      63

## 6   Consumer database vendors      75

# Acknowledgments

First of all, I'm grateful to Roland Phelps—Electronics Acquisitions Editor in the TAB Books division of McGraw-Hill—who believed in the book and encouraged the idea. And special thanks to David McCandless, also of TAB/McGraw-Hill, who did an outstanding editing job on my rough manuscript.

Once again, Floyd Ashburn and Jim Schaffitz of Compatibility Plus + in Springfield, OR, rescued me many times along the way.

Along the long journey from a title to a completed book, I've also had excellent company. Again I'm grateful for my wife, Dorrie, for her patience and understanding.

Many thanks to my named but unseen companions at various databases I queried, as well as their companies—all who helped me in many ways, gave freely of their time, and provided access to their databases. Among them are:

Robert C. Adams, Marketing Associate, DELPHI

Melanie Boodis and Karen Tulis, Client Relations, Telebase Systems, Inc.

Robin Chiappone, Customer Service Representative, Prodigy.

Marisa Gorczynski, Public Relations Assistant, Dow Jones & Company, Inc.

Martha Griffin, Program Manager, Communications, Prodigy Services Company

Rosemary Heffner from the EPIC Service of OCLC.

Carol Johnson, Director of Marketing, Portal Communications Company.

James M. Joseph, Manager, Public Communications, Mead Data Central.

Irene G. Jarrett and Gay Strane, both Customer Service Representatives, Chemical Abstracts Service division of the American Chemical Society.

Caitlin Kilday, Customer Services Representative of Orbit Search Service.

David J. Kishler, Corporate Communications, CompuServe

Jane B. Levene, Manager, Marketing Communications, MCI International, Inc.

Mark W. McCurdy, Account Executive, DataTimes

Patricia A. McParland, Marketing Communications Specialist of NewsNet.

Katherine S. Mulvey, Public Relations, Dialog and Knowledge Index.

# Introduction

I wrote this book to be used by researchers, scientists, managers, technical writers, physicists, engineers, chemists, designers, students, technicians, professors, computer designers/programmers . . . virtually everyone involved in any aspect of the engineering and science professions.

You need not be a computer expert to use this book. The computer is but a tool that will help you acquire the knowledge you seek. This book shows you—in a step-by-step, easy-to-follow manner—how to use this modern miracle to search through hundreds of thousands of articles and books in minutes and locate precisely what you need.

## More information than knowledge

Today we have much more information than knowledge. This book is dedicated to helping you locate and acquire the knowledge you need from the huge mountains of information stored in databases.

You are about to glimpse into the electronic libraries of the future, libraries that are not only here today, but libraries that will become a more and more vital part of your day-to-day activities.

No longer will you have to struggle, lost and frustrated, paging through outdated texts and printed material. No longer will you have to search for an obscure chemical formula or engineering data. No longer will you be discouraged by the fact that the book you want is checked out of the library, or is out of print. Now most engineering and scientific information is completely up-to-date, electronified, instantly available, and as near as the keyboard of your computer.

This is the age of the computer. But the computer is not a magician, it is merely an assistant, a valuable tool that can help you advance in your professional career. It cannot perform a single function without someone telling it what to do. This book will show you how to make it work for you.

## How to read this book

I designed *Using Online Scientific & Engineering Databases* to be read from beginning to end. The chapters form a sequence of logical activities that show you, step-by-step, what databases are, how they are constructed and what information they contain. Examples are given of how to access and search each of these types of databases to obtain specific engineering, scientific, or related information. Emphasis is on efficiency, minimizing jargon, and simplifying the procedures as much as possible.

To use this book most efficiently, first scan the Table of Contents for a quick outline of the book. Note the various topics covered. A variety of techniques is used to present the information in an easily readable manner. Look over some of the examples in the text. See what topics they cover.

Then begin with Chapter 1 and read the entire chapter. It gives you a good summary of the topics that will be covered and introduces you to the concept of online databases, what they are and what they can do for you.

The subsequent chapters introduce and explain the two basic types of databases that are available: Consumer and Technology.

Using this background, the book then covers specific databases and provides examples of accessing and navigating inside them, listing the information they provide, and how to respond to this information to obtain the data you seek.

When you read through this manual, be an active reader. Keep a marking pen nearby and underline or highlight the points you would particularly like to reinforce and download into your personal memory bank. This also helps you locate the important points that you may want to return to and review later.

This book was written not just to be read but—importantly—*to be used*. So, use it well and you'll find that your searches for knowledge will be easier, more thorough, and rewarding in many ways.

Let's get started.

# 1
# Engineers and scientists
## meet your new assistants

*Man is a tool-using animal.*
Thomas Carlyle

How would you like to have a dedicated and competent technical assistant who

- has an infallible memory (is capable of total recall)?
- is accurate, up-to-date, and completely knowledgeable in all branches of science and engineering?
- remembers all the details of millions of documents and has memorized all science and engineering formulas and data?
- is on call 24 hours a day, seven days a week, 365 days a year?
- is never ill and never tires?
- is not temperamental and is always willing and ready to do your bidding?
- works for a few dollars an hour?
- is as close as your telephone?

Sound impossible? Not if you take advantage of the many online databases that are available to every engineer and scientist with a computer, a modem, and a telephone line.

## A flood of information

The last decade of the twentieth century has seen 95 percent of all the scientific breakthroughs of human history. All of these vital breakthroughs have been thoroughly documented in writing, resulting in millions of articles, manuscripts, reports, documents, and books being published. More than one million books alone are published annually. The collections of large research libraries have doubled in the past 14 years.

Researchers at Bell Labs estimate that more information is printed in one weekday edition of the New York Times than a person in the sixteenth century processed in an entire lifetime.

We are, indeed, being inundated with information. But it is not information that we need. What we need is knowledge, facts, data. So the problem becomes how to locate those few kilobytes of knowledge you need in those bega-billion pyramids of information.

Modern computer technology has provided the solution and the means for making this important connection.

# Online databases

The rapid advances in the technology of online databases is radically changing forever the look and operation of our public and private libraries, the manner in which we store and access our scientific and engineering periodicals, our newspapers, magazines, and books, and the general way in which we obtain information. The hierarchy of an Online Database System is depicted in Fig. 1-1. Numerous database vendors market this vital and growing service. The repositories of this information are databases.

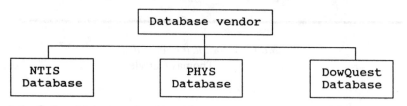

**1-1** Online database system hierarchy.

A database is a computer-readable electronic library. Each database has a large number of books, documents, or periodicals in its collection that are stored electronically. Companies and institutions are rapidly digitizing and storing much of the past, and most of the present published, as well as unpublished scientific and engineering information. They are also converting and storing the contents of newspapers and most periodicals in electronic databases that can be searched by anyone almost anywhere in the world, simply by using a computer and a modem. There are now over 5500 publicly available databases, including those online, on CD-ROM, on magnetic tape, and on diskettes.

To maintain proficiency in a field—whether it's mathematics, astronomy, physics, chemistry, or the many branches of engineering—you must have access to databases. To a large degree, electronic means of transmitting information is rapidly replacing the more traditional means of formally and informally exchanging scientific ideas and data via meetings and printed media. Electronic communication allows the speedy posting of new findings. Colleagues can now read a paper or report, whether in final or draft form, as soon as it is finished—and, sometimes, even as it is being written.

For example, scientists at Los Alamos National Laboratory have taken advantage of database technology by creating a new model, Electronic Data Publishing, for disseminating research information. Using this approach, scientific data bypasses technical journals and flows directly into a computer database, where it becomes immediately accessible to a worldwide community of researchers without having to wait for a lengthy publication and distribution cycle. This dramatic change in the way researchers share data also makes it possible to distribute data too massive in scope for publishing in conventional scientific journals.

Practically any type of information (text, graphics, data) can be stored in a database and searched online. In some databases, information is entered online even before it is published in a printed source. For example, information from the Commerce Business Daily is available online by 9PM the day before the printed publication is distributed. Because of the ease, convenience, and speed of electronic publishing, this trend will surely continue.

# Need for continuing education

Engineering and science continue to advance rapidly and are becoming increasingly complex. Learning about the latest technological advances is necessary so that professionals can keep abreast of the continual and often evolutionary developments in their professions. However, information is amassing so rapidly that we are being overwhelmed by its sheer volume. It is now physically impossible to manually review all technological developments simply by reading current periodicals and journals.

For example, STN International's Chemical Abstracts Service now compiles more than a quarter of a million abstracts a year. This huge volume of information makes manual searches a physical impossibility. Professionals need help in quickly and efficiently locating the specific information they require in these huge mountains of data.

Another factor emphasizing the need for continual updated knowledge is that, because of the exploding advances in technology, the "half-life" of engineering and science degrees is only five years. Engineers and scientists must continue updating their education throughout their entire careers. Because most professionals can't take a lengthy sabbatical from their jobs and return to college full-time, they must rely on published material, specialized seminars, and other means to continually update their education. However, too much printed matter exists for anyone to scan/review manually. Help is needed.

# The computer solution

The arrival of the personal computer and the continually decreasing cost of electronic memory arrived in time to solve the problems of massive information storage, easy access, and quick retrieval. Combined with a modem and a phone line, the personal computer has become the key for opening the doors and thus achieving access to the stored knowledge of all branches of engineering and the sciences.

This book will show you how to partake of this new and rapidly growing science of information access, as well as how to effectively use this new service to acquire many brilliant technical assistants with enormous, nanosecond-quick, infallible memories. You will learn how to access, search and locate any required information quickly, efficiently, comprehensively, and accurately. More importantly, the task can be accomplished for a minimum cost in time and money.

The overall approach used in this text is a "generic" one. The equipment and software described do not limit consideration to any specific product or vendor. Similarly, access to vendor's databases is described in general terms, although some vendors have unique qualities, so examples must of necessity derive from specific vendors. This generic approach is necessary because, although hardware, software, and vendor's databases will undoubtedly change radically with technological advances, the basic approaches to information access and retrieval will change very little.

# What's in a database?

A database is very much like a library except that the books, periodicals, newspapers, and documents in the database are "shelved" electronically. A computer can quickly scan and search any of the shelved documents in the library.

Each database usually represents either a given discipline or subject area (e.g., organic chemistry) or a specific class of documents (e.g., computer journals). Databases are managed by many different types of vendors including commercial companies, government organizations, institutional, and academic facilities.

A database can be a series of physics reference books, industry newsletters, geological periodicals, the daily news, stock quotations, detailed descriptions of electronic designs, or a computer-readable version of a chemical dictionary. Databases can include virtually any information (textual as well as pictorial) that can be converted to digital form (electronified) and stored in memory for retrieval by a computer.

Many of these electronic repositories are simply collections of abstracts and bibliographies from periodicals. Some databases contain specific abstracts collected and/or created by specialty organizations. Others are full-text databases that store the complete text of periodicals, books, newspapers, and documents. The variety, depth, and scope of available databases is staggering.

This book, however, will concentrate on detailing the databases of primary interest to scientists and engineers. This includes science and technology databases, as well as important business and personal databases that scientists and engineers need to access for their professional and personal pursuits.

## As near as your telephone

Databases can be accessed over common telephone lines. Now any fact is as close as your telephone. After you dial up one of these gigantic electronic libraries, you can search millions of documents in seconds and view (or print) the results on your home or office personal computer. For example, a doctoral literature search that might have taken six months a few years ago can now be accomplished in less than an hour. The results can be far more thorough, and the cost much less in both money and effort. A manual search can cost as much as ten to a hundred times or more than a computer search.

And some manual searches are a physical impossibility. Not only the sheer magnitude of the mountain of information, but also the lack of physical access to the books and periodicals makes many manual searches impossible when the documents are stored in a distant location.

## Why use databases?

> *There are thousands of books in the public library,*
> *but the one you want to read is always out.*
>
> Anon

Basically, scientific and engineering personnel need to access databases because

- you can search for and locate, at microsecond speeds, those few vital kilobytes of information you need in those gigantic pyramids of data.
- databases are easier to search, and searches are far more thorough than those with paper documents.

- you receive time-sensitive up-to-date information on new product developments, competition, business opportunities, customer requirements, etc.
- they are living libraries, growing as they are continually nurtured by time-sensitive information.
- databases are more flexible than printed records and can be updated at computer speeds.
- you obtain accurate, instantaneous answers.
- vendor's databases are much larger and diverse than public, personal, or private libraries.
- they can be accessed from virtually any place with a telephone.
- specialized databases exist for virtually every branch and every specialty of engineering and science.
- information is available when you want it. You need not be concerned that someone has checked out the book, document, or periodical you need to consult.
- the information is comprehensive, and you can research to any depth you require.
- you can query from your home or office. No longer do you have to waste time commuting, fighting city traffic, and dealing with parking problems.

# Summary of book

As illustrated in Fig. 1-2, this book will take you step-by-step through the procedures necessary to learn what online databases are, what they can do for you, and what hardware and software are required. The specific databases available to science and engineering professionals are described in detail, plus how to access and use them efficiently.

If you are "computer-literate," you might want to only skim Chapters 2 and 3. However, if you need more applicable background in computer hardware and software for online databases, read and study these two introductory chapters.

Chapter 2 provides a thorough grounding on the hardware—the "brawn" and muscle required to go online—giving you the necessary information to show you how to connect up with modern databases. Chapter 3 describes the "intellect" of the system: the software. Software provides the brains required by the hardware so that your computer can work as your dedicated technical assistant.

*Shareware* is also covered in Chapter 3. A unique marketing concept, shareware allows you to purchase a wide variety of high-performance computer software for a very low price (e.g., $3-5) so you can try it out and see how it works for you. This idea alone can save you hundreds to thousands of dollars in software.

Chapter 4 covers the anatomy of databases, how they are designed and constructed, and what types of information they contain. To be most useful, databases must be able to accommodate everyone from novice to expert. Learning how databases are structured makes access and searching easier for everyone.

Just as engineers and scientists must make detailed preparations before attending a project meeting, a design review, or a conference, so also must online researchers prepare their search strategy before accessing a database. Chapter 5 covers the basic preparations database researchers should make before logging on, including how to prepare your search

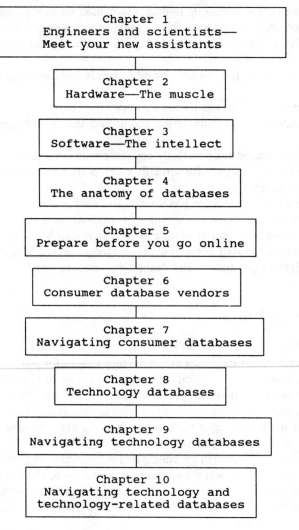

┌─────────────────────────────────┐
│         Chapter 1               │
│   Engineers and scientists—     │
│   Meet your new assistants      │
└─────────────────────────────────┘
┌─────────────────────────────────┐
│         Chapter 2               │
│   Hardware—The muscle           │
└─────────────────────────────────┘
┌─────────────────────────────────┐
│         Chapter 3               │
│   Software—The intellect        │
└─────────────────────────────────┘
┌─────────────────────────────────┐
│         Chapter 4               │
│   The anatomy of databases      │
└─────────────────────────────────┘
┌─────────────────────────────────┐
│         Chapter 5               │
│   Prepare before you go online  │
└─────────────────────────────────┘
┌─────────────────────────────────┐
│         Chapter 6               │
│   Consumer database vendors     │
└─────────────────────────────────┘
┌─────────────────────────────────┐
│         Chapter 7               │
│   Navigating consumer databases │
└─────────────────────────────────┘
┌─────────────────────────────────┐
│         Chapter 8               │
│   Technology databases          │
└─────────────────────────────────┘
┌─────────────────────────────────┐
│         Chapter 9               │
│   Navigating technology databases│
└─────────────────────────────────┘
┌─────────────────────────────────┐
│         Chapter 10              │
│   Navigating technology and     │
│   technology-related databases  │
└─────────────────────────────────┘

**1-2**  Summary of book.

criteria, how to save time and money, and how to quickly pinpoint a search to obtain all of the needed information in a minimum time.

# Two types of databases

Databases can be divided into two broad categories: *consumer* and *technology*.

*Consumer databases* serve the general public and cover a wide range of general-interest topics. Chapter 6 covers the major consumer database vendors, including Compu-Serve, GEnie, and Prodigy, and describes their services. Chapter 7 then describes how to access and obtain information from these consumer databases by providing examples of searches. Typical searches illustrate how to logon, search, and obtain the needed information in the most expeditious manner.

Chapter 8 tackles the over-5500 available different databases and reduces this unwieldy number to a practical list of well-equipped and comprehensive Technology Databases that serve all branches of the engineering and science professions. Chapter 9 provides examples of typical searches in these technology databases, using a variety of typical engineering and scientific problems that can be resolved with online databases.

Finally, Chapter 10 covers more technology databases, plus a diverse variety of technology-related databases that are important for both your professional and personal lives. If you encounter any terms you don't understand, check the comprehensive glossary of online terms in the rear of the book. A list of major online database vendors is included in Appendix A. Also, Appendix B provides a comprehensive list of major online engineering and scientific databases. Appendix C lists prevalent abbreviations in online systems. The Glossary defines terms commonly used in online database tasks.

# A search in a typical database

Next we're going to take a "trip" via telephone to a typical vendor and check out a database from the comfort and convenience of one's own home or other location. This trip does not require any technical knowledge on your part. It illustrates the ease and versatility of communicating with a remote location from your own home or office over common telephone lines. For the moment, we'll ignore the details of the equipment and hookup required to initiate this service and concentrate only on the procedure and the results. We'll logon to the GEnie system and check on the stock price of the company, Teledyne, Inc., to see how it's doing.

Assuming you've hooked your equipment up, to begin, dial the database's special number, or hit the appropriate keys on your keyboard so your computer telecommunications software can dial it automatically for you.

The next sounds you will hear will come from your computer as it beeps out the tones it is dialing over your computer speaker. Then you'll hear a ring. Next comes a connect-signal that sounds much like an ocean's roar. At that point the messages "CONNECT 2400" and "Input your customer number and password" (or some similar messages) will appear on your screen. After inputting the customer number and password, we'll receive this greeting:

```
** Thank you for choosing GEnie **
The Consumer Information Service
          from General Electric
          Copyright (C), 1991
```

*Note:* In case you're wondering, I've abbreviated some of the welcoming information and rearranged the menus to improve readability.

Next we'll receive this top menu:

```
GEnie    TOP      Page 1    GE Information Services

1.    [*]GEnie*Basic
2.    [*]GEnie News, Index & Information
```

```
3.   [*]User Settings/Billing Info.
4.   Communications (GE Mail & Chat)
5.   Computing Services
6.   Travel Services
7.   Finance/Business Services
8.   Online Shopping Services
9.   News, Sports & Weather
10.  Multi-Player Games
11.  Professional Services
12.  Leisure Services
13.  Educational Services
14.  Leave GEnie (Logoff)
Enter #, <H>elp?
```

To find out the price of any stock, input 7 after the <Help>? prompt and receive this
display:

```
Leaving GEnie*Basic Services
Entering the Business & Financial Services area.

GEnie  FINANCE    Page 600    Business & Financial Services

1.    About Financial Products
2.    Dow Jones News/Retrieval
3.    GEnie Quotes Securities Database
4.    VESTOR 24-Hour Investment Advisor
5.    GEnie Loan Calculator
6.    NewsGrid Headline News
7.    GEnie QuikNews
8.    Newsbytes News Network
9.    Charles Schwab Brokerage Services
10.   Schwab Investors' RT
11.   Air Force Small Business RT
12.   Home Office/Small Business RT
13.   Executive Desk Register
14.   Wall Street Journal (Mall Store)
15.   The Investment ANALY$T
Item #, or <RETURN> for more?
```

To obtain a quote, input 3 at the prompt and receive this display:

```
Entering the GEnie Quotes Securities Database area.
GEnie   QUOTES      Page 780

GEnie Quotes Securities Database

1.      Specific Issue Query
2.      Daily Market Indicators
3.      Portfolio Management
4.      Instructions
5.      Terms and Codes
6.      Rates
```

```
 7. [*]    Alternate Sources for Specific Issue Query
 8. [*]    Alternate Sources for Daily Market Indicators
 9. [*]    Alternate Sources for Portfolio Management
10.[*]     Closing Quotes Pricing Information
11.[*]     Dow Jones News/Retrieval Pricing Information
12.[*]     Investment ANALY$T Pricing Information
13.[*]     FEEDBACK
Enter #, <P>revious, or <H>elp?
```

To obtain a quote on a specific issue, input 1 and receive these choices:

```
STOP, EXIT, or QUIT exits the Gateway
Welcome to GEnie Quotes
GEnie Quotes DB Last Updated on 910726

Specific Issue Query
     1. Locate Issue
     2. Display Latest Activity
     3. Describe Issue
     4. View Issue History
Enter Choice?
```

To view the history of Teledyne, input 4 and receive these instructions:

```
At the Specifier? prompt, enter the issue specifier.
If you need help, type HELP.
Specifier?
```

Not knowing precisely what specifier means, input Help at the prompt and receive this information:

```
An issue is selected using one of four specifiers and optionally,
the type and exchange codes. The specifiers are:

<C>usip =         <N>ame =
<T>icker =        <S>ic =

Specifier?
```

Because you know the name of the stock, input N = TELEDYNE and receive these choices:

```
Specific Issue Query
     1. Locate Issue
     2. Display Latest Activity
     3. Describe Issue
     4. View Issue History
     Enter Choice?
```

To view the issue history, input 4 and receive this tally:

```
910725  <------ 910726 ------>    $
TICK    ISSUER      TYPE   CLOSE   CLOSE   VOL(00)   PE   DV   CHANGE
TDY     Teledyne    cm     18.37   18.50   661       33   0.8  + 0.12

Specifier?
```

Because the information we searched for has now been obtained, input TOP at the prompt to jump back to the Top menu:

```
GEnie        TOP          Page 1       GE Information Services
   1.   [*]   GEnie*Basic
   2.   [*]   GEnie News, Index & Information
   3.   [*]   User Settings/Billing Info.
   4.         Communications (GE Mail & Chat)
   5.         Computing Services
   6.         Travel Services
   7.         Finance/Business Services
   8.         Online Shopping Services
   9.         News, Sports & Weather
  10.         Multi-Player Games
  11.         Professional Services
  12.         Leisure Services
  13.         Educational Services
  14.         Leave GEnie (Logoff)
Enter #, <H>elp?
```

To logoff, input 14 and receive this signoff greeting:

```
Leaving GEnie*Basic Services
Thank you for choosing GEnie.
Have a nice day!
```

This is but a simple example of the enormous power available and the ease of access when you let your fingers do the walking for you as you research these enormous databases from your home or office.

Chapter 2 introduces you to the special hardware you need to make this important connection.

# Exercises

1. What types of databases do you need to access in your profession?
2. What are the disadvantages of using databases?
3. Select a specific database vendor you would like to access. Research the vendor's literature and determine which databases they offer and whether they offer full-text or abstracts.
4. What database vendors store and provide access to the specific periodicals you normally read?

# 2

# Hardware
## the muscle

*I think there is a world market for about five computers.*
Thomas B. Watson, Sr. (1943)
Chairman of the Board, IBM

Because the computer was conceived by humans, there is naturally considerable similarity between the creators and their creation. In a human, the body is the physical form, brawn, muscle. In a computer, it's the hardware, the printed circuit boards, the ICs, the disk drives that provide the physical form, brawn, muscle. Both the human body and computer hardware are physical entities that you can see and touch, but they are merely physical objects that only occupy space until they can be put to use.

In a human, the intellect is the invisible mechanism that enables the human body to perform awesome deeds. Stored in the human brain, the intellect enables the human to do such things as

- invent a large, multi-color-wall-panel TV.
- paint a tropical sunset.
- write a complex CAD program.
- postulate a theory of molecular physics.
- play a Brahm's piano concerto.
- design a space platform.
- create a chemical miracle.

In a computer, the invisible software stored in the computer memory is the intellect that empowers computer hardware to accomplish awesome tasks:

- perform complex scientific calculations in a microsecond.
- draw complex 3-dimensional presentations of space stations
- play fantastic digital symphonies such as Word Perfect, Lotus 123, SuperPaint, Bitcom, and nuBase.

This chapter will describe the muscle, the basic hardware you need to electronically connect to online databases. Chapter 3 will cover the software, the intellect that controls the muscle.

# Basic hardware

The basic muscle needed to go online and "let your fingers do the talking" is diagrammed in Fig. 2-1.

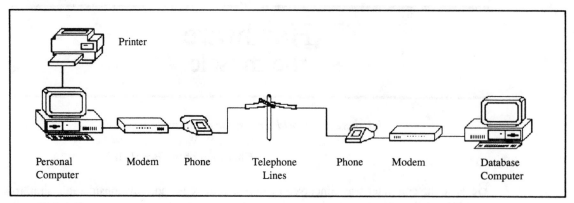

**2-1** Online system.

# Telecomputing

To go online, your computer system must be transformed into a "telecomputer"—a device capable of "computing at a distance."

When you query an online vendor's database computer located a remote distance from your computer, the host does most of the work. You compose your query on the keyboard, and then your PC dials the host computer, transmits the message over the phone lines, and tells the database computer what to search for. The database computer conducts the search you have requested and then transmits the needed data back to you.

# Personal computer

The single most important component in an online system is the personal computer. There are an estimated 60 million personal computers in the U.S., manufactured by nearly a hundred different manufacturers. However, most are IBM clones and Macintoshes. The IBM and its clones have a greater than ten-to-one advantage in sales over the Macintosh, so the IBM and its compatibles are rapidly becoming the defacto standard for many database vendors and users. However, almost any microcomputer (including Atari, Commodore, Texas Instruments, AT&T Unix, and even discontinued machines such as Osborne and Timex Sinclair) can be used to transmit and receive information by modem with many vendors.

The decision concerning which type to buy or use is a complex one. However, I'll provide the basic information you'll need to help make this important decision. You might already have a computer in your home or office, in which case I'll describe what peripherals and features to consider adding so you can go online. Or, if you're contemplating purchasing a computer, the information that follows will help you make that important decision.

# Greatest advance for engineers and scientists in modern times

No tool in recent history has had a more positive and revolutionary impact on engineering and the sciences—and has taken so much of the drudgery out of the professions—as the Personal Computer (PC). A PC is the single greatest science and engineering aid of modern times, not only for writing but also for complex calculations, database creation, graphics, scheduling, drafting, repetitive chores, and more. When I use PC in this book, I use that term to encompass all personal computers, including IBM and its clones plus the Macintosh, Atari, Commodore, etc.

The most widely used application of the PC (an estimated seventy-five percent) is as a word processor (WP). Time and again researchers have demonstrated that writing with a word processor not only encourages engineers and scientists to write, it also improves the quality of their writing.

A WP automates much of the mechanics of writing, simplifying it. Unlike using a typewriter, you don't have to hit the carriage return at the end of a line; it's generated automatically. No matter how fast or how slow you type, a WP can keep pace and flawlessly record everything you input. Text is automatically scrolled so you can watch the characters you input appear on the screen instantly. If you're an inept typist, you can—and should—forget all about errors when you're inputting your initial creative drafts. Later you can go back and easily edit out all your mistakes, without losing any of your original input and without having to retype the entire document (as in the olden days of the mechanical typewriter). In addition, what you have written is stored and can be easily recalled and edited, expanded, copied, printed out, or erased if you are finished with it.

# More positive about writing

Researchers have demonstrated that scientists and engineers who once dreaded writing have become much more positive about this necessary craft once they learn to write with a word processor. There is something comforting about the fact that what you write is not permanent and can easily be changed time and time again until the words say precisely what you intend them to say.

In addition, researchers have discovered that our short term memory lasts only about five seconds. A word processor can record your ideas much faster than you can input them, so your own typing speed—and not the computer's processing speed—is the limit in capturing your creative ideas.

Many WP auxiliary programs are available to help you create near-perfect text. Spelling programs, thesauri, and word counters are available. Electronic grammarian programs can review your writing for errors in grammar, the use of too many passive verbs, check sentence length, and the overuse and abuse of jargon, pretentious words, abstractions, etc.

Besides, word processors are the wave of the future. The days of handwritten or type-written drafts are nearly gone. Soon the only typewriters you'll be able to find will be in closets and museums. Before long, we'll deliver most of our writing as soft copy over Local Area Networks (LANs) and via modems over phone lines to our local, as well as to our more distant audiences.

# The war between Apple and IBM

If you are in a position where you can purchase or influence the purchase of a personal computer, and you need to choose between an Apple Macintosh or an IBM, you'll find it difficult to locatê unprejudiced evaluations and comparisons of the two. Both Mac and IBM proponents almost fanatically insist (or rationalize) that their computer is the best and claim there is no contest between the two. I don't agree with either side, though.

The long and often acrimonious war fought earlier among the many different manufacturers of computers has pretty much dwindled down to a precious two: the Apple Macintosh versus the IBM and its clones. I've been personally involved in these developments for over ten years, having first purchased an Apple II Plus, upgrading to an Apple IIe, and then purchasing an IBM XT clone that I later had converted to an AT clone. I've also purchased and have used my Macintosh Classic for some time. Thus, I feel I've had enough experience to form judgments. I also believe that my judgments are relatively unbiased because I still use and value both my Macintosh and my IBM in my profession as a science writer. Each has specific, unique capabilities, and (as could be expected) each has certain limitations. I've written some books and articles on my Macintosh and some on my IBM. I've found that each fulfills certain functions best.

The situation is similar to having two assistants. One might be a great technician and the other a fantastic mechanical designer. Alone their capabilities are limited, but the synergism of the two working together, each using his or her unique talents, results in much better and more creative products. You can achieve this synergism if you can utilize the capabilities of both the IBM and the Macintosh in your work as is presented in the next chapter. But first, let's take a look at them individually.

# First, the Macintosh

The Macintosh is much easier to learn to use initially with its easy-to-understand graphical icons (a.k.a. "GUI" or graphical user interface) and the very versatile, single-button mouse. Also, the Mac is much easier to use with a wide variety of software programs. Several studies have compared the efficiency and application of word processors and spreadsheets on the IBM and Macintosh systems and found that people who use the GUIs on the Macintosh were more accurate, had higher productivity, and suffered less frustration than character-based (IBM-clone) workers.

Another big advantage of the Mac that makes it easy to learn and use is that most Mac software programs (whether it's a word-processing, financial, or graphics program) use a similar menu bar across the top of the screen with similar entries. Once you learn what the specific commands accomplish in one program, you can use the identical commands for a wide variety of other software programs without having to learn an entirely new set of functions, nomenclature, and commands. Some diehards exaggerate that the Mac is so easy to learn that you don't even have to read the manuals.

The Macintosh excels the IBM by a giant margin for creating, manipulating, modifying, and using graphics. A wide and diverse variety of graphic drawing and paint programs are available for the Macintosh. Highly sophisticated graphics can be created. Paint programs can produce excellent, high-quality, color pictures. Object-oriented graphics can create complex drawings. You can choose between a wide variety of typefaces and fonts, easily adjust the style, and almost instantly see the changes you've made on the screen with a WYSIWYG ("What You See Is What You Get") presentation. The Macintosh is slightly more expensive than the IBM, but it's worth the extra cost if you use a lot of graphics. Many of my graphics are created by Super Paint, an excellent Macintosh graphics program. Much of my word processing text is written using Word Perfect on both the IBM clones and the Mac, both outstanding programs with enormous capacities. I doubt if I will ever use more than ten percent of these programs' total capability.

Another huge advantage of the Macintosh is that you can create and import graphics directly into your word processor and display them on your screen, right along with the text, so that you can size, position, and verify how your pages will look as you create them. With some desk accessories (such as the excellent combination of Desk Paint and Desk Draw, by Zedcor), you can edit and manipulate graphics from within the word processing program, import, and see almost instantly how the modified graphics and the page layout will look. It's always much easier to create and edit the accompanying descriptive text when it's so convenient to refer to the graphics on the same or an adjacent page.

Another desirable feature of the Macintosh is its ability to open multiple windows. With multiple windows open, you can switch back and forth, cut-and paste to transfer data, text, or graphics from one document to another, etc. With some programs, you can open up more than twenty-five windows.

However, one specific objection that I and many others have to the Macintosh is the Apple's persistent parochialism. By this, I mean that Apple has and maintains a complete and stifling monopoly on their computer hardware. No other company has been authorized to clone Macintoshes, so the prices on the Mac and its add-ons will continue to be a little higher than for comparable IBM products until Apple amends this policy. Fortunately, this doesn't hold true for Mac software. Stiff competition among many software developers has resulted in a wide variety of reasonably priced Macintosh software programs.

Unfortunately, only a limited variety of printers are compatible with the Macintosh. The Mac delivers a serial output, while most of the available low-cost dot-matrix printers require a parallel input. Thus, you might end up with two different printers, as I have, if you use both a Mac and an IBM. Or you can purchase serial-to-parallel converter electronics (usually slows down the printing) and use your Mac with a parallel printer. Alternatively, you can use a higher-cost, high quality printer; both the Mac and the IBM can drive ink-jet and laser printers.

# And now, the IBM

First of all, there are probably 10 or more IBMs in use for every single Macintosh. Because of this huge volume of usage and the ability of many competitors to build clone hardware, the IBM is lower in cost. It has considerably more and a much greater variety of software available for its machines. Because so many more IBMs are installed, some periodical and book publishers request that their manuscripts be delivered in an IBM-compatible format. If you have a computer where you work, it's probably an IBM.

Complementary software programs provide only limited graphics capability for the IBM. However, when graphics are imported into an IBM word-processing program, such as Word Perfect for DOS, you can't view the graphics unless you go through the annoyance of having to shift to a special viewing mode each time; also, this presentation is only a viewing mode where you can't modify the graphics. To use graphics effectively in a word-processing program, you should be able to view the illustrations, right along with the text, touch-up, move around, mask, and make minor modifications or size adjustments to the existing graphics. The recently developed Word Perfect for Windows provides some of these capabilities.

Another factor affecting the Mac/IBM choice is their relative "growth potential"—the ease with which accessory add-ons can be implemented later. Often when you first purchase a computer, you buy only the minimum you feel you can get by with. The more you use your computer, though, and as new add-ons are developed, you might decide to add more memory, a more complex graphics display capability, or increased capacity hard- or floppy-disk drives, a CD-ROM drive, or more. The IBM clones come out far ahead in this comparison because they usually have provisions built-in for adding many new and varied accessories inside the case. The growth potential of the Macintosh is severely limited inside the case. Except for simple memory upgrades, most Mac hardware add-ons must be accomplished by adding a separate chassis. In addition, because so many companies compete to add features to the IBM, the costs of most IBM add-ons is quite low.

If you're interested in a laptop computer, a number of competitive, continually improving, and highly versatile portable IBM clones are available. Macintosh has made few significant advances in the portable PC market.

Color is less costly on the IBM. Even though I write what later becomes black words on white paper, I still enjoy using my IBM color display because it seems to provide me with another writing dimension (maybe it's only psychological, but who am I to argue with a muse?). Because of its color capability, different colors and hues can be used to illustrate text on the screen that is to be underlined, bolded, cut and pasted, etc.

One objection to the IBM, which some computer dealers might view as an advantage, is that advanced versions keep coming out so frequently that by the time you have your IBM or clone installed, it's already out-of-date—a marketing technique they likely copied from the automobile industry. For example, I started out with a minimum IBM XT, later converted to a 286, then a 386 AT, added 3.5" and 5.25" floppy drives, a second hard disk, and a total of 4 megs of RAM, but I have always been at least two versions behind the latest. However, I have no urgent need to purchase the latest IBM clone, anymore than I have a burning desire to update my cars that are also a few years old. They serve me well, even in their "senior" years.

Finally, if you are fortunate to have access to both a Macintosh and an IBM, you can achieve the best of both worlds. You can create files on each computer and use a conversion program to transfer files from one to the other, translating the language between the two. Chapter 3 covers this important software capability.

# Basic requirements of a personal computer

No matter which type of computer you choose or use, it should have a certain minimum capability to function effectively in an online system. Among these minimum requirements are

- 640K RAM.
- serial output.
- one hard disk drive.
- one floppy drive.
- a speaker.
- graphics capability.
- a monitor.
- a clock.
- a modem.
- a printer.

These components, some of which can be mounted inside the computer chassis, will be presented in the following text.

A CD-ROM drive is also an excellent addition to a PC. CD-ROM drives are available in configurations that can be mounted inside the computer or as a separate chassis. As more and more CD-ROM disks become available and are more reasonably priced, CD-ROM drives will become standard equipment with a PC. CD-ROM disks make an excellent storage media for high volume static reference data. This topic is covered more thoroughly in Chapter 4.

## Random Access Memory

The amount of Random Access Memory (RAM) required depends on the type of programs you run. Some of the more complex telecomm programs use as much as 512 to 640 bytes (where a byte is equivalent to one key press or one character). Memory requirements also depend on how else you use your computer. For example, some word processing and database programs require at least 512K of RAM. Programs are becoming increasingly complex and more memory hungry, so it's best to invest in as large a RAM as your budget will allow. You need a minimum of 640K, with 2M being desirable and 4M or higher probably becoming standard for future software.

## Serial output

Your computer must be able to output parallel as well as serial data, so most PCs come with one parallel port and two serial ports. The IBM parallel port is usually your printer port. The "serial ports" on your IBM computer are usually designated COM1 and COM2 or RS-232-C interfaces. These serial ports are used when a two-way flow of data down a single wire (such as a telephone line) is required. Additional COM ports are provided by internal modems and I/O adapters. If you use a modem, a mouse, and a joystick, you'll need at least three COM ports. The Macintosh has been well planned and has adequate ports built-in.

## Disk drives

Disk drives are a necessity, not only for initial input of software into your system but also to store the data you create or for data you receive from a database. Printers are usually too slow to record database information at the same speed that you receive it, so it's necessary to store the data on disk so it can be accessed, printed out, and reviewed later.

Your system should have at least two disk drives. One floppy drive plus a hard disk has become a necessity for engineering and scientific applications. Memory capacity is rapidly used up because it takes about 2K bits to store a double-spaced page of text. Commonly used disks can store

- 180 pages on a 360K, 5.25″ disk.
- 600 pages on a high-density 5.25″ 1.2M disk.
- 360 pages on a 3.5″ 720K disk.
- 720 pages on a high-density 3.5″ 1.44M disk.

Graphics require considerably more memory—roughly 20 times as much storage space as text files, depending on the complexity of the graphics.

Hard disks range in storage capacity from about 20M to 100M or higher. The prices of high-capacity hard disk drives have become affordable, and the hard disk is becoming commonplace for most personal computers. It's surprising how quickly you can use up 40−80M storing programs and data.

The newer Macs are well designed and usually contain a hard disk and a single 3.5″ drive, adequate for most general applications.

A second floppy drive is common in IBM clones because of the slow but continuing conversion from 5.25″ to 3.5″ drives. And, as a smaller floppy drive (probably about 2″) becomes popular, IBM clones will likely still have two drives to continue to bridge the transition from one size to the next.

## Internal speaker

A speaker in your PC is essential, not only for some software programs but also for accessing online databases. When you dial a database vendor, it's reassuring to hear your modem "take the phone off the hook." Also, you can listen to the dial tones being beeped out over your speaker, the subsequent ocean roar that comes from the speaker when you have made a connection, or the busy signal if the phone number you've dialed is in use. If it weren't for those dial tones, it might be difficult determining why you're not establishing a connection. A speaker is usually included in a standalone modem or on an internal modem card.

## Clock card

A digital clock is essential for general use as well as for keeping track of your online time. For many PC functions, the clock "stamps" the current date and time on your files so you know when you last received or updated them. This also helps when you back up a hard disk because you can direct a backup program to backup only those programs that have been modified after a specified date, saving a lot of time, effort, and disks in the backup procedure.

The clock has a built-in battery to keep the clock ticking, even after you turn the power off in your computer. The clock requires very little battery power, so a battery should last a year or two before it has to be replaced.

## Graphics card

A graphics card must be added to some IBM computers to display graphics on your monitor. This plug-in card is essential if you query databases that transmit graphic images along with text, as more and more of them are doing. The graphics card is also needed to display charts, graphs, etc., on your monitor. Graphic cards are also essential for creating your own graphics for use with your reports and proposals.

A wide variety of graphic cards are available for the IBM and its compatibles. The more common in use are Hercules, CGA, EGA, VGA, and Super VGA.

The Hercules card has a resolution of $720 \times 350$ pixels but displays only 1 color. The lowest in cost, it displays well formed text characters and high resolution graphics, but has some difficulty running some color programs.

The CGA (Color Graphics Adapter) graphics card has a resolution of $640 \times 200$ pixels when operating in a two-color mode, and a resolution of $320 \times 200$ pixels when displaying four colors. The cost is higher than for a Hercules, but it is still the lowest cost and most widely used color system available. The CGA is only marginally adequate for online databases.

The EGA (Enhanced Graphics Adapter) graphics card, the next step up in the ladder of improved performance and (of course) higher cost, has a resolution of $640 \times 350$ pixels and can display 16 colors. Text characters are well-formed, and the card displays high resolution graphics.

The next most expensive is the VGA (Video Graphics Adapter) card, with a typical resolution of $640 \times 480$ pixels when operating with 16 colors, and $320 \times 200$ pixels when operating with 256 colors. The VGA has the fastest operation and displays the most colors. VGA also has the advantage that it is downwards compatible with EGA and CGA, so it supports a wide range of programs. However, the VGA offers only a small improvement over the EGA.

The top of the graphics hierarchy is the Super VGA card. It has a resolution of $800 \times 600$ and $1024 \times 768$, depending on the driver and the amount of RAM on board. The Super VGA is also downward compatible with the VGA, EGA, and CGA. If you're involved in CAD/CAM, you need this superior resolution. The Super VGA gives you 2.5 times the useable display area of the VGA. I used a CGA card for a couple of years; but when I saw the incredible resolution and beautiful colors of the Super VGA, I quickly traded up to a Super VGA.

Excellent graphics capability is built-in the Macintosh. No special add-ons are required for the Mac, except possibly for additional RAM for complex graphic or desktop publishing programs.

## Monitor

The monitor must be compatible with the type of graphics card you use. I used a monochrome monitor for nearly five years; but after I purchased and used an IBM color monitor, I know I could never again be content with an IBM monochrome. The reason is difficult to explain, but the addition of color to even a text document makes all displays more "colorful" and pleasing to the eye for me. Conversely, I'm fully content with my monochrome Macintosh that I use for graphics and other complex word processing tasks.

If you're limited in budget, you can squeeze by with a monochrome. If not, you'd enjoy a color monitor for your IBM clone. Most modern computer programs can be run using either a monochrome or a color monitor. Color is available for both the IBM and Mac machines. However, a color Mac is much more expensive than a color IBM.

Screen sizes vary from $12-14''$, with 12 being adequate for most online applications unless you're using CAD/CAM, high-end drawing packages, or desktop publishing. For these more detailed applications, a $16''$ or larger monitor is desirable. Your monitor must have a resolution compatible with your graphic card or the card's resolution is wasted. However, higher resolution monitors (e.g., $1024 \times 768$) are expensive.

## Modem

A language barrier exists between a computer and a telephone system, so a "language translator" is needed so the two can "talk" to each other. The computer speaks digital (the language of 1's and 0's), whereas the telephone lines (designed to carry the human voice) speak analog (the oscillating type of waveforms covering the range of frequencies from about $200-3300$ Hz). The device accomplishing this two-way signal translation (digital-to-analog and analog-back-to-digital) is a modem (**mo**dulator-**dem**odulator).

The modem *modulates*—converts the computer's digital information into analog information for transmission over the audio telephone lines. The modem also *demodulates*—converts the analog information it receives from a database back into the digital language, the mother tongue of the computer. Modems are required on both ends of the system: at the personal computer end, and at the database vendor's end. Modems, being very formal in their operation, first introduce themselves to each other by asking each other questions (i.e., they "handshake" to determine which signalling, error-correction, and data compression protocols they should follow before they send data).

**Two types of modems**   Two basic types of modems are available: external and internal. They offer essentially the same features.

An *external* modem is a separate, stand-alone package mounted in its own housing. It's typically about the size of a giant paperback book. It connects to the computer via a cable and can be used with computers from a variety of manufacturers. An external modem doesn't require an expansion slot inside your computer. It usually has LEDs on its front panel so you can monitor the progress of your call. However, an external modem costs slightly more than an internal modem. An external modem uses up shelf space alongside your computer and requires hookup cables. Some computers, such as the Mac, do not have provisions for an internal modem, so an external is the only possible choice. An external modem can function with virtually all IBMs and Macs and can be moved from one computer to another.

The *internal* is a full modem mounted inside your computer, so it can't be easily moved from one computer to another. The internal modem does not have indicator lights as the standalones do. An internal draws some power from your computer, but it does not use up valuable shelf space. An internal is an especially good choice for an IBM and its clones because considerable competition in this market has resulted in prices appreciably lower than for external modems.

From a functional standpoint, external and internal modems operate virtually the same. If you have the room inside your computer, I'd recommend an internal modem. Once installed, its operation becomes transparent and you can forget about it.

I have an internal for my IBM clone and an external for my Macintosh. As far as I'm concerned, they're both "invisible." As long as they operate reliably, I don't even need to see them.

**Modem requirements**  Although diverse types of modems are available from a variety of manufacturers, a modem should have specific fundamental characteristics regardless of the computer it is used with. First of all, the modem should be "Hayes Compatible," which means that it should use the Hayes Smartmodem register set. Hayes Microcomputer Products has made such a powerful impact on modems that its basic operating characteristics have been adopted by much of industry to become the *de facto* standards for modems.

A modem should be able to operate in a half- or full-duplex mode. Half-duplex is a one-way-at-a-time transmission, much like a phone conversation where only one person can speak at a time. With half-duplex, signals can travel in both directions, but only in one direction at the same time.

With full-duplex operation, transmission can be accomplished in two directions at the same time. Full-duplex is made possible by transmitting data at one frequency and receiving data at a different frequency at the same time. Most modems now available can operate in both full- and half-duplex modes.

**Modem speeds**  Typical modem speeds now in use are 2400 and 9600 bps, which translate roughly to 240 and 960 characters per second. Other higher speeds are also available (e.g., 19,200). The higher speed equipment is relatively expensive and might not be available in the databases you'll be using. However, as prices are continually reduced on high speed modems, 9600 is likely to be the next standard for telecommunications. Note that most modems that operate at 9600 can also shift down and communicate at 2400 bps, or even as low as 1200 and 300 bps.

If there were no other considerations, everyone would probably opt for the highest speeds because data can be transmitted and received in a minimum time and for a minimum cost. However, some vendors charge more for higher speed access, and the higher speed modems are considerably more expensive because they are more complex. Because of inherent physical limitations, full-duplex operation at 9600 bps is normally impossible over ordinary phone lines. Then the higher speed modems must use the complex process of echo cancellation, which requires that a built-in digital signal processor (DSP) be included, increasing the modem cost.

Still, online charges are not always a direct ratio of speed. For example, if it costs only twice as much to operate at 9600 than at 2400, the higher speed would be a bargain because you'd be receiving information at four times the speed for only double the cost, thus reducing the amount of connect-time for which you have to pay.

Another consideration in modem selection is the number of COM ports that can be accommodated by the modem. If you have a mouse, a joystick, and a modem, purchase a modem capable of working on any of the 4 COM ports.

**Hardware error correction in modems**  Other difficulties come with higher modem speeds. One problem that becomes more severe at the higher speeds is that errors can occur during transmission of data. If you encounter a few errors when text is being transmitted, it probably would be of little consequence. However, if you are having a software program, a stock quotation, or a design formula or procedure downloaded and you lose one bit, your design or program won't work or your quotation could even mislead you to a financial disaster. Error correction techniques are used to help prevent this.

Error correction techniques check each received transmission to see if any errors have occurred. A variety of error-correction techniques have been built into current modems. The major ones currently in use are MNP1-4 and V.42. MNP1-4 is a series of four correction protocols that were devised by Microcom (MNP stands for Microcom Networking Protocol) and that are incorporated in current modems (the numbers indicate specific versions or classes). V.42 is an internationally established standard protocol that has been approved by CCIT and is also incorporated in current modems. Some modems offer both types, while some offer only one. You should make sure your modem has both capabilities. Both the transmitter and receiver must have the same capability (e.g., both must have V.42 capability) for these techniques to be used.

The operation of error correction techniques is basically the same. The sending modem performs a mathematical calculation on the transmitted data and transmits this calculation along with the data. The receiving modem receives the data and performs the identical calculation. If the two numbers match, the receiving modem sends back an "ACK"(or **ack**nowledgement) that the data was received correctly. If they do not match, the receiving modem sends back a "NACK" (or negative **ack**nowledgement) that states that the data received was corrupted and requests that the data be retransmitted. The sender then retransmits the data.

Software error control is also available in telecom programs as presented in the next chapter. However, hardware error control has two advantages over software error control: it is more efficient because there is no drain on the CPU, and it applies error control to everything, not just to file transfers.

Unless your office sends and receives a great deal of data via a modem, a 2400 bps modem should be adequate to minimize phone costs. Also, if the modem has built-in error correction and data compression (see the next heading), it can transmit data at a throughput equivalent to 4800 or 9600 bps—two to four times faster than the base speed. However, if you are going to send and receive considerable material and complex graphic images, you should opt for the highest speed you can accommodate.

**Data compression**  Reducing the size of the files to be transmitted saves money because the amount of online time is reduced in direct proportion to the amount of compression. Existing data compression techniques can compress files from one-half to one-fourth their unpacked size.

Data compression techniques take advantage of the considerable redundancy existing in the data and use abbreviations whenever possible. The more redundant the data, the better the compression that can be achieved by using an algorithm to encode the pattern of frequently repeated letters, words, or pixels.

MNP5 and V.42bis are the two most widely accepted hardware compression standards that are built into modern modems. In an ideal situation, MNP5 can compress data to about half its original size, whereas V.42bis (the first international standard established for data compression) can do much better, compressing data to one-third to one-fourth its original size. When data are compressed before transmission by one of these techniques, modem throughput can be effectively doubled or quadrupled; thus, a 9600 modem can effectively increase its throughput to 19,200 or 38,400 bps. The data are still transmitted at the 9600 rate, but it effectively arrives at two to four times the modem's rate.

The amount of compression that can be achieved depends on the type of data the file contains. Random data, for example, cannot be compressed because there is no redundancy. However, spreadsheets, ASCII text, graphics, assembly language, program source code, etc. can be compressed from nearly 3:1 to as high as 4:1.

If data is previously compressed by a software technique, such as PKZIP or STUFFIT (covered in Chapter 3), hardware compression techniques cannot be effectively used to further compress the file. Modems with built-in MNP5 compression will impede transmission rates when handling precompressed files. Thus, if you are going to use precompressed files such as PKZIP and if you have MNP5 in your modem, turn the MNP5 off. However, the V.42bis modem detects precompressed files and automatically turns its compression off without having to be concerned about it.

**Summary of modem requirements**   Here's a summary of the factors to keep in mind when selecting modem hardware:

- If you procure a 2400 bps, make sure the following are included (the slower rates are needed if your modem is on a noisy phone line, they should all shift down in speed until they reach a reliable rate at a commonly accepted protocol):
  ~ V.22bis for the 2400 bps modulation standard.
  ~ V.42 and MNP 1−4 for error correction.
  ~ V.42bis for data compression.
  ~ Bell 212 for 1200 bps.
  ~ Bell 103 if you want 300 bps.

- If you procure a 9600 bps, make sure it has all of the above, plus
  ~ V.32 for 9600 bps modulation standard.

- If you need to communicate with Europe, you should also have these European standards:
  ~ V.22 for 1200 bps.
  ~ V.21 for 300 bps.

- External or Internal configuration, capable of accommodating 4 COM ports.

- Half- and full-duplex operation.

## Printer

When you receive information from a database and display it on your monitor, it usually scrolls by too fast to read. Thus, if you're having trouble locating and analyzing the data you need when conducting a search, you can store the input data on disk, go off-line, print it out, and pause to study it and change what you were doing wrong. After modifying your search strategy, you can log back on to the database and continue with your search. A printer also provides a permanent, readable record of any information you obtain from a database and want to preserve for later reference. Your printer should have a built-in buffer of about 4−8K or more so that it can store data at a high speed and then print it out at its lower speed. Also, your printer should be able to print graphics. The more you use a computer, the more applications you'll find for graphics, not only for tables but also for simple block diagrams, graphs, and figures.

Printers are available with either 11″ or 16″ width carriages. Eleven inches is by far the most common and is adequate for most applications. Printers can accommodate about 80 characters per line for an 11″ carriage and 132 characters for a 16″ carriage. However, software is available that permits printing with a smaller font, so you can print 132 characters with an 11″ printer. You should be able to select these printing modes by software, as well as be able to choose these from front panel switches on the printer.

Two basic types of printers dominate the market: dot matrix and laser. The dot matrix has cornered about ninety percent of the market, principally because the more versatile laser printer is about five to ten times more expensive than a dot matrix printer, not only in initial cost but also in the cost per page.

One other printer occupies a small part of the market: the inkjet printer. Made by a few manufacturers, the ink-jet sprays ink on the paper through tiny holes. The inkjet is a silent printer, which is especially desirable in heavily populated offices. It delivers crisp text output and prints high density graphics. Typical printing speed is about 240 characters per second. The inkjet costs somewhat less than a laser printer.

**Dot matrix printer**   Dot matrix printers have printing heads containing from 9 to 24 tiny pins, arranged in a matrix that can be individually and collectively controlled. The pins in the print head are activated and strike the paper in various programmed combinations through an inked ribbon to form characters, dots, special symbols, and graphics.

Draft printing speeds vary from about 120 to 360 characters per second. Super-fast models can print over 500 characters per second. Naturally you pay more for the higher speeds; but unless you're doing a lot of printing, speeds as low as 120 characters per second are adequate for most purposes.

The emergence of the dot matrix printer as being the printer of choice has been brought about by two factors. The development of 24-pin printing heads has improved the quality of dot matrix printers to what is called "near letter quality" (or NLQ) and is virtually indistinguishable from that of an impact printer. Secondly, software programs are available that allow the low-cost 9-pin printers to print and overprint characters in two or three successive passes so that the resulting characters are also letter quality and are equivalent to an 18- to 27-pin dot matrix print head. The quality of both techniques is excellent; however, the 9-pin printer, in making the two to three passes, is slowed down in printing speed by a factor of two to three. For most purposes, though, particularly if your printer has a buffer, the slower printing speed (often about 25 to 50 characters per second) might not be a detriment. You should be able to activate this letter quality printing from either the front panel switches on the printer, or from the software in your computer.

Another requirement your printer should meet is the ability to print what is called the "IBM character set." This character set permits the printing of fairly complex graphics, plus a variety of special symbols not available in other character sets.

**Laser printer**  The laser printer uses a laser beam, directed by a rotating mirror, to impress an image on normal paper. The laser printer can handle four different paper sizes: letter, legal, executive, and A4, as well as envelopes. Also, it can print in both the landscape and portrait modes.

Because the laser traces out characters with a narrow beam, by properly programming you can print a wide range of internal fonts and virtually any character, image, or graphics that the laser driver program can accommodate. The speed of the laser printer is fast and ranges from 4 to 12 pages per minute, putting it a quantum leap ahead of the dot matrix. However for most personal uses, the high price tag ($1000 to $2000 or more) is a considerable deterrent to its widespread use. It is likely, though, that the price will eventually come down to less than $500, a price that many individual personal computer owners are willing to invest.

However, one hidden cost in the use of a laser printer is not only the cost of the paper but also the cost of the printing cartridge because it must be refilled after printing a given number of pages. This can result in a cost of a few cents per laser-printed page. There are, however, companies that can reload your cartridge for a nominal sum to significantly reduce this recurring cost per page.

## Facsimile

Another peripheral rapidly gaining in acceptance is the facsimile machine, or fax, as it is commonly known. Much like a modem, a fax transmits information over phone lines. However, its respective formatting and methods of transmission are different, and a fax machine can communicate with other fax machines all around the world. Whereas the modem is principally concerned with text and limited graphics, the fax transmits scanned images, much as television does. If you will be transmitting or receiving documents, graphs, illustrations, etc., you should consider acquiring fax capabilities.

Two basic types of fax configurations are used: internal and external. The internal fax is contained on a board mounted in a slot inside your personal computer. The external fax is a stand-alone chassis that you mount near your PC. Their modes of operation are radically different.

The internal fax is less costly but can only transmit data that exists in your PC. However, for many applications, this might be all you need a fax for. It converts the data you create with your personal computer into a special format, called a *bit map*. A bit map is an image of your document that is composed of black and white dots, much like a black and white TV picture. These dots are transmitted over your phone lines in a serial order to a receiving fax machine that, in turn, reconstructs them back into an image resembling the original image that you can then view on your monitor or print out on your printer.

The internal fax can also receive data from distant fax machines or from PCs equipped with internal fax boards. Received faxes are stored as images on your disk and can be recalled and printed out on your dot matrix or laser printer, rather than the less-desirable thermal paper.

The external or standalone fax is more expensive but has much more capability. With a standalone, you place your paper document in the fax machine. The document may contain text, graphics, illustrations, or a combination of them. The standalone scans the document and converts the document into a series of black and white dots (ones and zeroes).

These ones and zeroes are then transmitted over the phone line in series. The reverse operation takes place in the receiving fax machine, the ones and zeroes being converted back into black and white dots. The receiving fax then prints the dots on special paper (usually thermal), reconstructing the original image.

Most stand-alone fax machines print the recorded image on thermal-sensitive paper. Thermal paper is hard to write on, though; it curls, is fragile and thin, and the image slowly fades in readability. Incoming faxes can, however, be photocopied onto plain paper and should be if they are to be filed away for reference.

A variety of more expensive alternate fax machines are also available and will eventually be replacing the thermal fax machines. Among them are laser and LED printers using dry toner, special devices that connect to a laser printer, and ink-jet printers, all of which print the fax image onto plain paper.

Because of its ability to scan and transmit photos, graphs, illustrations, forms, etc., as well as text, the stand-alone is a much more versatile and useful fax configuration. A stand-alone takes from 10 to 40 or more seconds to transmit a letter-size page. Faster machines are also available at increased cost.

Stand-alones also have many optional features such as automatic data feeders for feeding in multiple sheets, automatic paper cutters, automatic dial-back for busy numbers, etc. However, unless you will be transmitting many faxes, a bare-bones minimum fax will be adequate for most applications.

All fax boards for PCs come with software. Most software sends ASCII and PCX graphics; TIFF graphics is common. A variety of file types may be supported, including specific word-processor formats.

## Fax/modem

If you need to communicate by both fax and modem, consider installing a combination fax/modem board in your PC. A combination fax/modem board costs only a little more than an internal modem board and combines the capabilities of both facsimile and telecommunications on a single board. The board manufacturer usually provides the requisite modem and fax software.

Fax/modem boards can transmit data you create on your PC to distant fax machines or to other PCs with a fax/modem board. It has much the same capabilities as the internal fax board.

Make sure your fax/modem board has an internal, on-board processor and memory. With this combination, you can receive a fax in the background at the same time you're using your computer without your computer slowing down appreciably.

Purchase a fax/modem board that can both transmit and receive faxes. Some boards are transmit only and are of limited application.

# LAN

A Local Area Network (LAN) is a physical network setup so two or more computers in a single location (such as an office building or series of labs) can communicate with each other and so they can also share costly peripherals, such as a laser printer. The LAN includes the cabling that interconnects all of the equipment, plus the associated electronics and software that makes the intercommunication possible. The LAN regulates the flow of data to each unit on the network. Three of the most popular LANs are ARCnet, developed by Datapoint; Ethernet, developed by Xerox; and Token-Ring, developed by IBM. Ethernet and ARCnet are the most popular topologies because they're relatively easy to install, accommodate growth well, and provide good performance. The specific configuration to install depends on your specific application: distances, number of terminals, speed of transmission, the type of cabling to be installed, etc.

The hardware part of the LAN consists of the cabling system that interconnects all of the PCs together on the network and a Network Interface Card mounted in each PC to provide a high-speed interface between the PC and the network. The cables may be coaxial, twisted pair, or fiber optics. Some LANs use radio transmission rather than cable runs. Coaxial cable is usually preferred; however, fiber optic cable is becoming more and more popular.

Small LAN networks can serve from two to ten PCs, while large LANs can handle hundreds of network PCs, along with bridges, routers, gateways, and communication servers. Naturally, the more PCs that are served, the more expensive and the more complex are the LANs.

# Phone lines

Regular telephone lines are usually suitable; but if you're going to telecommunicate a lot, a separate line is needed, with a different and unlisted phone number.

If you have call-waiting, a separate phone line might be a necessity because the beeping tone that signals call waiting on the line might garble your data, or it might disconnect you from an online service. To disengage call-waiting, dial *70. You also can input ,*70 on your computer keyboard when you enter a phone number into your telecom dialing directory. The comma is necessary because it instructs your modem to take a two-second break before it dials the number you want, long enough to make sure that the dial tone has begun. If you have a pulse phone, insert the code 1170, before the dialing prefix, area code, and phone number. Don't forget the comma.

If you are employed by a company where many individuals will be using online services, special phone lines are a necessity. For modest usage, dial-up lines are adequate. However, if you anticipate that more and more individuals will be using the online systems and as modems speeds continue to increase, you should procure modems that can communicate over two-wire dial-up lines as well as four-wire leased lines. This allows you to start with a dial-up strategy and later move to a dedicated leased-line arrangement as necessary.

# Recommended computer system

My recommendations for a computer system for online engineering and scientific database use and for general engineering and scientific organization use are listed in Table 2-1.

Now that you know the basic hardware or "brawn" requirements, you can read Chapter 3 to learn how to give your personal computer some intellect so it can accomplish many miracles for you.

**Table 2-1   Recommended hardware.**

**Computer**   IBM or IBM compatible with 4M of memory.
Super VGA Graphics card with 512K of memory.
One 3.5" floppy.
Hard disk with 40M of memory minimum.
(Additional 5.25" high-density floppy and
     a second hard disk are desirable).
CD-ROM drive (Saves hard disk memory).
Mouse, Internal speaker, and clock card.
Four serial ports.

A Macintosh with a minimum of 2M of RAM if you
     utilize considerable graphics in your work.

A CD-ROM drive is also desirable.

**Monitor**   Super-VGA color monitor preferred.
Black and white adequate for Macintosh.

**Printer**   Laser printer for correspondence and final drafts
     of reports, etc.
Dot matrix 24-pin printer, for routine drafts and
     for backup of your laser printer.

**Modem**   Hayes compatible, 2400 bps speed (9600 bps if you
     will be transmitting and receiving a considerable
     amount of data)

**Phone**   Separate dedicated phone line desirable

**Fax**   Standalone fax if you will be transmitting a
     lot of images such as illustrations, graphs,
     charts, hand sketches, etc.

Fax/modem board if you must transmit information
     stored in your PC to other locations that you
     might not be able to communicate with via a modem.

# Exercises

1. Which PC is the most suitable for your profession: IBM or Macintosh? Why?
2. Select a specific model of an IBM or Mac PC. What minimum features would you need to add to your PC to accomplish the tasks you envision your computer to accomplish now and in the next five years?
3. What other features would you like to add if cost were not a consideration?
4. What are the advantages of hardware file compression?

# 3
# Software
## the intellect

*Well-informed people know it is impossible to transmit*
*the voice over wires and that were it possible to do so,*
*the thing would be of no practical value.*

Editorial in Boston Post, 1865

Software is the "intellect" that enables your computer program to perform a wide variety of functions for you. With the proper software, your computer can, in turn, become a design assistant, a proposal grammarian, a mathematician, a scheduler, a consultant, a research specialist, an accountant, a communicator, a skilled chess opponent, a draftsman, a program manager . . . the list is virtually endless.

## Basic software required

To function in an online mode, the bare minimum you need, in addition to your PC hardware, is a telecommunications software program that lets you "talk" on the telephone.

Because over fifty thousand computer programs are available for the IBM PC alone and with thousands of Mac programs available, making software choices is a very complex decision. This chapter will help you select the proper software to perform the telecommunication functions and any related tasks you want to assign to this hard-working, indefatigable, willing assistant with a perfect memory.

## General requirements for a software program

Before I go into the details of the individual software programs, there are certain basic or generic requirements every software program should meet.

First, will the software perform all of its functions properly with your system? This might seem to be an obvious and unnecessary question, but we often purchase programs and find out too late that the program required more memory, a special plug-in board, a specific type of printer, a greater or lesser operation speed, a hard disk, supplemental programs, etc., that we didn't count on. So, first and foremost, carefully check the basic hardware that the software requires to make sure your computer setup meets them.

The next question is also vital: "Is it easy to use?"

Most people who use computers have neither the time nor the patience required to spend many hours of study before they can even begin to use a program. If a user is required to learn and memorize a completely new set of complex commands to use with each new program, the software has lost much of its appeal. Computer programs should be designed and programmed so they can be run by an easy-to-use menu or icon system that minimizes the number of key commands a user has to input. As much automation as possible should be built into each program. Help screens should be easily and instantly available, no matter what mode you're operating in. Help should be *context-sensitive*—it should provide immediate solutions for the specific problems the user is puzzled about at the moment.

Another highly desirable asset of a well-designed program is that installation of the software should be largely automatic, requiring very little or minimal technical input from the user. Examples of good installation programs are ones that direct you to "Insert Disk One in Drive A, type 'Install' at the prompt, and then hit Enter." The installation process should then be largely automatic from that point.

# Documentation requirements

Closely allied with the ease-of-use criteria just presented is the availability of good documentation. Often this documentation is written by the same people who programmed the software; that is unfortunate. The type of organization required to write a computer program is radically different from that required to write a user document.

When a software program is written, programmers use certain standard and well-established commands, procedures, and techniques that have been developed to accomplish specific logic functions within the computer. Functional software modules are utilized to perform needed computer functions. For example, a computer subroutine might be written to sort a group of words alphabetically, to perform a calculation, to draw a line, to trace an arc, to fill in and compute values in a spreadsheet, etc.

However, to the person using this program, these functions should be transparent. The user does not need to know, and probably doesn't care to know, how that particular function is accomplished inside the computer. The user is interested in results, not the methods used to obtain the results. When people turn on their television sets, they only want to see a movie or watch the news. They don't have to know how the TV signal was generated, transmitted, received, and converted to an audio-picture in their television set.

A computer program is written from the viewpoint of the computer, in a language the computer can understand, as if one were inside the computer.

However, a user's manual should be written from a user's viewpoint, from outside the shell of the computer. A user wants to compose text on a monitor, edit it, and then send it out to modem for transmission to another computer on a network or to a database vendor. The user is not interested in the subroutines it takes to make a character appear on a screen, nor how a stream of characters is sent to another computer or to a database. The user only wants the computer to automatically display all of the characters s/he inputs on the screen and then, by pressing one or two keys, output that information to a modem or a network.

# A tutorial and an operator's manual

The best way to learn a new program is usually through an on-screen tutorial. Properly written, a tutorial leads users, step-by-step, through typical examples that are similar to what they will encounter when using the program. A tutorial is a much more effective method than attempting to learn the program from a printed text. This does not mean to imply that a written text is unnecessary because a tutorial is only a one-time explanation of the commands and operating modes. A user's manual, with detailed explanations, numerous graphic illustrations, charts, and tables is essential to refer to so you can refresh your memory, learn special modes, and troubleshoot effectively, among other things.

A user's manual should summarize the commands and briefly explain what each does. It should also summarize the operation and the basic characteristics of the program: how much memory is required; how to start the program; how to end it; how to save, print out, or transmit the data generated; etc.

Troubleshooting is also a vital part of printed documentation requirements. Troubleshooting should list the most common error messages that address the most common problems, their symptoms, and how to correct them.

Some user manual writers skimp on the table-of-contents and the alphabetical index. These are essential in all documentation. The index in particular should list topics not only under their most common term but also synonyms for common terms. A comprehensive Glossary should define all new or unusual terms as used specifically in the text to satisfy a wide range of user backgrounds. It's much better to have a glossary and index with many more terms than are needed than to skimp on these important parts of a manual.

Finally, the paperwork accompanying the software, should include a customer registration card. This serves a number of purposes: if bugs are still present in the program (this is not an unusual occurrence), as a registered owner you are informed of how to correct these bugs and you may receive updated disks. Also you'll be on the mailing list to receive offers to update the software periodically as the software developers add more and more capabilities to their programs. And many software companies distribute a newsletter periodically that provides suggestions on how to better use their software.

# Does it do what I need it to do?

"Does the program accomplish everything I need it to do?" is another vital question to answer before you invest your money in software. This is the most difficult question to answer strictly by attempting to analyze the software's performance to determine if it accomplishes what you want it to. Too many unknowns must be answered in such a situation. An untold amount of software has been purchased, failed to deliver on its claims, and been retired to the buyer's closet, never to be called on again. But this important question can be solved. Many software vendors now offer their programs on a 30-day trial, with a money-back guarantee if you're not satisfied with the software. This is a trend that should continue; take advantage of it.

Another solution has resulted from a unique marketing concept called "shareware." I highly recommend it and have used it for some of my software purchases.

# Shareware—an important
# and unique software concept

Many software programs sell in the several hundred dollar range; however, some low-cost alternatives exist. Software programs are available through a unique marketing concept called "shareware," where you can not only purchase low-cost software, but you also can try it before you buy it.

Shareware is created by individual entrepreneurs who develop software programs and offer them to the general public on a trial basis. Since shareware authors do not go in for fancy packaging and costly, expensive advertising, their programs can be purchased for a fraction of the cost of commercially available programs.

Shareware is initially offered to computer users for little more than the cost of the individual disks, usually less than five dollars per disk. The authors often include an instruction manual on the same disks as the software, a manual the user can print out and use when evaluating the program. The user can test the program on his or her own computer. If the user decides to continue to use the program, he or she is requested to send in a modest "registration fee" that might range from about ten to around a hundred dollars for a complex program. For this registration fee the user receives:

- A printed and more detailed instruction manual, complete with illustrations, and additional information.
- The opportunity to contact the author for help.
- Updates as the program is improved. Often the author will provide a more sophisticated version of the software than was on the initial demonstration program disks.

This revolutionary marketing concept is participated in by authors who write programs for both the IBM and the Macintosh. There are many more shareware programs for the IBM than for the Macintosh. IBM shareware programs include fairly complex word processing, database, and spreadsheet programs, while complex Mac shareware programs are much more limited.

Here are some of the best sources for purchasing shareware:
For the IBM:

PC-SIG, Inc.
1030D East Duane Av.
Sunnyvale, CA 94086
(800) 245-6717
(800) 222-2996 in California

The Public Software Library
P.O. Box 35705
Houston TX 77235-5705
(800) 242-4PSL

California FREEWARE
1747 E. Avenue Q
Palmdale, CA 359-2189
(800) 359-2189

Software Excitement
P.O. Box 3097, 6475 Crater Lake Highway
Central Point, OR 97502
(800) 444-5457

For the Macintosh:

EDUCORP
531 Stevens Av. #B
Solano Beach, CA 92075
(619) 259-0255 for information
(800) 843-9497 for orders

BMUG
1442A Walnut St. #62
Berkeley, CA 94709-1496
(415) 549-BMUG

# Downloading software

Another excellent source of software is downloading public domain, shareware, and other software programs from libraries of online databases. Most of the general consumer databases, and many bulletin boards, have wide varieties of software that you can download via your modem. Most are available for only the cost of the online time required to download.

Most telecomm software programs can accomplish this download function. To do this, choose a file protocol transfer that you and the database vendor have in common; XMODEM, YMODEM, ZMODEM, and KERMIT are the most commonly used.

The specific procedure may vary from one vendor to the other, but they usually require the same basic information. The general procedure (assuming you're logged on to the vendor) is as follows:

1. Select the SIG (Special Interest Group) forum or whatever library the vendor stores the software in.

    Ex. IBM SIG

2. Select the protocol you have in common with the vendor. While error-checking protocols are not vital when downloading straight text, they must be used when you're downloading software programs because the loss or garbling of a single character might make the program inoperable.

    Ex. XMODEM

3. Specify the directory in which you want to store the downloaded program in your computer. You can use the vendor's file name or assign your own.

    Ex. C: \ temp \ Newname

4. Select the software program you want to download, then sit back and relax. The vendor will inform you of the progress of the download and tell you when it is complete.

Some database vendors have simplified and largely automated the downloading procedure. CompuServe, for example, presents a series of easy-to-use menu choices for accomplishing this download. America OnLine has one of the best menus and procedures for downloading software, although their library isn't as extensive as some of the giants.

# Menus

One of the most useful software programs to purchase for any computer is a menu program of the type illustrated in Fig. 3-1. A menu program is at least two orders of magnitude easier to use than to try to remember and input all of the required complex DOS or operating system commands. A simple, text-based menu automates most of the computer's operation.

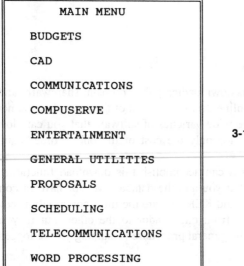

```
┌─────────────────────────────┐
│        MAIN MENU            │
│                             │
│   BUDGETS                   │
│                             │
│   CAD                       │
│                             │
│   COMMUNICATIONS            │
│                             │
│   COMPUSERVE                │
│                             │
│   ENTERTAINMENT             │
│                             │
│   GENERAL UTILITIES         │
│                             │
│   PROPOSALS                 │
│                             │
│   SCHEDULING                │
│                             │
│   TELECOMMUNICATIONS        │
│                             │
│   WORD PROCESSING           │
└─────────────────────────────┘
```

**3-1** Typical Main Menu presentation.

The Main menu should be installed so it is activated and displayed on your monitor when you turn your computer on. To select one of the entries listed on the menu, simply move the cursor to highlight the entry you want (using either the arrow keys or your mouse), and hit the Enter key or the mouse button. The computer then brings up the desired program for you without you having to input a number of complex computer commands. Or it might take you to a submenu that gives you additional menu choices using the same simple procedure.

Unless you're deep into programming or are a computer hacker, you don't have the time, nor probably the desire to spend an inordinate amount of time learning and memorizing numerous system operating commands (e.g., dir, assign, format, etc.), commands that you will undoubtedly forget from time to time and have to look up and try to recall how you activated them some time ago. A good menu program eliminates this problem and replaces these easy-to-forget system commands with a series of menus of possible choices that can be selected merely by your hitting a few keys and watching the action take place.

After evaluating a dozen menus, the best one I found and the one that I use constantly is the following:

Menu Works Advanced, by PC Dynamics
31332 Via Colinas, Suite 102
Westlake Village, CA 91362

This modestly priced program is easy to install and will automatically add to the menu over 2500 popular software programs as it scans your drives and automatically creates ready-to-use menus. Once this is done, you can activate your programs simply by using the arrow keys and the Enter (or Return) key or your mouse. You can assign passwords for system security, maintain a log of all system usage, and generate a variety of formatted reports showing users, times, dates, activities, and project codes. It also has built-in and user-defined help.

# Windows

In a determined attempt to make the IBM emulate the easy-to-use Macintosh, with its standard icon or picture menus, Microsoft Corporation labored long and diligently to develop a program called "Windows." Announced with much fanfare and promotion, Windows has been enthusiastically endorsed by some and summarily rejected by others. Although lacking in features in earlier versions, Windows has been continually updated and will certainly continue to be improved. With the power and finances of Microsoft behind it, Windows will likely become a defacto standard for many present and future versions of IBM and its clones.

Even its detractors reluctantly admit that Microsoft Windows is an example of an excellent installation program. To install, you simply put Disk #1 in your A or B drive, access the drive, and input

Setup

The installation program takes over from there. Most of the installation is automatic, with the program searching for and determining the type of computer you have and other pertinent data. All you must input is specific data that Windows can't determine for itself, such as the printer you're using, which port it's connected to, etc.

Windows requires a large memory—at least 2M to operate efficiently, with 4M being preferred. It works sluggishly with the slower IBM XT clones and requires an AT or higher to function satisfactorily. Plus, the software you use under Windows has to be compatible with Windows. Windows has a number of built-in features such as an elemental word processing program, a calendar, a notebook, a database and a color paint program that are useful utilities.

# Scientific/mathematical word processors

Although many popularly used word processors (e.g., Word Perfect and Word) can accommodate most technical writing assignments, few can accurately generate and properly display complex scientific and mathematical symbols. Some of the more full-featured word processors, such as Word Perfect, have a limited capability to process these special symbols. Here is an example of about the maximum complexity that text word processors, such as Word Perfect, can generate:

$$\frac{2x}{y} + \sqrt{\frac{\pi^2-1}{(y-1)(x-1)}}$$

However, the process required to generate these symbols in conventional text word processors is rather lengthy and complex. If you are required to create more complex mathematical symbols (e.g., integral signs, chemical structure, etc.) and equations, you should procure a scientific word processing program. You need a program that is easy to use and one that creates and displays your symbols and equations as they will appear in the text when printed. The best I've found that accomplishes these goals is TCI's $T^3$ Scientific Word Processor.

For the IBM, TCI's $T^3$ Scientific Word Processor is the world's most widely used scientific word processor. $T^3$ is easy to learn and also serves as a general purpose word processor. An on-screen picture of the keyboard is available as a pop-up. You can use this massive program to write mathematical equations, create chemical structures, import graphics, and use various fonts. It provides many foreign language capabilities including Cyrillic (Russian), Greek, and accented characters for almost all European languages. $T^3$ is the one I strongly recommend for the IBM.

For the Macintosh, I recommend MathWriter. It's a WYSIWYG presentation and, like so much of the Mac's software, it's easy to learn and a pleasure to use. MathWriter automatically sizes and centers mathematical symbols, italicizes variables, formats tables and matrices, and shows on-screen renumbering of both equations and references to equations. The interactive library for storing and retrieving repeatedly used text, graphics, and mathematical expressions is available from the keyboard or a mouse.

# Graphic programs
# —pictures save words and explain better

The content of a message is embodied in its words and its graphics. But most people who write are "word-oriented." By that, I mean that they use only words to discuss or illuminate topics that could be much better explained with a proper combination of words and graphics. Illustrations not only help explain what are often difficult technical concepts, but they also break up the forbidding task of tackling a solid page of closely spaced words expounding on a topic. Graphics provide better understanding, as well as much needed

"eye-relief."

Graphics or illustrations have, until recently, been difficult to create for many engineers and scientists who are required to write as part of their jobs. As graphic programs become easier and more convenient to use and more versatile in their application, graphics will serve an increasingly important role in engineering and scientific documentation.

Chemists, for example, tend to think and write in pictures—successful chemists usually have strong visual imaginations. Chemists used to have to draw their own structures with plastic templates or have a skilled technical illustrator convert their rough sketches into publication-ready illustrations. But modern computer programs (for example, Chem-Draw) simplify this process by offering large libraries of chemical clip art, drawing tools, etc. Illustrations can now be created by chemists and placed directly in word processor text.

Another source of graphics is "clip art." Both the Mac and the IBM can import clip art directly into many of their programs. A wide variety of software clip art, ranging from office equipment, to computers, to people, to chemical lab equipment, and to objects of all kinds is available for use by both computers. Engineers and scientists require more than clip art, however. They also require the ability to draw figures, circuit diagrams, symbols, block diagrams, modify clip art, and more. For these tasks, versatile graphics programs are needed.

## Graphics programs for the Mac

Because of its ease of use, the Macintosh is by far the best computer for creating graphics. A number of excellent graphics programs are available for the Mac: SuperPaint, Canvas, MacDraw and many others. The one I use and recommend is SuperPaint. Don't let the name confuse you: SuperPaint is excellent for bit-map drawing as well as object-oriented graphics. I also have a graphics program for my Mac that functions as a Desk Accessory (DA). A DA is especially useful because you can call up the program while remaining in a word processing program. You can use the DA graphics program to construct your illustration and then import the graphics directly into your word processing document. I use and recommend Desk Draw and Desk Paint (both from Zedcor)—two excellent and easy-to-use complementary DA graphics programs.

Both Microsoft Works and Word Perfect for the Mac have built-in graphics programs that can be called up. Elemental graphics, such as block diagrams, etc., can be constructed with these programs and inserted right in with the text. Clip art can also be imported into these programs.

A few elementary Mac shareware programs are also available. Here's the few I've tested:

- XVT Draw
- Minicad (a good one)
- MusicPaint. You can also use this one to create sheet music.

## Graphics programs for the IBM

There are not as many easy-to-use graphics programs for the IBM. One of the best is Draw Perfect, a low-cost program produced by the Word Perfect Corporation and that also works well with Word Perfect. Draw Perfect has an elemental graphics capability for simpler illustration tasks but is severely limited for constructing complex graphics.

For near-drafting quality drawing, TurboCAD and DesignCAD 2D and 3D are excellent and low-cost Computer Aided Design programs.

The best IBM shareware graphics program I've tested is FLODRAW, available from most shareware vendors. FLODRAW was developed by

George Freund
P.O. Box 203
Mentor, OH 44061.

Freund's program also converts FLODRAW graphics to a PCX file that can be imported directly into and used with such word processors as Word Perfect.

# Telecommunications

Telcommunications software, or "telecomm," is the special software that enables your computer (which speaks digital) to make the necessary "language" translation so your computer can "talk" analog over the audio-frequency telephone lines.

But before we get into the details of telecommunications, here are some important definitions:

**Baud rate**   The correct definition is the number of discrete signal events per second occurring on a communications channel. Even though it's technically incorrect, baud rate in online systems is usually referred to as bits per second (bps). Because it takes roughly 10 bits to transmit a single character (a letter, a space, etc.), the character rate equals the baud rate divided by 10.

**Hayes compatible**   Modems that are Hayes compatible use the Hayes command set, sometimes referred to as the "AT command set" because it uses the prefix AT to grab your modem's attention. Originated by Hayes Microcomputer Products, the AT command set has been so popular that it has become the de facto standard for modems.

**File transfer protocols**   A number of different protocols are used to transmit data via modems to ensure correct formatting and accuracy of the data. Error-checking protocols are not as important for text as they are for transmitting chemical formulas, software programs, numbers, etc.

**CCITT**   International Consultative Committee on Telephone and Telegraph. This international committee establishes the standards that ensure international telephone systems connectivity. Specific standards are identified by the letter V, followed by a period and a number (e.g., V.32). When the suffix bis follows the number (e.g., V.32bis), it denotes a revision of a protocol, not necessarily an extension of the previous version.

## General requirements

For online operation, a modem should have the following minimum capabilities:

- Auto-dial, re-dial, manual dial, and a busy notification
- Handle various protocols
- Receive and transmit text files
- Emulate various terminals
- Generate script files
- Running record of on-time
- Auto answer

**Autodial, redial, manual dial, and busy notification** Your modem should be able to dial another computer without your having to manually input the number each time. Your telecomm software should store all the telephone numbers you need to dial so that all you have to do is switch to a dial menu and tap the proper key to automatically dial into the online vendor system you selected. The ability to continue to redial a number until it's available is another important feature. Some modems have a "number-linking" or "chaining" capability that you can set up to automatically dial a series of numbers, one after the other, skip to the next number if one number is busy, then return and redial the previously busy number(s). Your software program should also allow you to dial numbers manually when you need to dial a number you use infrequently. And your software should also output a busy signal when your call doesn't go through when the line is busy.

Telecomm software should be able to accommodate a variety of file transfer protocols. A file transfer protocol is a group of standardized methods used to exchange data between different computers. Among the most popular are XMODEM, YMODEM, KERMIT, ZMODEM, and MACBINARY. Insist on XMODEM, KERMIT, YMODEM and ZMODEM as a minimum and MACBINARY for the Mac.

These error-correcting techniques check to see if the data has been corrupted during transmission. This is accomplished by the transmitting modem performing a mathematical computation on each block of data and sending this calculation along with the data. The receiving modem performs the same calculation on the incoming data. If the two numbers match, the receiving modem sends back an *ACK* or positive ACKnowledgement signal. If they do not, the receiving modem sends back a *NACK*—a Negative ACKnowledgement signal—and requests that the corrupted block be retransmitted.

**Capture and transmit files** The ability to both capture and transmit files is necessary, not only for transmitting information to a database, but also so you can capture your two-way "conversation" with the database for later display, analysis, and printout.

Because different databases set up their systems to emulate specific terminal types, your software must be able to emulate a variety of terminal types. Terminal emulation options give your computer the ability to respond to the special screen-formatting commands and characters coming from the database computer. The most common are TTY and ANSI. You should insist on TTY, VT-102/52, and ANSI, which will enable you to logon to just about any popular service or BBS.

A Script file lets you set up a mini-program to automate some of the functions of your telecomm program. A typical script program will automatically dial your database phone number, wait 5 seconds, input your account number, wait another 2 seconds, then transmit your password, wait another second, transmit another command, etc.

Another script feature uses your computer clock. It can be set up to dial a data bank, query for a specific topic, then send or receive a message at a specific time.

Your software should also be able to provide you with a log, a running record of on-time. It's surprising how quickly you can use up fifteen minutes in a database before you realize how long you've been on.

An auto-answer capability gives your personal computer the ability to automatically answer and accept incoming data when your computer is unattended. If you request information to be delivered to your computer during off-hours, or if you want to converse with other computer users, your software should have this ability.

## IBM telecomm programs

Here's a summary of some of the more common IBM telecomm programs:

- Bitcom Deluxe. It's a commercial program, is easy to set up, has support for 4 serial ports, accomplishes text or binary file transfer, has good terminal emulation, has script or action files that you can use to build your own logon procedures, and has good documentation.

- Boyan. It's available as shareware, has extensive scripting, phone books, chat mode, few terminal emulations, log of online activity. However, the documentation is poor.

- Crosstalk. It has a Procomm-like dialing directory, excellent script language and extensive list of terminal emulations, and good documentation. It can translate at speeds from 110 to 115,200 baud and has all major file transfer protocols. It's an easy package to use. It works under Windows, TopView, or DESQview. XMODEM and KERMIT protocols, and can use either menu or commands for operation.

- Mirror III. It's a strong program with many features: pull-down menus, auto-dial, auto-answer, chain-dialing, keyboard and mouse operation, plus more. It covers most file transfer protocols, MNP 5, wide range of terminal emulations, has a text editor, supports MNP 5 session/data compression protocol, has a good scripting language with learning procedure for creating automatic logons. It has good online help and is easy to install.

- Procomm Plus. It's a commercial version of a shareware product and is a good choice for beginners and pros. It has good documentation, and it generates script file by learning your logon sequences. Procomm Plus has a wide range of file transfer protocols and terminal emulations, mouse support, chat mode, a large dialing directory, a text editor, an activity log, a good user interface and extensive help. Works from 300 to 115,200 baud.

- QMODEM. It has an easy-to-use dialing directory, queue dialing, a good text editor, excellent online help, a limited list of protocols and emulation, and a good script language. The documentation is poor.

- Smartcom. It's easy to use, has a clear and comprehensive menu structure or keystroke operation, mouse support, good scripting, an excellent file manager, good online help and text editor. Still, it's difficult to set up and has few emulations.

- Telemate. It's a low-cost shareware product (costing about $40 to register) and is an excellent, full-featured, and flexible telecomm program. It's easy to learn and easy to use. Telemate includes a separate editor, viewer, and mouse driver accessible through menus and windows. It also has multi-tasking features, a clipboard, and a wide-variety of protocols and terminal emulations. The script language is powerful and easy to learn. Telemate is an outstanding program!

- Telix. It's a shareware product of which commercial versions are available. It's inexpensive, has many protocols, has a good dialing directory, and is easy to set up.

### Macintosh telecomm programs

Some of the more common Macintosh telecomm programs are:

- Microphone II. It's easy to use, flexible, has good scripting, good documentation, and supports XMODEM, YMODEM, ZMODEM and KERMIT and MacTerminal 1.1. It can operate modems at any speed from 50 to 57,600 baud. It also has VT102 and VT52 emulations.

- Smartcom. It's an excellent user interface that utilizes on-screen icons. It's easy to learn and use, it has a learn mode with good scripting, and it has online help and good documentation.

- White Knight. It's a commercial version of the popular Red Ryder shareware product. It's a full-featured telecomm program that uses on-screen icons for all major functions. White Knight has an on-screen clock, powerful scripting, and a learn mode for scripting. It also has enhanced terminal support including VT102, and it supports XMODEM, YMODEM, ZMODEM and KERMIT protocols.

# Teaching the Macintosh and IBM to speak to each other

As mentioned earlier, the IBM and Macintosh each perform specific functions better than the other. So if you own or have access to both computers and are able to put this combination to best advantage, how can you obtain the best of both worlds? Is it possible to accomplish certain functions on the Macintosh and transport them to an IBM, and vice versa?

It *can* be done, and I have made good use of this capability in writing this and my other books. I'll give you some possible methods of doing this.

First, a couple of definitions. Transferring a file is simply moving a file from one computer to another computer. The file is transferred in the same format as it originally existed, with no file conversions being made.

However, if you want to move a file from a Macintosh to an IBM, transferring the file usually isn't enough because the two computers don't speak the same language. Their disks are formatted differently; and fonts, underlining, etc., are not defined the same. What is also needed is a "translator." Much like a foreign language translator, a software translator changes the IBM language into the Macintosh language or vice versa. For example, if you move files either from IBM Word Perfect to Macintosh Word or the reverse, the language translator changes not only the text but also most of the formatting from one program to the other so that little information is lost in the translation.

You can follow two basic methods for this translation:

- You can connect an external cable between two computers.
- You can use one computer to read and/or write on a disk written on by the other computer.

For the first method, you must connect an external cable—called a "null-modem" cable—from the serial port of one computer to the serial port of the other. Software is required in both the sending and receiving computers to accomplish this transfer, but the transfer is quick and accurate.

For the second method, you store files on a floppy disk and then physically transport the disk from one computer's disk drive to the other computer's disk drive. The Macintosh has a unique program called "Apple File Exchange" that helps implement these translations. Used in conjunction with the excellent and versatile "Apple SuperDrive," the Macintosh can read and convert IBM files to Macintosh compatible files and vice versa. The Macintosh can also format and read disks in both the IBM and Macintosh formats.

## Apple File Exchange program

The Apple File Exchange program translates files that are in the ASCII format (a basic format without underlining, bolding, etc.) or a DCA/RFT format, (Document Content Architecture, used by some IBM word processing systems; and Rich Format Text, a text format developed by Microsoft, which retains formatting information). The AFE can also transfer text that uses the same word processing format for both computers; for example, Word Perfect for the IBM can translate to Word Perfect for the Macintosh and can also translate IBM Draw Perfect graphics.

One of the best translators to accomplish the more complex translations from one program on the IBM to a different program on the Mac (or vice versa)—and also the one I use—is MacLink Plus, developed by

DataViz, Inc.
35 Corporate Dr.
Trumbull, CT 06611

MacLink Plus provides a set of 150 translators that will translate virtually any IBM format to any Macintosh format and vice versa. In using the Maclink Plus, however, there is one problem I learned the hard way in trying to translate some Macintosh Word files to IBM Word Perfect. Make sure your Word file does not use large or unusual type fonts, or the program will bomb. Change all of your Word text files to a single and small font (like 10 or 12) before you accomplish the translation.

So there is a way to have the best of both the IBM and the Macintosh worlds. You can do whatever is best accomplished on one computer and translate it to the other computer.

## LAN software

LAN software, known as NOS (Network Operating System), is the intellect that controls all of the intercommunication on the Local Area Network. The software stores the files it receives and gives the individual PCs access to specific files. The software also permits and sets up communications (E-mail) from one PC to one or more PCs that are tied into the LAN.

LAN software also controls access to the various shared peripherals such as a laser printer or CD-ROM. Some software programs also contain scheduling software and telephone directories for everyone on the network to use.

# Viruses

Not only are people afflicted by a variety of viruses, but in the past few years a wide variety of human-generated computer viruses have been infecting computers throughout the world. These viruses can slow down a computer, cause it to do odd things, and even completely destroy a disk memory. Some are timed so they only take effect after a specific period of time has elapsed. However, you can observe certain precautions and utilize certain antidotes to prevent these disastrous infections.

First of all and foremost, do not buy any software with such an inexpensive price that it appears too good to be true. If it's too good to be true, it probably is.

There are a number of excellent antidote programs that can be installed on your PC and that will inoculate your computer against many viruses. However, just as in the human world, new viruses will undoubtedly be popping up from time to time when unprincipled hackers are turned loose on systems.

The best remedy for long-term protection against viruses is to make sure you use only quality software from well-established software companies. Restrict access to all your PCs to the proper responsible personnel, and most importantly of all, backup your work on floppy disks frequently when you are inputting data. I generally keep a disk in one of my floppy drives and back up every document whenever I make significant changes. It takes a little extra effort, but it ensures that I will always have the latest version of my data stored on a reliable medium.

# Utility software

If you have trouble remembering (and who doesn't) all of the DOS commands you have to use and need a quick reference, I recommend Resident Expert for All Versions of DOS, an excellent software program by

Parsons Technology
375 Collins Rd. N.E.
Cedar Rapids, IA 52406-3120
(800) 223-6925.

This hypertext program not only helps you make better use of the more familiar commands with its excellent descriptions, it also leads you to use many functions and commands you never knew existed. Easy to use and quick to respond, Resident Expert can be loaded as a TSR and will occupy 69K of RAM (17K if you have expanded memory). Hypertext consists of many DOS topics linked together with keywords or selection menus. You jump from one topic to another to reach your term and then receive an easy-to-understand description of the term and its application.

# Recommended software

Table 3-1 lists the software I recommend for a typical PC for engineers and scientists.

Now that you have a good background in hardware and software, let's take a look at the anatomy of databases—what their insides look like.

**Table 3-1   Recommended software.**

**Textual Word Processing**
Word Perfect for the IBM.
Word or Word Perfect for the Macintosh if you're going to do a lot of writing.
If your writing efforts are modest and you want an easy program to learn, consider Q & A Write for the IBM and MacWrite for the Macintosh.

**Scientific Word Processing**
TCI's $T^3$ Scientific Word Processor for the IBM.
MathWriter for the Macintosh.

**Graphics**
Draw Perfect for the IBM for simple graphics, TurboCAD or DesignCAD for near-drafting quality. SuperPaint for the Macintosh.

**Menu**
Menu Works Advanced and Windows for the IBM. The Macintosh already has its own excellent menu system.

**Telecomm**
Procomm Plus for the IBM for routine telecomm, Telemate for sophisticated telecomm tasks. Microphone for the Macintosh

**LAN**
I can't recommend specific LAN hardware or software because it depends on your specific configuration.

# Exercises

1. List ten features that all software programs should have and explain why they should have them.
2. List ten capabilities that a telecomm program should have and explain why they are needed.
3. What are the advantages of using graphics in writing?
4. What are the advantages and disadvantages of using Shareware?
5. Why should you pay a registration fee for Shareware?

# 4

# The anatomy of databases

*There is no reason for any individual to have a computer in their home.*
Ken Olson, President of Digital Equipment Corporation, 1977.

Just as skilled engineers and scientists must know and understand the intimate anatomy of the equipment they're designing or testing, or of an experiment they're conducting, so also must the searcher for scientific knowledge understand the intimate anatomy and details of databases to properly utilize them. This chapter presents a short course in the anatomy of electronic databases.

The hierarchy of an online system is depicted in Fig. 4-1.

Online systems are comprised of the worldwide collection of computerized electronic libraries that are managed by Database Vendors, such as Dialog, BRS, and CompuServe. Online Databases are organized collections of information that can be accessed electronically from a computer located at a remote distance. Typical online databases are:

- INSPEC. Offers worldwide coverage of the literature in physics, electrical and electronics engineering, computers and control, and information technology.

- Chemical Abstracts. Offers worldwide coverage of the chemical sciences literature from over 9000 journals, new books, conference proceedings, and government research reports.

- COMPENDEX PLUS. Offers combined coverage of the COMPENDEX and EI Engineering Meetings databases, with about 2.6 million records.

- Scientific & Technical Books & Serials in Print. Offers comprehensive subject selection of books and serials in scientific and technical fields. Over 160,000 book titles and more than 23,000 titles of serials are included.

- Dow Jones Quotes. Contains current stock quotes for all major companies.

- National Newspaper Index. Contains front-to-back indexing of major nationally distributed newspapers and newswires.

Databases are created and periodically updated by companies, individuals, academic institutions, corporations, government agencies, etc. These databases are then leased to database vendors who, in turn, charge users for accessing their databases.

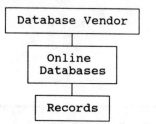

**4-1** Online database systems hierarchy.

Each database consists of from a few to as many as a million individual records. Each individual record is a complete set of information, such as an abstract of a journal article, or the full-text of a physics reference book, or a numeric listing of stock values during a company's history, etc. The individual record is the level that contains the information you will be searching for.

# Basic components of a record

Each record usually contains the three basic components listed in Fig. 4-2.

The first component of a record is usually a bibliographic citation (bibcite) that gives the title, the author, the publishing media, the date, and similar reference information about the article, or the information, or the facts cited. The body—or second component of each record—is an abstract, a summary, the complete text, or the complete set of facts.

The third component of each record contains the list of keywords or descriptors that describe or accurately summarize the contents of the database. These keywords or descriptors are the words you should use when you search the databases to quickly locate the specific records you need. Creating, applying, and using various combinations of one or more keywords are vital concepts in the use of online databases and will be covered in detail in this and later chapters.

The three components just listed are not always included in this one-two-three order; they might be scattered throughout the record. However, most records do have all three basic components.

```
* Bibliographic citation

* Body (abstract, summary, full-text, or facts)

* Keywords (or descriptors)
```

**4-2** Components of a record.

# Types of databases

The basic types of online databases are diagrammed in Fig. 4-3. Some database vendors provide all three types, while others specialize in only one type.

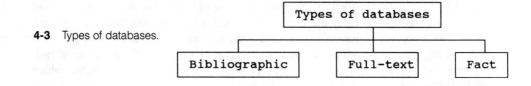

**4-3** Types of databases.

## Bibliographic database

A Bibliographic type of database is comprised of a number of individual records similar to the bibliographic record illustrated in Fig. 4-4. The simplest of the three types, it was the most common when databases were first used. Each bibliographic record contains reference information as the first entry. As a minimum, a bibliographic record includes a reference or citation to a publication, magazine, or journal article, news story, patent, conference paper, etc. Many also contain, in the body of the record, an abstract or summary of the information contained in the referenced article. The bibliographic type of database usually concludes with a list of keywords.

In the sample record of Fig. 4-4, the name of the database is Magazine Directory, which has been copyrighted and supplied by the MDC Corporation. The Magazine Directory might contain tens of thousands of bibliographic records of articles from hundreds of other magazines. Lines 2−4 in the figure provide reference information about where and when the article was published, etc.

The second component of the record contains a summary or an abstract (I've abbreviated it here) of the text of the referenced article. The third and last component of the record lists the keywords a searcher should use to locate and access this specific record for review.

```
MAGAZINE DIRECTORY (Corp. MDC)

Sons of Norway. (Minneapolis, MN)

Viking Influence on Ireland v17 p34(4) May 1992

Illustration, photograph

   The Viking influence in Ireland resulting from the

raids of these fearless warriors is mirrored in the

many names of the cities, etc...

KEYWORDS: Vikings--Ireland--History--Cities--Names
```

**4-4** Bibliographic record.

## Full-text record database

The second major type, the full-text record, has essentially the same basic information as a bibliographic record, except that it contains the full-text of the article, the book, or other documents in place of the abstract or summary. Because of the continually decreasing cost of computer storage and to meet the needs of researchers, more and more vendors are offering full-text records in lieu of abstracts and summaries. This trend is likely to continue. For some types of records, such as key engineering and scientific documents, full-text records are essential. Some full-text databases also provide an abstract which searchers can review to help them determine whether or not they wish to access the full-text of the record.

## Fact record database

The third type of database, the Fact Record, is illustrated in Fig. 4-5. It is also comprised of essentially the same three Record components: Reference Information, the Body (Facts) of information, and a list of keywords that can be used to locate the database record. In a facts record, however, the keywords are usually scattered throughout the record.

As you can see from Fig. 4-5, most of the content in the facts record consists of a listing of stock price quotes over a specific period of time for an imaginary company named Chemical Equipment Supplies. Only a few keywords are needed for this type of record. You only need to select the proper database, and then key in the name of the company and the period for which you want the stock quotes displayed.

```
         ENGINEERING EQUIPMENT SUPPLIES

Vugip: 3847596        Exchange: N           Ticker: MES

   Date        Volume      High/Ask     Low/Bid      Close/Avg

   1/12/92    1,234,456    112 1/8      110          112 1/8

   1/13/92    1,928,560    112 3/8      110 5/8      110 3/4

   1/14/92    1,876,340    109 3/4      110 1/4      110 7/8

   etc.

   Prices available: 3/13/77 through 1/18/92

   Last page !
```

**4-5** Sample facts record.

# What goes into a database?

Continuing with our anatomy of databases, let's review some records and see what information is incorporated in each and, knowing this, how the records can be efficiently searched for this information.

The first component of all types of database records usually contains reference information for that record. For bibliographic and full-text records, the reference information is in a fairly standard format. It usually lists the title, the author, where the original information was published, etc. It might also list the source, the company involved, the date, and any other pertinent information for the facts that follow.

The second component of bibliographic records is also fairly standard in content. Most contain either a summary or an abstract that has been compiled by professional abstracters or by the author. It summarizes the content of the full-text that it references and that forms the basis for the record.

However, the second component or body of a facts-type of record contains the tables, the numeric data, the listings, or other factual information. Or it might contain a summary or a factual writeup about a company, an organization, or a product, etc., that has prepared by a professional abstracter.

The third component of each type of record is a list of the keywords used by the database computer in a search. Applying one or more carefully selected words, the keywords summarize the various topics the specific record covers to help the database computer quickly locate that record. In some instances, a combination of numbers and words (e.g., SIC: 3851) might be used as keywords for searching. The keywords are usually at the end of the record, although sometimes they are scattered throughout the record.

## How databases are built

To build a database, all of the straight textual information and data (including the keywords and descriptors) in a record are first input in a serial or reading order and are stored as a direct or "vertical" record in a database in the manner illustrated back in Fig. 4-4. This vertical record is what you will read when you access and view (or print out) a specific record.

Next, to expedite the computer search, this same information is then alphabetized and the rearranged words are stored in the same database in alphabetical order in a second record, called an "inverted" record. This inverted record is an alphabetical index that performs essentially the same function that an index does for a book.

All of the words from the vertical record, except some common words, called "stop words" or "noise" (see section on "Stop words" later), are stored in this inverted record, along with their location in the record. This alphabetical word arrangement makes it much easier and quicker to search the files since sophisticated computer programs can zero in very quickly on an alphabetized list.

## Categories of keywords

Two basic categories of keywords can be used for searching as diagrammed in Fig. 4-6.

The controlled vocabulary category restricts a search to using only the keywords that are included in a special thesaurus—a limited or controlled set of words that has been created for that particular class of database. Controlled vocabulary keywords may be created in a number of possible ways. For some databases (e.g., chemical), all of the possible keywords are listed in a limited chemical thesaurus. Some of the thesauri currently in use include the Library of Congress Subject Headings (LCSH), the Sears List of Subject Headings, and the Standard Industrial Classification (SIC) Codes. A wide variety of thesauri have been developed for other databases. They are usually available online for you to review to help you create keywords for searching.

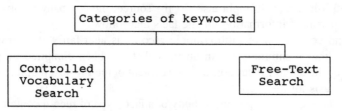

**4-6**  Categories of keywords used for searching.

A free-text search, however, permits a search to be conducted with any one or with several words that are stored in the record that the user chooses to search. At first thought, you would think that a free-text search would be the best and easiest type to use. However, because of the widely varying connotations of words, different or incorrect word spellings or abbreviations, and the existence of so many synonyms in our word-rich English language, this technique is often fraught with uncertainty. In free-text searching, access is provided to the reference information plus the keywords, as well as the full-text.

# Stop words

To expedite searches, database vendors specify a list of common words that should not be used in searching. These words are common and frequently used words that only clutter up a record and contribute nothing to a search. These words are called "stop words" or "noise." Dialog's stop words, for example, are the following: "an," "and," "by," "for," "from," "of," "the," "to," and "with." Each database has its own list of stop words and their lists might vary from nine to more than fifty stop words. Check with your database vendor for their list of stop words.

Stop words or reserved words still can be used in searches, but they must be specified differently than the normal keywords. One technique used is to enclose the phrase containing the stop words in quotes. For example, if you wanted to search for a book or article called Love and War, you would specify "Love and War" in quotes as your search terms.

# Search strategy

Essentially online searching consists of asking the computer to look for the occurrence (or absence) of specific words or groups of words in the text, title, or keyword references in a database record. You input your keywords, connected by simple search terms, and the computer quickly scans through all the records in the database to locate not only the words, but also precisely the position in which the keywords you input appear in the record.

An online search should be a journey from the general to the specific. Plan all of your search strategy using this approach. Start out with broader, more general keywords that will help locate a large number of records. Then you should gradually and selectively narrow your search down to the few records that most closely match your specific keyword combinations. In this way, if you finally end up without any references cited, you can back up and try different combinations.

To initiate a search, you input one or more keywords that describe as accurately as you can the topic or topics you are searching for. When you enter the keywords, the database computer makes a quick search of the database(s) you have chosen and locates all of the records that contain the keywords you have specified. The database computer returns with a list of the number of "hits," which specifies the number of different records that contain the keywords you have entered.

For example, assume you input the keyword "computer" into a database for software. The database computer searches all of the records in the database or databases you have elected to search. If the word "computer" appears in 1000 of the records in the database that was searched, the computer would reply that your search resulted in 1000 hits or citations.

This number of hits gives you an approximate idea of how effective your search has been. If you end up with something like 1000 or more hits (as you would most likely with such a common word as computer), it is obviously impractical to scan that many records to locate the specific reference(s) you are seeking. But this large number at least indicates that your search is in the proper databases that cover "computer."

Assuming you next input the word "graphics" and receive 500 hits, again a number much too large to use, but it does tell you that many of your records cover "graphics." For your final search, you combine the two and input "computer AND graphics" as your keywords to search with. This tells the computer to search for records that contain both terms. The computer then returns with 10 hits (see Fig. 4-7).

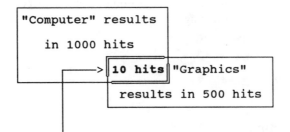

The combination of the keywords in records containing both terms (computer AND graphics) results in only 10 hits.

**4-7**  Hits resulting from combined terms.

At the other extreme, if you end up with no hits or with too few hits, you have to change your strategy to further broaden your search.

Therein lies the basic strategy for searching online databases: inputting the proper keywords, or combinations of keywords, so you can locate your topic, and at the same time not receive too many or too few hits. A number of tools and procedures are available to help you organize your search strategy to achieve the proper number of hits so you can locate your needed information as quickly and efficiently as possible. These techniques are described next.

# Basic input information to use

Specific fundamental inputs that can be used to help you locate specific records are the following:

- Author
- Title
- Publisher
- Country of publication
- ISBN Number
- Company name
- Corporate source
- Document type
- Journal or periodical name
- Language the article is printed in
- Publication date or range of dates

If one or more of these facts is known, they can be used singly or in combinations to quickly zero in on a database to find the specific record(s) you need.

# Keyword combinations/exclusions

Created by the English Mathematician, George Boole, Boolean Algebra is an excellent technique for expanding and contracting a computerized search. The basic Boolean terms used in database searching are:

- AND
- OR
- NOT

## Boolean AND function

The AND function is used when searching with a combination or group of keywords. The AND function narrows your search; i.e., it retrieves only records in which *all* of the search terms appear. For example, consider a search for records in which "Macintosh," "color," and "graphics" occur. (Usually it doesn't matter whether you use upper or lowercase or a combination of them.) Figure 4-8 diagrams the strategy you could use.

For your first search, as diagrammed in Fig. 4-8, you input Macintosh and receive 145 Hits, a large number of records that contain the keyword "Macintosh." For your second search, you input Graphics and receive 264 hits, another large number of records containing the search word "Graphics." For your third search you input "color" and receive 121 hits, another large number. By analyzing the first three searches, you see that you have successfully located records that contain each individual keyword. So your next step is to see how far down you can narrow your search by using the AND Boolean function to determine how many records contain all three terms. For your next search, you input all three terms, joined by the AND function (Macintosh AND Graphics AND Color), and receive 9 hits, a small and workable number of hits.

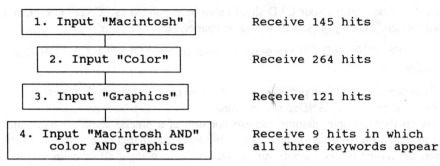

| | |
|---|---|
| 1. Input "Macintosh" | Receive 145 hits |
| 2. Input "Color" | Receive 264 hits |
| 3. Input "Graphics" | Receive 121 hits |
| 4. Input "Macintosh AND" color AND graphics | Receive 9 hits in which all three keywords appear |

**4-8** Use of Boolean AND Function.

At this point, if you still have too many hits, you'll have to add another clarifier—such as "bit-map" or "vector graphics"—to narrow your choices down to a manageable number, such as less than ten or twenty.

However, if you receive too few or no hits for the three keywords, you have to back up and expand your search, perhaps by limiting the search terms to:

SEARCH FOR: Macintosh AND graphics

or you could limit your search to:

SEARCH FOR: Macintosh AND color

Then, depending on the number of hits you receive for the various AND searches, you can try other combinations to zero in and locate the specific references you need.

As another example, if you knew that a periodical article you wanted to search for was published in the year 1992, was in the English language, and was written by a Dr. Arnold Berg, you could limit your search to the one or more articles authored by Dr. Berg during that year by using this combination of keywords with the AND function:

Publication year = 1992 AND Language = English
AND Author = Berg, Arnold, Dr.

The records containing all three of these keyword combinations would then be accessed and you would be given the number of hits. (In actual practice, standard abbreviations are used for the qualifiers; e.g., PY for Publication Year, LA for Language, and AU for Author.)

## Boolean OR function

To use the Boolean OR function, you might need to experiment by adding a number of different synonyms, acronyms, or names to help locate your information. Synonyms play a large part in retrieving good results. The OR function broadens your search; it retrieves records in which any of the search terms appear.

As an example, assume you are looking for a three dimensional CAD program and searched for "3-D" AND "CAD" and received no hits, so you must expand your search strategy by using the OR function. Because 3-D might be listed as "three-dimensional" or "three-D," you should expand your strategy to search for "3-D OR three-dimensional" or "three-D." And perhaps your CAD should also be expanded as "CAD" OR "Computer Aided Design." Then your search would be changed to:

SEARCH FOR: (3-D OR three-dimensional or three-D) AND (CAD OR Computer Aided Design)

Your search would then provide you with the number of records that contain any combinations of the pairs of ANDed search words.

As another example, assume you are not sure of a precise chemical name and you want to search for information on a new compound designated by a number of different names, depending on the manufacturer. You would then input all of them as your keywords using this format with the OR function:

SEARCH FOR: Mentone OR Prepazone OR Diaphone

The computer would then quickly scan the applicable databases and give you the number of hits, the number of records that contain either "Mentone" OR "Prepazone" OR "Diaphone" in their text or listed as keywords.

## Boolean NOT function

Finally, the NOT function (sometimes it's called a "BUT NOT" function) can be used to exclude one or more keywords in a search. The NOT function excludes some unwanted elements; it eliminates records in which certain search terms appear, reducing the number of hits.

Assume you want to search for information on a graphics program that is an object-oriented (OR vector) program but is not a bitmap or paint program. You could use this search strategy:

SEARCH FOR: Graphics AND (object-oriented OR vector) NOT
(bitmap OR paint)

The three basic Boolean operators—AND, OR, and NOT—are relatively easy to apply and are extremely useful in conducting search strategy. They can be used in any combinations with keywords to repeatedly narrow or broaden your search.

## EXPAND

Another extremely useful searching aid that some vendors offer is the EXPAND command. The EXPAND function lets you view a portion of a database index so you can see exactly which closely-related terms are included and how they are entered into the index. Assume that you do not know the precise spelling of a chemical name, the correct abbreviation of a corporation name, the complete name of a software product, or the precise name of an individual. This is where the EXPAND function comes into use.

For example, suppose you want to locate references to articles that were written by Adeline Butz. The author may use A. Butz or Addie Butz, or Adeline H. Butz or some other combination as her official designation. So to expand and search for the correct combination, you would input this command:

EXPAND: Butz Adeline

The database computer would search and list the number of hits for all possible combinations of the name, such as Butz, A.; Butz, A. H.; Butz, Adeline H., etc. You could review these citations and combine them with other information you know (using Boolean logic or other tools) such as the topic of the article (TOPIC=oysters, Adeline Butz's scientific specialty), the date, or range of dates, the name or partial name of the journal, etc. and narrow it down to locate the specific Adeline Butz you are searching for.

## Synonyms

Another technique to apply when constructing your search strategy is to use synonyms and other related terms. Although you might refer to your Chevvie as a car, an author might have called it a motorcar, an automobile, a Jenny, a motorized vehicle, or some other synonym.

Authors, being creative individuals, make full use of our English language and can often assign unconventional names to conventional objects. So consider the alternate use of synonyms and other related terms, particularly in conjunction with the Boolean OR function when creating your search strategy.

## Wild cards/truncation

Another very important search tool is the application of a "wild card"—the use of "truncation" in your keyword searches. Computers are very literal in their searches and need direction when searching for word variations. The specific wild card symbol used and how it is applied varies from one database vendor to another. I'll use a question mark as a wild card for my examples here.

If you are uncertain about the spelling of a common word (disk or disc) or chemical (chlorperazine) or foreign word (clinique), the complete name (Abel/Barrow's, Inc.), the exact abbreviation (Co. or Corp.), or the punctuation (online or on-line), etc., you can use one or more wild cards to help guide your search. Most systems let you specify whether the wild card signifies a single letter, a specific number of letters, a prefix or suffix, or an unknown number of letters.

Assume, for example, that you want to locate some information on telecommunications. You might find the information under telecom, telecomm, telecommunications, telecommunicate, etc. To apply a wild card to locate all of the variations to your search, you simply input the letters in the root of the keyword which you are certain of and insert a question mark to account for the unknown letters in the word. The remainder may be one or more letters. To use the wild card approach, you would then input:

SEARCH: teleco?

The database computer would then locate all references to all versions of this root word and display a list with the number of hits for each specific variation of the root word. Then, by analyzing the hits and by further restricting your search using Boolean techniques, you can pinpoint and locate the precise information you need.

But be careful with wild cards. You could try to search for tele? and get hits on telephone, telegraph, television, telepathy, and dozens of other variations.

# Range searching

Another search clarifier is the application of range searching. For example, assume you are searching a database that has records covering documents published from the years 1979 to the present time. That could be an enormous group of records to search, possibly many millions of documents.

Assuming you know the approximate date of publication or just want to know what given situation existed over a specific period of time, you can narrow your search down by using a range search by inputting:

    PUBLICATION YEAR = 1986 1988

or you could input:

    PY = 1990

to limit it to a single year.

# Proximity or positional operators

Another excellent but somewhat more complex search tool is the application of proximity or positional operators. These are used when you want to search for information that includes two or more keywords and where the keywords might or might not be near to each other in the text. The proximity operator lets you input two or more keywords and search for records in which these keywords are located within a specific number of words from each other.

For example, suppose you want to locate information on articles dealing with petroleum and Texas. You would first estimate that the two words should be within five words of each other in the record. You would then input:

    SEARCH FOR: petroleum(5N)Texas

The database computer would then search the requested database records to locate all records in which the two words were within five words of each other in the text (meaning they probably had information about Texas petroleum) or in the list of keywords, and in any order.

Other variations of this technique can specify that the keywords must be in the same paragraph, in a given order, in any order, adjacent to each other, only listed as keywords, etc.

# Powerful techniques

All of the search methods covered in this chapter are extremely powerful techniques. They can be used singly or in combinations. Relatively logical to apply, they are easy to learn and manipulate once you begin experimenting with them. But don't be overwhelmed by the variety and scope of search tools available, use only those which work most effectively for you.

You might end up with only a few favorites that you actually use repeatedly. However, you do have many alternative methods to experiment with and to choose from. When you consider the alternative—a manual search—you can see that we have advanced many quantum leaps into the art and science of searching for knowledge with the use of computerized databases.

# Selective Dissemination of Information

Selective Dissemination of Information (SDI) is another special feature that many database vendors also offer. Assume you are concerned with all of the continuing developments in the field of oil exploration in Alaska. The SDI feature lets you store your search strategy for this topic on their system indefinitely. Then, each time new information is input into the database covering oil exploration in Alaska, the database vendor's computer automatically searches the databases and stores this information in a special file. The vendor will then provide you with a printed copy of the new information, or some vendors let you access this special file the next time you logon to their service.

There is an extra charge for this service, but if you need to follow all of the continuing developments on any specific topic, it's a powerful capability you should consider.

# Portable databases—CD-ROMs

Another rapidly growing type of database is the *CD-ROM* or Compact Disk-Read Only Memory. The "Read Only Memory" part means you can read the disk but you can't write your own data on it. However, CD-ROM is a portable database because it exists on a physical compact disk that can be handled and transported from one place to another. It is a rugged media. There is no wear on the disk because it is read by a laser beam. CD-ROM functions much like the audio compact disk used to play music in your home, except that the CD-ROM permanently stores text and graphics information from reference books or other sources. CD-ROM has more error-correction built into it than the commercial home audio CDs, and its stored information is organized in a special way to provide an easy random access to that information. CD-ROMs contain information that cannot be changed, however, much like a printed book cannot be changed, so it is much akin to a publishing media.

The CD's storage capacity is enormous. A single CD-ROM 5″ diameter disk can store about 600M of information. That's equivalent to about 500 books of 400 pages each, or about 200,000 pages of text. For graphics, it can store up to 4000 color photographs, 1000 typefaces, or 3000 illustrations.

For example, Grolier's entire online 21-volume encyclopedia uses less than $1/3$ the storage space of a CD-ROM. More storage space is required for graphic information (usually as much as 20 times more than is required for text files), so incorporating visuals significantly reduces that number.

With the proper interface, you can quickly search CD-ROMs for information using the same search techniques described earlier in this chapter. Instead of having to physically handle and page through a number of reference books, you can input the proper search terms into your computer and have the information you searched for displayed almost instantly on your monitor. Then you can read it, or print it out for a hard copy record.

For example, suppose you need to find the address and phone number of a specialty chemical production equipment manufacturer in one of the Midwestern states. You don't have to search through a huge pile of city phone books and other reference books in the library. You only have to place the proper disk in your CD-ROM drive, input the complete or partial data you know, and have the updated information displayed for you in a few seconds.

CD-ROMs provide much the same basic search capability as vendor's databases. You can usually search for title, author, subject, dates, etc., conduct Boolean searches, and use proximity criteria. You can view graphics, scan articles, and skip between hits.

## To add to your computer

To be used with your computer, a CD-ROM requires a special disk drive that can be placed externally or mounted inside your computer. If you're willing to give up one of your disk drives, some CD-ROM drives can be mounted in the standard disk drive slot inside your computer chassis.

In addition, special hardware and software are required for your computer to be able to "converse" with the CD-ROM. Not only do the hardware and software require a significant investment, the cost of the CD-ROM disks can range from about $100 to as high as $10,000. However, the future trend is toward including CD-ROM drives as standard equipment built into a computer, and as more CD-ROM drives are installed and as more and more disks are sold, the cost of the disks will be reduced. These disks are available for both IBM and Macintosh computers.

The choice of available subjects stored on disks is diverse and growing. But CD-ROMs should only be considered as storage for static data, the same as print media. They do have the advantage of requiring much less storage space and are much easier to use to locate specific information than print media.

CD-ROMs are most useful for reference material that you use frequently, such as engineering reference books, directories, dictionaries, atlases, or encyclopedias. They are periodically updated by supplying a new disk (usually every three to six months, at additional cost), so the information is seldom up-to-date. However, they do store an enormous amount of reference information in a tiny space.

Here is a sample of CD-ROM disks available. This list will undoubtedly continue to grow:

- Grolier New Electronic Encyclopedia stores the full text contained in the 21 volume Academic American Encyclopedia and more than 1000 VGA images.

- McGraw-Hill Science and Technical Reference Set—A textual and graphic database consisting of over 7000 articles from the printed McGraw-Hill Concise Encyclopedia of Science and Technology and over 98,000 terms and over 115,000 definitions from the Third Edition of the McGraw-Hill Dictionary of Scientific and Technical Terms.

- National Technical Information Service contains bibliographic references and abstracts for government sponsored R&D and engineering reports.

- Jane's All the World Aircraft available from Jane's Information Group, provides on-screen pictures and the ability to quickly search through the incredible amount of data included in the disk.

- Magazine Rack contains articles from more than 325 popular magazines and periodicals, more than 100,000 articles (73 percent of them full-text) covering general interest, business, health, and computers.

- Time Table of History: Science and Innovation includes over 6000 stories culled from 75 reference works on a time line from 5000 B.C. to the present.

If you have certain basic reference material that you must access frequently, consider adding a CD-ROM drive to your computer. Both CD-ROM hardware and software will continue to be improved in the future, not only in quality and quantity but also in making search techniques quicker and more efficient. But be sure suitable CD-ROMs are available before you invest in a CD-ROM drive.

# Bulletin boards

A Computerized Bulletin Board (BB or CBB), while not strictly a database, is a service that most database vendors, as well as individual entrepreneurs, have established for fun or profit. BBs range in size from setups in individual's homes to the huge BBs maintained by the largest vendors, such as CompuServe and Prodigy. There are over 30,000 bulletin boards in the U.S. alone, and many exist in foreign countries.

A Bulletin Board is an electronic medium set up to serve as a central point for the exchange of information. The exchanged information can range from notes from one person to one or more persons, to long reports from one group to another group or company.

A BB is a public message board used much like a bulletin board in a company or organization to make announcements to a select group of people. All the messages you send to the bulletin board are "posted" on the electronic bulletin board for all users to access and review. BB announcements are usually posted for only a limited time and then erased.

Another important feature that most BBs have is a library of computer software. You can download free or low-cost copies of this software for your own use. Downloading is the process whereby you transfer the software program stored in the BB to your own computer, where it can be stored and used later. BBs provide a wide variety of public domain, shareware, and user-supported software for both the IBM and the Macintosh.

Bulletin Boards are set up for specific topics, ranging from sports, to computers, to astronomy, to photography, to genealogy, etc. Bulletin Boards can exist as separate entities, or they might be a key part of a conference setup as described next.

# Conferences (Forums or RoundTables)

Conferences (also known as forums, RoundTables, or SIGs—Special Interest Groups—I'll use the word "conference") are another important service that most database vendors also offer. Each conference group usually has its own bulletin board that is used as the medium for electronic conversation.

A conference is much like a continuing record of a series of person-to-person conversations in that one user may make a comment or ask a question. That input is stored and can be reviewed by one or more users who, in turn, adds his or her comments or questions. This information is continually added to and provides a running dialog of many user's comments covering a particular topic, or specific aspect of a topic, over a period of time.

Conferences are available on such diverse topics as Aviation, Medicine, Science/Technology, Education, Writing, and Software. And there are many subdivisions within the main categories (e.g., Science Fiction, Poetry, Hockey, Graphics, Non-fiction Writing, Scuba Diving, Tandy Computers).

After you join a conference devoted to a specific topic, the next time you logon you will probably be greeted by your name and be given summaries of any new developments that have occurred since your last visit. If you're active in the conference, you might have messages waiting for you which you can download, review, and reply to as necessary.

# E-Mail

E-Mail (Electronic Mail) is mail that is transmitted electronically from one person to one or more persons via a computer and a modem. Although not specifically a database, E-Mail is an important capability that virtually all database vendors also provide. An estimated 12 million people use E-Mail.

Using E-mail, you can send notes, questions, comments, etc., on virtually any topic over a network of some sort. The database vendor will then "post" your message by storing it in the recipient's private mailbox so that only the addressee can receive the message.

When recipients logon to the system some time later, check for mail, and receive an affirmative answer, they then input their personal password to gain entry to their electronic mailbox and read or download the message. E-Mail is different from mail sent to bulletin boards in that E-Mail is private and sent from one person to one or more persons. Only the recipients who have the password can open their mailbox and receive the message.

Some E-mail systems can send graphics and computer programs from user to user. Many modern companies use E-mail to send information to their employees located at remote locations. One company, MCI Mail, for example, is unique in that it is designed exclusively for the transmission of electronic mail.

Significant advantages of E-mail are that

- it's convenient. You can send a message whether or not the recipient is present.
- you can send it to one person, and only that one person can access your message.
- you can send mail and read your own mail at any time convenient for you. The "electronic post office" is open most of the time.
- you can send messages as short as a memo and as long as a report.
- it saves time, you often receive a reply to a query in a day or so.
- you can contact many of the world's experts in many topics ranging from computer technology to oil exploration.
- you can reach a worldwide audience.

- they are inexpensive to use—for some you pay only for the phone charges.
- it's not essential that you and the person with whom you are communicating be with the same database vendor. Some vendors, such as Portal, have special interservice "gateways" that allow E-Mail to be sent from a user on one service to a user on a different service.

# CB simulator

So named because it emulates the Citizen-Band Radios that permit real-time conversation among many parties, the CB Simulator is the computer version of CB Radio, combined with a variation on Bulletin Boards and Conferences. Your "conversation" on the CB Simulator, of course, is limited to what you can input from your PC keyboard; however, it does permit simultaneous, real-time, back-and-forth typed conversations among several users.

CB Simulator operates quite differently from E-Mail. E-mail is much like sending a letter in the mail. You write down your question, transmit it to a bulletin board, and then in a day or so you receive a reply. The reply might not be adequate, or your question might be misunderstood or even ignored. So if you're in a big hurry, time is not your ally with E-mail.

However, CB Simulator functions much differently in that you receive instantaneous answers. The major advantage of CB Simulator is the instant feedback and interplay you receive. This person-to-person interaction helps you refine and rephrase your questions to obtain the needed information, without having to wait a long time for answers.

Many of the major vendors offer this capability, although it may be designated by different names. Some vendors offer a one-on-one type of conversation, while others offer open-channel or line-seminar types of formats. The CB Simulator is an extremely useful capability that, after using it to make some online acquaintances, you will find more and more applications for.

In the next chapter, I'll cover the importance of making detailed preparations before accessing a database.

# Exercises

1. Which of the three types of databases do you need in your profession?
2. Give an example of a Boolean AND search with three keywords.
3. Give an example of a Boolean OR search with four keywords.
4. Give an example of a Boolean NOT search using two excluding keywords.
5. What are the advantages of using the CB simulator service?

# 5

# Prepare before
# you go online

*Learning without thought is labor lost;*
*thought without learning is perilous.*
Confucius

To function effectively, engineers and scientists must make extensive preparations for meetings, conferences, design reviews, experiments, and field tests. To search effectively, so also must a database searcher prepare before he or she queries a database.

"Think before you act" is a very important aphorism that especially applies to online searching. Proper planning before you logon to a database is essential to not only help you expeditiously locate the knowledge you seek, but also to help eliminate the "frustration factor" of getting lost among the megabytes of information. This chapter will show you what preparations to make and how to make them.

## Signing up

The procedure for signing up with database vendors is fairly standard. The names, addresses, and phone numbers of a number of key database vendors are listed in Appendix A. All vendors have an information number you can call; many have 800 numbers. Also, you can write them to obtain their signon requirements. Some vendors advertise and summarize their signon procedures in computer periodicals so you can signon using that information.

Here's what you usually need before signing on:

- The database vendor's online access phone number, which is different from their information number.
- The basic facts about yourself and/or your company: address, phone number, etc.
- Your preferred method of billing. The most common is to be billed on one of your charge accounts.
- A password that is unique with you and not too obvious so others can guess what it is. Some vendors assign you a password when you sign up.

Be careful when you choose a password. Unfortunately, a few unprincipled individuals are skilled in—and make a practice of—stealing passwords, and then use someone else's account to run up charges. In choosing a password, be cautious. Don't use your initials, or something obvious such as ENGRBILL or SCIENTIST. And don't post your password near your computer where others can see it. You should change your password every few months to further frustrate any unprincipled hackers.

You can usually utilize most of the alphanumeric characters in any combination in a password. It's best to devise some random set of characters, such as RT7UIP, to use as a password (upper- and lowercase are not important with most vendors). And be sure to record your password on paper and store it in a safe place.

Some vendors make signon very simple by providing a "front end" software program that stores and dials the vendor number and gives you a chance to create a password (or they might assign you a temporary password). The database vendor collects and records basic information about yourself. You are then given an account number that will also be used during signon. The front end program stores your account number and automatically transmits it to the vendor so you won't have to input all of the information manually each time you signon. However, front end programs (e.g., CIM) will only let you logon to the specific vendor who supplied the particular program (e.g., CompuServe).

Many general purpose telecom programs (e.g., Bitcom) function similarly and help you generate automatic signon sequences. A script file automatically outputs all of your signon information, including your ID number and stored password (the password is blocked out from you or anyone viewing your screen during signon) so you won't have to input the information manually each time you logon.

If you lose your password, all is not lost. You can call the database vendor and they'll mail your password to you, but it might take a few days to receive it.

## Types of databases

Two basic classes of database vendors are:

- Consumer
- Technology

Vendors that supply consumer databases include databases that serve the general consumer public. Typical consumer database vendors are CompuServe, Prodigy, and GEnie. They cover a wide and diversified range of business, news, sports, recreation, software, and personal topics.

Technology database vendors (such as Dialog, Mead, Orbit, and BRS) have a large number of databases. However, their databases are concentrated in a much narrower and special interest spectrum. Technology database vendors cover the various fields of engineering and science, management, technology, finance, business, medicine, and law.

## Consumer database vendors

Although consumer database vendors cover a varied spectrum of consumer-oriented topics, they also have a number of databases that are of interest to engineers and scientists for both their professional and personal lives. Consumer databases

- are relatively easy to access and to navigate.
- are low in initial cost and in cost per hour of use.
- cover a wide range of topics.

- make excellent practice media.
- are equipped with a variety of both IBM and Macintosh software that can be downloaded.
- are well populated with forums and RoundTables for discussion on virtually any topic, many in the fields of science and engineering.
- have experts available for free consultation on virtually all phases of computer software and hardware.

You should join one or more of the consumer database vendors to acquaint yourself with the varied content of their databases, their format, how to access and download their information, how to search for specific topics, and, in general, how to navigate databases. The basic techniques of access and navigation are very similar for both the consumer and technology databases, so what you learn from the low-cost consumer databases can be used to advantage in expediting and making your technology database searches quicker and more thorough.

Sign up with one or two consumer database vendors and login to their services. Check out what they offer and explore them. Leave a message at one of their bulletin boards, check a movie review, and read the latest news. Just as you were trained in your engineering and science courses, the best method of learning a new procedure is to study about it and then practice it yourself. That's also the best way to learn about databases. And Help is always just a keystroke away when you navigate databases.

Later, as you become more familiar with the processes of accessing and querying various consumer databases, you will be better prepared to investigate and decide which of the technology databases you feel most comfortable with and which have the specific knowledge you seek.

# Which technology database vendor to choose

If you're not sure which technology database vendor has the information that most closely relates to your specialty, a number of approaches are possible. First of all, most major technology database vendors let you search for your topic(s) over all of their databases simultaneously, or over any group of databases that you specify. Most major database vendors also provide access to a computer searchable database index (e.g., DIALOG has DIALINDEX, BRS has CROSS) that helps you determine which databases to access by measuring the relevance of each database to your topic(s).

Another potential source is the appropriately named DATABASE OF DATABASES (available from DIALOG), which provides detailed and updated information on all major publicly available databases. Geographic coverage is worldwide and includes databases in English and other languages. Each record contains the name of the database, synonyms, information about the producer of the database, accessibility, subject matter and scope, and a wide variety of other elements including file size, update frequency, language, language of source material and similar information. Dialog's online database is the electronic version of the printed *Computer-readable databases: A directory and data sourcebook—science, technology, medicine* and *Computer-readable databases: A directory and data sourcebook—business, law, social, humanities.* Both are published by the American Library Association and Elsevier Science Publishers.

# Published directories

Alternatively, you can review published online database directories. Here are some of the most comprehensive:

- Computer-Readable Databases: A Directory and Data Sourcebook by the American Library Association, 1985. Two volumes cover about 5300 databases. Volume 1 covers science, technology, and medicine. Volume 2 covers business, law, social sciences, and humanities.
- Cuadra/Elsevier Directory of Online Databases published by Cuadra Associates, provides comprehensive and timely information about online databases since 1979. The directory lists over 3700 databases offered through 555 online services. Updated quarterly with a complete reissue every six months.
- Data Base Directory by Knowledge Industry Publications in cooperation with the American Society for Information Science (1984 +). Annual. Contains alphabetical listing of databases with subject and producer indexes.
- Datapro Directory of On-Line Services by Datapro Research Corporation. (1985 +). 2 v. A looseleaf news and reporting service designed to provide up-to-date information on the online industry.
- Federal Data Base Finder is a directory of free and fee-based databases available from the federal government.
- Knowledge Industry Publications, Inc. also outputs the IDP Report, a bimonthly newsletter.

# Gateway systems

Another excellent method that will help you select the right database is to use a "gateway database vendor." A gateway database vendor provides an ad-hoc connection, or path, between you and many other database vendors. This gateway hooks you up with up to a dozen different vendors and you can query and search all of the different vendors using the gateway vendor's method of searching.

For example, EasyNet (covered in detail in Chapter 8) is an excellent gateway database vendor. Developed by Telebase Systems, it can connect you up with Dialog along with 11 other online vendors, giving you access to over 850 different databases while still operating within the easy-to-use EasyNet service. EasyNet is marketed under its own name, as well as under a number of different names, including:

- ALANET PLUS on the American Library Association
- InfoMaster on AT&T Easylink Services
- Life Science Network on BIOSIS
- IQuest on CompuServe
- SearchMaestro on The Defense Technical Information Center
- Personal Health Abstracts, ANALYST for GEnie
- REFERENCEMASTER for Master Data Center

EasyNet is available online 24 hours a day, seven days a week. EasyNet charges $11 per search. In addition, databases accessed via EasyNet may carry additional surcharges from $2 to $25, so the total cost for a search may be higher. However, they do provide a running total of your online charges (minus access time) so you can carefully monitor your up-to-the-minute charges.

Many of EasyNet's databases offer the full text of periodicals and newspapers. Easy-Net conducts the actual search and displays the results for you. It accesses these services using a single, menu-driven or command mode interface.

EasyNet lets you make your own choices, and you can select and search any of their 850 databases. You can specify the database you want to search, or EasyNet will help you identify an appropriate one. If you need more help, EasyNet displays a series of menus and online descriptions of each database in case you're not sure which one you need. SmartScan, another search option, selects potential databases to search, based on the search term or terms you input. And you don't need to learn the other vendors' search commands; EasyNet accomplishes most of the command translations for you.

Another advantage of using a gateway is that you don't have to go through the trouble of signing up with the other vendors to use their databases. And if you're searching for an obscure topic and have no idea where to begin, a gateway gives you a wide access to a diverse group of databases.

EasyNet also offers a number of abstract-only databases. Often an abstract or summary has enough information to help you decide if you need to see the complete article. Frequently reviewing the summary or abstract will completely answer your question. Some EasyNet databases offer both an abstract and the complete text.

EasyNet allows 240 characters for a search term. It also recognizes the Boolean operators AND, OR, and a wild card character, so you can string (using ANDs and ORs) five or more words together to make your search as specific as possible.

# Front-end software

Some database vendors provide front-end software that has been specifically created to simplify accessing and searching their databases. This software is supplied by the vendor at a reasonable cost (with some it's included in the cost of the sign-up) and is easy to install on your computer. This software is designed to simplify and expedite searching by automatically performing some of the steps required for the search process. Good front-end software can reduce many searches to basically hitting a few keys on your keyboard. However, front-end software is limited to serving only a single database vendor.

More and more vendors are beginning to offer this front-end software, and this positive trend will undoubtedly continue. Front-end software performs all of the repetitive signon information required to logon. The software usually provides a set of menus that makes it much easier to select a particular vendor's database and to navigate once you are inside a database. These programs are designed to guide you through the search process, step-by-step, by displaying menus of options and by using English commands. They help you select a database and always have Help functions readily available.

CompuServe, for example, offers CIM (CompuServe Information Manager). A windowing program with mouse support, CIM utilizes CompuServe's online graphics format. It incorporates pull-down windows, light-bar cursors and dialog boxes, and has built-in error correction. CIM offers a number of features that simplify much of the navigation around CompuServe. Also, some of your preparatory search strategy can be accomplished offline to save on connect time costs. CIM's major disadvantage is that it is slow to use because of the graphics mode it uses for display. And slower menus mean more time online and a more expensive connect sequence. You can get on and off faster with a conventional telecomm program, but navigation with such a program is more difficult. CIM has much room for improvement and probably will be updated more in the future. I advise that you try both the menu and the command modes, as well as a telecomm program, and see which one works best for your purposes. Nonetheless, I feel the easier menu mode is often worth the slight added cost.

GEnie's front-end program is Aladdin—software that functions similarly to CompuServe's CIM. You can find Aladdin on many different bulletin boards, or you can obtain it directly from GEnie.

Prodigy has an Interactive Personal Service Start-up Kit that is also easy to install and automates much of the signon and navigation within the databases.

Dialog has DialogLink for IBM compatibles, which can also be used with its Knowledge Index. It handles autologon chores and helps you create search strategies offline. DialogLink then conducts your search immediately at signon, meaning less online time. Other features let you capture, store, print, and display the information you obtain in the searches.

Meade also has an excellent front-end program for accessing their LEXIS/NEXIS and other databases. The software automatically logs you on and provides considerable assistance in implementing your searches.

# Basic search strategy

It's difficult to overemphasize that the most important single key to easy, efficient, and comprehensive searching is detailed preparation before you go online. Prep your search strategy in considerable detail. Write down the concepts, your notes, the keywords, the synonyms, and the groupings you intend to use. Check the spelling of all names, places, technical terms and foreign words. Use wild cards judiciously. You will be charged for every minute of online time, and it is often difficult to make decisions quickly when you are unprepared and suddenly confronted with a series of menus or commands that you don't understand. If you prep properly and do your "homework" before you go online, your entire trip will be expedited and more rewarding.

First of all, note and make a record of the vendor's basic commands. You should have available in front of you and know the following information as a minimum:

- The telephone number to call to go online
- Your password
- Your account number
- The procedure needed to logon in case you're doing it manually
- Which command to use to quickly disconnect from the service (BYE or LOGOFF or EXIT are typical disconnecting commands)
- Which command to use to backup one menu

- How to select specific databases
- How to record your online "conversation" on your hard disk for later review
- What costs are involved in accessing the databases
- Search terms that have been carefully chosen
- A planned search strategy

## Basic commands to know

Before you go online, review the basic commands and have them nearby for ready reference. If the vendor supplies a quick reference chart, post it near your computer. The two
most important are the commands and information you need to logon, and the commands
you need to logoff, in case you have to disconnect in a hurry. Also, you have to maintain
continuous contact with the vendor by continuing to input information. Some vendors are
impatient and may disconnect you if they don't receive a response within a given time.

Make sure you do a complete logoff from the vendor's service using the vendor's
accepted procedure. If you just turn off your modem, it may be an expensive way to disconnect. Sometimes a vendor may take five to ten minutes to find out that you're no longer
connected and you will be billed for this unnecessary online time.

## Local access numbers

Unless you live in a remote location, you don't need to make a long-distance phone call to
access a vendor's database. Instead, you can dial a local access number and use a communications service to access the vendor's computer. Typical communication services
available are Tymnet and SprintNet. However, there are still phone charges to consider
when using a communications service, and these can range from about $3 to $10 per hour
which the database vendor normally adds to your bill.

The local access phone numbers are usually listed in one of the printed manuals that
you receive from the database vendor, or you can usually call the database vendor's 800
number to obtain this information. Alternatively, when you are online for the first time,
the database vendor can supply you with a local access number.

## Recording your online conversation

Many telecomm programs have a provision for recording your entire online two-way conversation with a database vendor. Online information is invariably delivered to you at
much too fast a rate to print in real-time. Also you shouldn't normally spend your costly
online time reading long articles or pondering data on the screen.

I recommend that you always activate your telecomm's recording function so you can
save your entire two-way conversation on disk for later review if necessary. If you find out
you don't need the information, it's easy to erase. And if you need it to study and analyze
it, you can print it out later and peruse it at your convenience. You can also use this information to critique and modify your search criteria.

# Cost savings

As long as you are logged on, an online database service keeps totalling the cost, much like a meter in a taxicab. The online meter keeps running and the charges keep adding up as long as you are online. Make sure your telecomm program has a built-in clock that tells how long you have been online. Time sure flies when you're absorbed online.

And, just as a cab driver will charge you extra to take you to special places, so also will a database vendor assess a surcharge to take you to special databases. So time is money when you're online.

Before choosing or signing up with a service, check some of the ads in the computer magazines available at the newsstand or at your public library. Database vendors frequently have special discount offers for signing up with their service and also offer some free online time when you sign up. Some vendors offer discount rates if you sign up for an extended period, while some have special corporate or company rates for organizations or groups.

If the vendor offers an online tutorial or free tour—as many of them do—take advantage of it. If you have a telecomm program that captures all of your online conversation (such as BitCom or Procomm), you can capture and print this tutorial for later review and study. Some vendors market training videos. These, however, have the disadvantage that you might find yourself running back and forth between your VCR and your computer, but they do provide some background and information you can view at your own pace. A tutorial is preferable, however, because it's interactive and the best way to learn.

If you want to send E-mail or some other type of message, compose it before you go online and either print it out or store it where you can quickly recall it and transmit the message when you go online. Make notes of what you are going to do before you logon.

Although some vendors assess different charges for different modem speeds, it's usually cost-effective to use the higher speeds, especially if you're downloading much material. For example, if the cost for a 9600 baud connection is twice the cost of a 2400 baud hookup, the 9600 is cost-effective because you receive the data at four times the speed, requiring only one-fourth the online time. If you have considerable material to download, and if the cost differential is significant, you might be able to accomplish your initial explorations at the lower speeds, set everything up, make notes, and then logoff and log back on and use the higher speed to download your material.

If you'll be transmitting and receiving considerable graphics, the higher speeds are essential because graphics might require from 10 to 20 times longer to transmit than text.

Different database vendors offer identical databases but not necessarily at the same surcharge. Check the publication lists of different vendors to see which databases they offer. If the database you want to use is available from a number of vendors, compare rates and see which offers the best services.

Many vendors also offer reduced rates for access to their databases during non-prime-time hours. Some vendors will provide non-prime-time access to all of their databases, while some vendors limit access to a selected few databases. These cost savings are substantial and worth considering. Off-hours are usually from about 6PM to about 8AM, and all day weekends and holidays. Check with the individual vendors for this specific service.

# Choose your search words carefully

Before you go online, study a "seed" article. Read an article that is relevant to your topic to become familiar with the terms, the names, the companies, the spelling, and the people's names. This can give you effective and alternate keywords to use for searching.

Also, make a list of synonyms and alternate spellings. Make judicious use of Boolean operators, truncation, proximity and other search functions. If the database uses a thesaurus, review a printed version or obtain access to their online thesaurus to find the proper words to use for your searches.

# Practice databases

If practice databases are available, as they are on Dialog, BRS, and others, use these lower-cost practice databases for training purposes before you use the full-cost databases.

CompuServe has a free Practice Forum. There is no charge for access time when you're in that forum, and if you spend some time in learning how to navigate around CompuServe, it's an excellent investment. The Practice Forum is also a good place to test out your hardware system to make sure you have the optimum hookup. In this Practice Forum, you can save time by using commands (GO OAG) instead of menus because it takes time to generate and display the menus. The GO command is a much faster method of navigation. Keep a list of commands near your computer to refer to without wasting online time.

# Compressed files

To save both memory storage space, and to reduce the time required to transmit information, some database vendors use various techniques to compress their files. These compression schemes can typically reduce the file storage required to about half of its original size. Common compression schemes in use are ARC, and PKZIP for IBM files and STUFFIT for Macintosh files. These files are usually designated by a suffix, such as TELLEL.ARC or TELLEL.ZIP for IBM files, and TELLEL.STUFFIT for Macintosh files.

Programs for un-compressing these files are readily available and relatively simple to use. Typical of these are PKUNZIP.ZIP and ARC-E.COM for the IBM and UNSTUFFIT for Macintosh files.

# Universal search procedure

Figure 5-1 illustrates a universal search procedure that can be followed for most databases.

For the first step, before any search is started, select the keywords, synonyms, and combinations that will be used in a search.

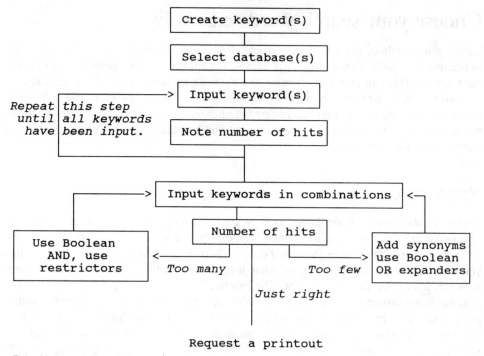

**5-1** Universal Search Procedure.

For the second step, select the database, or the group of databases you need to access. This can be accomplished by studying the database descriptions in the database vendor's literature, or by using one of the database Help screens to find a suitable database.

For the third step, once you are in the database, input the first keyword, or group of keywords to see how many hits result from that search.

Repeat the third step until all the keywords have been input and suitable hit lists have been created.

It's usually best to start out by using each individual keyword separately to make sure that you receive some hits for each keyword. Once you are assured of hits for each keyword, then you can combine them with Boolean logic as required.

Next, input the keyword combinations you have derived in the first step and note the number of hits you received. If you receive too few, use synonyms and the Boolean OR or other expanders to broaden your search and increase your number of hits.

If you receive too many hits, use the Boolean AND, plus other restrictors (e.g., range of dates, periodical name, language, author, organization, etc.) to limit the hits.

Continue with either the expanders or restricters until you receive what you feel is a reasonable number of hits. Then you can request a printout of the abstracts, or whatever type of listing is available. From this listing, you can then either download the full-text version or order a copy of the full document.

# Cost savings summary

The cost of using databases can be significant; some databases cost as much as $200 to $300 per hour, so minimizing online time is essential. Many databases also assess extra charges for display fees, offline prints, etc. However, a number of techniques and methods can be used to minimize online costs. Because cost is such an important consideration, here is a recap of the cost savings tips:

- The most obvious and effective cost savers are to thoroughly preplan your search strategy before you go online and to learn how to quickly navigate once you are online by using the command modes rather than the menu modes. When you're preparing your search strategy, consult a thesaurus for synonyms for your search terms in case you must expand or modify your strategy when you're online.

- Using online services during non-prime-time, although it might be inconvenient, can also result in significant cost savings. And logging on to a non-prime-time subsidiary service, such as Dialog's Knowledge Index or BRS After Dark, provides access to many popular databases at significantly reduced rates.

- Keep the vendor's quick reference charts, notes, and navigation commands nearby so you can quickly refer to them when you need to check some command or function after logon. Know how to logoff quickly in case you get stuck and need to do a little offline research or contemplation. Record your online sessions so you can view or print them out to help you decide what to do next.

- Use the fastest modem speed that you can. Alternatively, you may want to use a modest speed (1200 or 2400) and a less expensive connect time rate when you are first browsing or spending time searching for a topic you want to download. Once you have located it, logoff and then log back on at the higher speed to perform your download at this higher speed.

- Many databases are available from more than one database vendor, and they contain the identical information. Compare costs and determine which provides you with the most service for the least investment.

- If you don't search specific technology database vendors often, use a gateway system—such as Telebase's EasyNet—to access them. That way you won't have to pay for signing up with many different vendors.

- If you or your organization uses a specific database vendor often, negotiate volume discounts with the vendor. Some offer flat rates for files most heavily used and flat monthly and maintenance deals.

- Make sure you are using only the special services you need for each database vendor. Monitor which services you are using and eliminate those you don't use.

- Be sure you use the lowest cost telephone service. Most database vendors offer local telephone access through such networks as TymNet and SprintNet.

- Make sure you do a complete logoff from a database vendor. Sometimes it might take the vendor as long as 10 or 15 minutes to discover that you are no longer connected, and you must pay for this dead time.

- If you're downloading text, download it into your computer's hard disk rather than reading it in real time on the screen. Once recorded, you can logoff and read it at your leisure on the screen or print it out for a permanent record.

- If you're going to upload a message or communication, compose it when you're offline, and then go online and transmit it.

- If you have a large file to upload, use a compression program to decrease its size before transmitting. Or, if your modem has this capability, activate it.

Next we'll take a look at some typical consumer databases and see what they have to offer engineers and scientists.

## Exercises

1. What are front-end software programs and what do they do?
2. What are gateway-vendors and what service do they perform?
3. How do the Consumer and Technology database vendors differ in what they offer?
4. What basic commands should you have available for reference before logging on?

# 6

# Consumer database vendors

*For the things we have to learn before we can do them,*
*we learn by doing them.*

Aristotle

The three most popular, diverse, and largest consumer database vendors are Compu-Serve, GEnie, and Prodigy. These databases serve the general consumer public. However, they also have considerable information of interest to managers, engineers and scientists, and technical personnel.

## CompuServe

CompuServe, the oldest and one of the largest of the trio, has the most comprehensive and diverse selection of databases. Here are the basic facts about CompuServe:

- Subsidiary of H & R Block

- Access via CompuServe network (local or 800 number) or local Telenet number.

- Prime/Daytime service: 8AM to 7PM weekdays. (All times are your local time). Standard/Evening service: 7PM to 5AM weekdays, all day Saturdays, Sundays, and announced CompuServe holidays. Service from 5AM to 8AM on weekdays is on an as-available basis billed at the standard/evening service rates.

- Startup cost around $40, but they often have special signup offers.

- Current time billed in one-minute increments, with a one-minute minimum. Cost does not include communication surcharges and database surcharges.

- $2 per month membership support fee

| BAUD Rate | Cost per Hour |
|-----------|---------------|
| Up to 300 | $6.30 |
| 1200/2400 | $12.80 |
| 9600 | $22.50 |

CompuServe also has an option for a flat monthly fee of $7.95 for about 30 information services.

- Text-based, with graphics in selected product areas, mouse-compatible, has software downloads for Apple II, Macintosh, IBM and its clones, and Commodore 64.

CompuServe has an excellent, easy-to-use, front-end program, CIM (CompuServe Information Manager) for MS-DOS and Macintosh. Both simplify navigating in and around the CompuServe databases. CompuServe has a Practice Forum (use GO PRACTICE to access it) that you can use to practice using CompuServe commands without incurring connect-time charges.

The Top or Main Menu of Fig. 6-1 summarizes the basic databases and services that CompuServe offers. The entries in this menu, and in all of the submenus designated by FREE, are free of usage charges (communications charges still apply). The other menu entries are available as outlined in the rate information earlier.

```
    1. Member Assistance (FREE)

    2. Find a Topic (FREE)

    3. Communications/Bulletin Boards

    4. News/Weather/Sports

    5. Travel

    6. The Electronic MALL/Shopping

    7. Money Matters/Markets

    8. Entertainment/Games

    9. Hobbies/Lifestyles/Education

   10. Reference

   11. Computers/Technology

   12. Business/Other Interests

   Enter choice number!
```

**6-1** Typical CompuServe Main menu.

As you will note from the above list, much of the information is directed toward the general consumer. CompuServe is much like Readers' Digest, a general-interest, consumer magazine directed to the general public, as contrasted with a specialty database vendor, such as Dialog, which caters to specialized interest audiences.

The first time you logon to CompuServe, take their free Guided Tour to become acquainted with the wide variety of services they offer.

CompuServe offers both menu operation and command access to its databases. At first, you'll probably use menus to navigate around the service. However, as you become more skilled at using the database, you can save time (and money) and go directly to the area you need by using the commands.

## CompuServe top menu choices

In the paragraphs that follow, the GO command (which is enclosed in square brackets [ ]) skips over all the submenus and takes you directly to the CompuServe area of your choice.

MEMBER ASSISTANCE, [GO HELP], selection 1 from the menu of Fig. 6-1, puts you in contact with the Customer Service Department to check on your charges, change your password, change your billing options, view a directory of members, review a daily report of events occurring elsewhere on the service, or review news reports for the world of computers.

FIND A TOPIC [GO INDEX] presents an index of features found on the service that you can use to search for databases relating to specific subjects. You can utilize the FIND command at most of the ! (exclamation mark) prompts.

COMMUNICATIONS/BULLETIN BOARDS [GO COMMUNICATE] contains the CompuServe Mail service, a "real-time" CB Simulator, CLASSIFIEDS, many discussion forums, clubs, and special interest groups and a FEEDBACK feature that lets you leave messages for Customer Service.

NEWS/WEATHER/SPORTS [GO NEWS] provides news and sports reports from a number of major wire services and from newsletters produced by various sources, such as AP Online and Hollywood Hotline. The Executive News Service is a special feature providing an electronic "clipping" service for stories of interest to you from the AP, UPI, and other news wires. Local weather reports are available from most National Weather Service Stations and Accu-Weather, which displays weather maps just like the TV stations use.

TRAVEL [GO TRAVEL] allows you to make reservations with three popular full-featured airline services: EAASY SABRE, the Official Airline Guides Electronic Edition, and TRAVELSHOPPER. These services offer the same information used by travel professionals all around the world. You can examine flight schedules, compare fares and book your air, hotel, or car rental reservations.

The ELECTRONIC MALL [GO MALL] provides 24-hour-a-day, 7-days-a-week, free shopping in the Mall with access to over 100 stores and to over a quarter of a million name-brand products. This online shopping service can be addressed by product category, product code, model number, etc. Access to the mall is free of connect-time charges.

MONEY MATTERS/MARKETS [GO MONEY] includes stock market quotes and information, as well as brokerage services, tax and insurance information, corporate reports, earnings, and economic discussion forums.

ENTERTAINMENT/GAMES [GO GAMES] offers a wide variety of online fantasy, adventure, roleplaying, sports, and parlor games that can be played individually or with other CompuServe members.

HOBBIES/LIFESTYLES/EDUCATION [GO HOBBIES or GO HEALTH or GO EDUCATION] offers a wide range of services, from health topics to cooking to personal finance and home banking. There are also health and fitness forums, and features on hobbies, the arts, music and literature.

REFERENCE [GO REFERENCE] provides access to many comprehensive electronic reference services including Grolier's Academic American Encyclopedia, Peterson's College Database, Marquis Who's Who, Books in Print, Dissertation Abstracts, and U.S. Government publications, as well as numerous bibliographic references.

COMPUTERS/TECHNOLOGY [GO COMPUTERS or GO TECHNOLOGY] provides a number of discussion forums where members can converse about specific kinds of computers and software. It also contains a research and reference section and directions for using your own Personal File Area (to store your personal information) on CompuServe.

BUSINESS/OTHER INTERESTS [GO BUSINESS or GO PROFESSIONS or GO INTERESTS] is a database for corporate executives and other professions such as law, health, aviation, engineering, and data processing. Newsletters, periodicals, discussion forums, and a wide variety of information features are available for these professions.

Here are the basic operations for navigating within CompuServe:

- The prompt at which you are required to input a command is an exclamation mark !.
- Every command must end with a carriage return (or Enter).
- Carriage return (or Enter) is displayed on the screen as <CR>.
- Pressing on the carriage return (or Enter) at the prompt brings you back to the previous menu if there isn't a next page. If you're at the end of an article, it returns you to the previous menu.
- T or TOP takes you to the TOP menu (first page) of CompuServe (see Fig. 6-1).
- M or MENU takes you to the previous menu.
- H or ? or HELP displays a CompuServe command summary or instructions for the specific area of the service you have accessed.
- F goes forward a page.
- B goes back a page.
- BYE or OFF disconnects and signs you off from CompuServe.
- GO *Word* or GO *Page* takes you directly to a service identified by a word or by a page by skipping all of the intermediate menus. To go directly to the communications menu that contains communication databases, for example, you input GO COMMUNICATE.
- FIND topic (e.g., FIND Computers) finds all index references to a topic and displays a menuized list with corresponding page numbers.

These commands do not always apply when you use CIM. Instead, members use menu bars, dialogue boxes, etc.

## Submenus

Choosing menu selections from the top menu will often take you to submenus.

**Communications/Bulletin boards** For example, if you select 3, Communications/Bulletin Boards from the top menu of Fig. 6-1, the submenu shown in Fig. 6-2 is displayed.

From this menu, you can take advantage of the FREE Practice Forum that will help you learn what is available on CompuServe and will give you some excellent online practice for no extra charge. As you will note from reviewing the menu choices, a large and diversified number of other useful services are also available from this menu.

**Reference** Another excellent choice from the top menu of Fig. 6-1 is option 10, Reference. This choice provides you with the submenu in Fig 6-3.

```
┌─────────────────────────────────────────────────┐
│                                                 │
│   1 CompuServe Mail                             │
│                                                 │
│   2 CB Simulator                                │
│                                                 │
│   3 Connectivity Services                       │
│                                                 │
│   4 Forums (SIGs)                               │
│                                                 │
│   5 Practice Forum (FREE)                       │
│                                                 │
│   6 CompuServe Classifieds                      │
│                                                 │
│   7 Online Membership Directory (FREE)          │
│                                                 │
│   8 Ask Customer Service (FREE)                 │
│                                                 │
│   9 PARTICIPATE                                 │
│                                                 │
│  10 The Convention Center (tm)                  │
│                                                 │
│  11 Member Recommendation Program (FREE)        │
│                                                 │
│  12 Specials/Contests (FREE)                    │
│                                                 │
│  Enter choice !top                              │
│                                                 │
└─────────────────────────────────────────────────┘
```

**6-2**  Communications/Bulletin Bds. submenu.

```
┌─────────────────────────────────────────────────┐
│                                                 │
│   1 IQuest                                      │
│                                                 │
│   2 Academic American Encyclopedia              │
│                                                 │
│   3 Business Database Plus                      │
│                                                 │
│   4 Demographics & Government Information       │
│                                                 │
│   5 Consumer Reports                            │
│                                                 │
│   6 Computer Library                            │
│                                                 │
│   7 Magill's Survey of Cinema                  │
│                                                 │
│   8 Magazine Database Plus                      │
│                                                 │
│   9 Name/Address/Phone Directories             │
│                                                 │
│  10 Books in Print                              │
│                                                 │
│  11 Health Database Plus                        │
│                                                 │
│  12 Newspaper Library                           │
│                                                 │
│  Enter choice!                                  │
│                                                 │
└─────────────────────────────────────────────────┘
```

**6-3**  Reference submenu.

IQuest, for example, is the gateway to the important Telebase EasyNet Service. Easy-Net will be covered in Chapter 8.

Computer Library provides access to Computer Database Plus, which is a service that lets you search for and retrieve computer-related articles from more than 130 magazines, newspapers, and journals.

The menu also lists a number of other databases of interest to engineers and scientists.

**Computers/Technology**   Selecting the computers/technology option from the Top menu of Fig. 6-1 displays the submenu in Fig. 6-4.

This submenu is the home for a number of discussion forums about specific kinds of computers and software. It also contains a research and reference section and directions for using your own Personal File Area on CompuServe.

```
 1 Software Forums

 2 Hardware Forums

 3 Connectivity Services

 4 Magazines/Elect. Newsstand

 5 Science/Technology

 6 SOFTEX (sm) Software Catalog

 7 Personal File Area

 8 Research/Reference

 9 CompuServe Software Information

10 Electronic Mall Merchants

11 Online Today

Enter choice!
```

**6-4**   Computers/Technology submenu.

**Science/Technology**   Selection 5 from the menu of Fig. 6-4, Science/Technology, results in the submenu of Fig. 6-5.

Note the wide variety of discussion forums that are available at this level. Many of the forum participants are experts in their particular field who are willing to share their knowledge.

**Business/Other interests**   Selection 12, Business/Other Interests, from the top menu of Fig. 6-1, results in the submenu of Fig. 6-6. This section is for executives and other professions, such as law, health, aviation, engineering, and data professions. Newsletters, periodicals, discussion forums, and a variety of informational features are available for these professions.

As you can see from the earlier menus, the scope of CompuServe is wide and varied.

```
 1  Space/Astronomy

 2  Computer Training Forum

 3  Consumer Electronics Forum

 4  Engineering Automation Forum (LEAP)

 5  Ham Radio Forum

 6  Online Today Readers' Forum

 7  Photography Forum

 8  Graphics Forum

 9  Science Fiction/Fantasy Forum

10  Magazine Database Plus

11  Online Today

Enter choice!
```

**6-5**  Science/Technology submenu.

```
 1  Aviation

 2  Business Management

 3  Data Processing/MIS

 4  Media Services

 5  Engineering/Technology

 6  Health Professions

 7  Legal Services

 8  Market Quotes/Highlights

 9  Other Interests

Enter choice!
```

**6-6**  Business/Other Interests submenu.

## CompuServe software download

A diverse variety of software programs can be downloaded from the libraries of Compu-Serve's more than 300 forums. To find a forum that features your equipment, type FIND and your computer brand (e.g., FIND IBM).

Many useful programs can also be found in the hobby-related and professional forums on CompuServe.

Libraries are separated by subject to make locating specific software files fast and easy. If you can't locate a specific program, leave a message in the forum addressed to the forum manager (or sysop). PC MagNet, for example, features a utilities database that enables you to download programs to your IBM PC or compatibles.

To determine which protocol to use for downloading, check your software documentation. If the protocol is not specified, the members or the managers of your computer forum can help you determine which protocol is best for your computer and software. Finally, the online help file on protocols covers the most common CompuServe protocols used: CompuServe B, XMODEM, and KERMIT.

Two basic types of files are stored in forum libraries: ASCII and Binary. ASCII files are text files that can be read in a forum online by typing R (for READ) followed by the file's name. For example,

R Filename.TXT

Or you can download them and read them offline.

Binary files are usually programs, although these are sometimes in an archived or compressed format, designated by a name such as FILENAME.ZIP. You can download them and unarchive them with a program called PKUNZIP.EXE, which can also be downloaded from the forum libraries.

There are two ways to retrieve data from CompuServe: ASCII capture, and error-checking transfer. ASCII capture is the procedure by which you tell your telecomm program to capture all of the back and forth conversations between you and CompuServe. You can then load them into your word processor and read or edit them and print them out if you must. This technique is usually adequate for downloading small text files.

An error-checking transfer is needed if you are going to download a software program, because a single glitch on the telephone line can cause the loss of a single bit that could make the program inoperative. You should also use an error-checking transfer for long text files.

Once you have located the file you want to download, type

DOWN filename.txt

and select a protocol that your telecomm program supports. Your computer will then display the progress of the download—the number of bytes or blocks received so far. When the download is completed, press the Enter key to continue any other activities you want to pursue.

CompuServe will be accessed in Chapter 7 to demonstrate its ease of use and variety of information.

# Prodigy

Here are the basic facts about Prodigy, a database that has over one million subscribers and is growing:

- Joint venture of IBM and Sears Roebuck and Co.
- Macintosh and IBM compatible.

- Access via an 800 number or local Prodigy number.
- Startup cost about $50, special signup arrangements are frequently available.
- 1200 or 2400 bps, Hayes-compatible for IBM and Macintosh.
- Cost per hour—no cost.
- Flat rate of $12.95 ($9.95 per month if you sign up for one year) is charged, regardless of how often you use it.
- Graphic based displays, VGA/MCGA/EGA/CGA/Hercules or compatible graphics card is needed for IBM.
- DOS 2.0 or higher and at least 512K of RAM for the IBM; 4.1 and higher and at least 1MB of RAM for Macintosh is necessary.
- Mouse-compatible.
- No software downloads.

Prodigy is a very different type of database vendor. You have to use its proprietary, though excellent software program, for logging on and navigating within Prodigy. It is one of the easiest online systems to use. You can purchase a Prodigy startup kit at many computer and book stores around the country, often at a discount, or contact Prodigy directly to sign up.

The costs are very low because much of the cost is subsidized by the advertisements accompanying each screen, just as ads pay for your radio and TV programs.

When you logon using their software, you'll receive a graphic screen with basic information on the top two-thirds of the screen and a menu across the bottom that lists the menu choices. They are MENU, PATH, and JUMP.

The MENU command presents a series of overlaid menus for you to use. The first menu, called the Guide Menu, is depicted in Fig. 6-7 and gives you the following choices.

Each of these headings then can be further broken down into a series of submenus to work your way through.

**6-7** Prodigy Guide menu.

```
* News & Features

* Living

* Shopping

* Money

* Travel

* Computers
```

News & Features from the Guide Menu of Fig. 6-7, for example, provides a submenu with the following self-explanatory choices:

- Information
- Newsroom
- Business
- Sports

- Weather
- Consumers
- Extra Extra

Whenever you are in a specific menu and want to back up one menu, hit the Esc key or click your mouse in the ESC icon on the screen.

The Living submenu choice from the Guide Menu of Fig. 6-7 provides these choices:

- Information
- Entertainment
- Funhouse
- Under 21
- Lifestyles
- Health
- Travelog
- Computing

The Health submenu, from the Living submenu above, for example, provides another submenu with these topics: Health Spa, Psychology Today, Health Topics, Health Quiz, and Health News.

The Money submenu choice on the Guide Menu of Fig. 6-7 provides a submenu with these choices:

- News/Markets
- Features
- Credit/Loan, Insurance, Banking, Investment, Real Estate and Resources Services.

The Travel submenu choice from the Guide Menu of Fig. 6-7 provides these choices:

- Features
- Weather
- Airlines
- Hotels/Condos
- Cars/Rail
- Trips/Tours

To learn how to make your travel reservations, an EAASY Tutor is provided.

Finally the Computers menu selection from the Guide Menu of Fig. 6-7 is divided into two major topics:

- Hardware—Systems, Accessories, and Furniture
- Software—Productivity, Entertainment, Education, and Publications

Once online, you can navigate using either the cursor keys on your keyboard or your mouse. Help is always available. You can use the menus or the JUMP commands for navigating. To locate something, hit the JUMP key at the bottom of the display, and you'll be presented with a menu where you can input a word (e.g., software), and then the program will jump you to another submenu to further define your search. Using the Jump screen, you can also page down through the list of all the available JUMP words to help you quickly narrow down your search. Or you can use the FIND command where you type in a subject you're looking for (e.g., stocks), and the FIND option will locate all the places where that subject is covered.

The function keys can also be used with Prodigy. F1 brings up Help, F5 brings up the original Guide Menu or Main Menu, F6 brings up the Jump screen, and F8 the Find.

One other interesting feature is the PATH command, which is available at the bottom of the screen. When you use this command, you can either travel a path through a series of menus that Prodigy has set up, or you can modify the path for your own personal use. For example, if after you logon each time, you want to travel a specific path from News & Features to Computers to Money, you can easily modify this PATH listing to accommodate any personal path you create.

Although most of Prodigy's services are family oriented, it is an excellent service to use for becoming familiar with online systems since it's so economical and easy to use. And there are several services (e.g., EAASY SABRE, hardware and software reviews, financial services, American Academic Encyclopedia, banking, news, bulletin boards, sports, etc.) that are of special application to engineers and scientists.

# GEnie

The smallest of the trio, GEnie (General Electric Network for Information Exchange) is a bargain. It is also growing and has many forward-looking ideas. Here are the basic facts about GEnie:

- Subsidiary of General Electric
- Any computer can telecommunicate
- Access via an 800 number or local number
- 300, 1200, 2400 or 9600 baud
- No signup fee, no monthly minimum
- 300–2400 baud—Cost $18 per hour prime-time, $6.00 non-prime-time
- 9600 baud—Cost $30 per hour prime-time, $18 per hour non-prime-time
- Aladdin front-end program available at no cost
- Flat fee of $4.95 per month for unlimited access to many of its services during non-prime-time (6PM to 8AM, your local time, all day Saturdays and Sundays and selected holidays)
- Text-based
- Has software downloads
- Available for IBM and Macintosh

GEnie has a number of RoundTables comparable to the Forums of CompuServe. Most RoundTables have libraries attached, with software programs and information files available for access. Thousands of utilities, games, business programs, etc., can be obtained from these libraries. GEnie also has a bi-monthly magazine for all subscribers that provides up-to-date information on the latest services it offers, plus other helpful information.

The typical top menu of Fig. 6-8 lists the basic services provided by GEnie. Note that the GEnie Star*Services are available without a surcharge and are indicated by an asterisk [*] in front of the applicable menu listing.

```
┌─────────────────────────────────────────────────┐
│   1. [*] GEnie*Basic Services                   │
│                                                 │
│   2. [*] GEnie News, Index, & Information       │
│                                                 │
│   3. [*] User Settings/Billing Info. Services   │
│                                                 │
│   4.     Communications (GE Mail and Chat)      │
│                                                 │
│   5.     Computing Services                     │
│                                                 │
│   6.     Travel Services                        │
│                                                 │
│   7.     Finance/Business Services              │
│                                                 │
│   8.     Online Shopping Services               │
│                                                 │
│   9.     News, Sports & Weather                 │
│                                                 │
│  10.     Multi-Player Games                     │
│                                                 │
│  11.     Professional Services                  │
│                                                 │
│  12.     Leisure Services                       │
│                                                 │
│  13.     Educational Services                   │
│                                                 │
│  14.     Leave GEnie (Logoff)                   │
└─────────────────────────────────────────────────┘
```

**6-8**   GEnie Top menu.

Selection 1, GEnie Basic Services, provides a submenu that lists the basic services that are available without a surcharge. They include GEnie Users' Bulletin Board and the Aladdin Support BBs. The GEnie Aladdin package can be used on IBM PCs and compatibles; it automates the normal functions of accessing and capturing information from GEnie. A copy of the Aladdin software can be obtained free of charge from this Bulletin Board. Other services available with a surcharge include Entertainment, Travel, Money Matters/Personal Finance, Hobby and Leisure Services, Education Services, Games, News, Weather and Sports, and Shopping.

The GEnie News, Index & Information selection provides the latest news about the service, a calendar of events, an index of the services, phone access numbers, system tips and information, and general information about the operation of the service. It also provides up-to-date information about new commands, products, services, and system charges.

User Settings/Billing Info. Services provides rate and usage information which you can review and utilize to update your user settings, change your password, and your billing method.

Selection 4, Communications (GE Mail and Chat), provides the ability to Send/Read GE Mail, an electronic mail system that lets you send and receive letters to other GEnie users using your computer. Also provided are This Week In History, the ability to send or receive computer files, and a schedule of events.

Computing Services presents a wide spectrum of hardware and software RoundTables that include IBM, Macintosh, Tandy, Apple, Atari, Commodore, and Amiga systems. Here you can obtain expert advice from other GEnie members at no cost.

For air travel, Travel Services provides travel information from both American Airlines EAASY SABRE and the OAG (Official Airline Guide). With these services, you can check schedules, book your flight, compare costs, check the weather, etc. You can also rent a car and book a room with this service.

Finance/Business Services lets you access GEnie Quick News, Dow Jones News/Retrieval, get GEnie quotes, use the GEnie personal loan calculator, track your stock portfolio, contact a brokerage, and get advice and information on business, investments, finance and real estate.

Online Shopping Services provides electronic access to dozens of stores and a quarter of a million products at reduced prices. Products can be price compared and ordered with this service.

A topic of interest to everyone, News, Sports & Weather, provides up-to-the-minute world, local, sports, business, entertainment and computing news. You can also create your own clipping service to automatically select electronic articles in your field of interest.

Individual and group games are available with the Multi-Player Games selection. It provides a mix of old classics and new games, and you can discuss the latest strategies and obtain advice in the Games RoundTable.

Professional Services provides valuable contacts in the fields of law, medicine, photography, writing, religion, and many other fields.

Leisure Services contains RoundTable information covering a wide variety of hobbies ranging from writing to genealogy to scuba diving to automotive to science fiction to movie and book reviews.

Educational Services provides access to the Grolier's Academic American Encyclopedia, and an education RoundTable. Leave GEnie (Logoff) disconnects you from the GEnie service. Navigating through the GEnie system is largely handled by menus and submenus. They have excellent guides for navigating through the system. Even so, there are a number of word commands that you have to use within some of the databases to obtain what you want. In summary, GEnie is a very economical system, fairly easy to navigate in, and has a wealth of information about a wide range of topics.

The GEnie system will be accessed in Chapter 7 to demonstrate the procedure for making an airline reservation.

# Other consumer databases

A number of other consumer databases also offer complementary services. Among the most popular are

- America Online
- DELPHI
- MCI Mail
- Portal

## America Online

This very friendly database vendor service, offered by America Online, Inc., accommodates both Macintosh and IBM users. Menu-driven, it is easy to navigate. America Online (AOL) has no protocols to memorize if you want to send or receive files, no navigation commands to remember, and no dull text-based screens. Their pull-down menus and colorful icons can be accessed with your mouse or your keyboard.

America Online is a low cost service with a $7.95 monthly fee, which includes two free hours of service time per month and 10 cents per minute (24 hours a day) for additional time used. They have an excellent "front-end" software program (i.e., the software interface you see as a user). It's one of the best of all the database vendor front ends. AOL offers a free software kit for signing up, which is available by calling (800) 827-6364.

America Online has a graphic interface: for IBMs, you need either a Hercules, EGA, or VGA monitor, and you also need a mouse. America Online offers a variety of services including software and hardware reviews, product reviews, buyer's guides, E-mail, EAASY SABRE, clip art, online encyclopedia, bulletin boards for technical support, multi-player games, travel reservations, stock quotes, huge software libraries, sports news, and "chat" features throughout. They have tens of thousands of software programs that can be downloaded. One special interest area exclusive with AOL is the Microsoft Small Business Center where you can learn about running a small business. Help is also available from computing experts.

## DELPHI

Another of the smaller, consumer database vendors, DELPHI, is a service of General Videotex Corporation. DELPHI is well-known for its friendliness. They have members not only in the U.S. but in over 40 foreign countries. DELPHI has a $5.95 monthly fee. Online charges are $6 per hour after the first hour each month. Note that telecomm charges apply for some methods of connecting to Delphi from your local area. A surcharge of $9 per hour is added for Tymnet access and $12 per hour for SprintNet access during prime-time. DELPHI also has a 20/20 Advantage plan where you get 20 hours online for $20 and $1.20 per hour after the first 20 hours each month.

DELPHI's Special Interest Groups (SIGs) for the IBM PC and for the Macintosh provide a link to experienced users with the expertise to help you solve virtually any hardware or software problem you encounter. And these knowledgeable consultants don't charge for their time. Delphi has a substantial collection of over 10,000 public domain and shareware software programs that can be downloaded. XMODEM, YMODEM, ZMODEM and KERMIT protocols are available.

Also available is financial information designed both for business users and individual investors. Stock and commodity price quotes are also available. They also have a Disabilities Forum designed for the handicapped and for individuals interested in issues faced by the disabled community.

DELPHI also offers electronic messaging, UPI News, weather and sports, travel (OAG and EAASY SABRE, reservation and information), press releases, shopping, movie reviews, a reference library (Grolier and Kussmal Encyclopedias), and games.

DELPHI also has a gateway to Dialog, which is listed as Research Library (Dialog)($) on their Reference submenu. This Dialog gateway gives you a "pay as you go" option so you don't have to sign up with Dialog to query their databases. If you only have occasional use for Dialog, this might be an ideal method of access. However, you still have to pay DELPHI's surcharge (35 cents per minute or $21 per hour during both prime and non-prime-time) in addition to Dialog's database charges.

## MCI Mail

MCI Mail, MCI's worldwide public electronic mail service, gives you access to electronic mail, fax, and Telex from your PC or terminal. You can also send messages via hardcopy for postal or courier delivery throughout the world.

You can use MCI Mail to integrate diverse messaging systems, collect information, distribute updates and price changes, connect with public databases . . . the applications are practically endless.

Here are a few examples of how you can use this service in the engineering and science professions:

- Send laboratory test results across town from your laboratory to another laboratory.
- Announce your laboratory's new chemical breakthroughs to corporate sponsors in Taiwan.
- Communicate with IEEE members concerning legislation activity and industry news.
- Make travel and other reservations.
- Communicate with a colleague in France or other foreign countries.

MCI Mail also offers gateways to office automation, LAN and PC environments, and has been at the forefront of establishing public network interconnects. MCI Mail can be accessed through a toll-free number in the U.S. and through packet-switched networks from over 90 countries worldwide. Message costs vary by length and delivery method.

## Portal

The Portal Online System is a general-purpose communications service for business, groups, and individuals. It provides online users with a wide variety of services such as international E-mail, Usenet access, Public Domain Software Libraries, conferencing, meetings, and chat lines. Here are the basic facts about Portal:

- Account startup $19.95 (one-time charge).
- Monthly use $13.95.
- Long-distance access through the SprintNet data network, from $2.50 per hour off-peak (6PM to 7AM your local time).

Portal's databases can be accessed by either menus and commands. At first, you'll probably use menus, but as soon as you become familiar with the service, you can switch over to command operation, navigating with GO and the name of your destination, saving both time and money.

Here's Portal's main menu.

One very handy feature the Portal menus provide is that the navigation commands that can be input at each stage are listed at the bottom for easy reference. Another feature I like is that when you have dropped down a couple of submenu levels, Portal indicates the com-

```
---------
Main Menu
This is a Portal directory menu. To move to an item, enter its
number, then Return. To move up one level, enter 'done'. To return
to the top directory menu, type `top'. Type `help' anywhere on the
system for more details.
---------
0  -  Home [directory]
1  -  Using Portal [directory]
2  -  Portal Activities at a Glance [directory]
3  -  Organizations [directory]
4  -  Computer Groups [directory]
5  -  Gateways [directory]
6  -  Meetings [directory]
7  -  Services [directory]
8  -  Special Interest Groups (SIGs) [directory]
---------
page mail help top logout set go done
Command:
```

plete path down from the top or main menu. For example, Main menu/Services/UPI Newswire tells you that you are at the UPI Newswire menu, which is down two levels from the Main menu. Sometimes when you are navigating via menus with other database vendors, you can get lost and forget how you got to where you are.

Portal has gateways to many other communication networks, including UUCP, Internet, and Bitnet. UUCP is used primarily by people at companies in technical businesses and many educational organizations. Internet is used mainly by government and research organizations doing work for the government. Bitnet is used by colleges and universities. You can use the service to send a communication to your professional associates all over the country, and in many cases it will arrive at their desks in under an hour.

Usenet is a distributed conferencing network used by millions of people all over the world. It is useful for exchanging information about many computer-oriented topics, as well as non-technical topics.

Conferencing lets you exchange messages or files with other users. You can carry on a discussion or you can create "libraries" of information. Conferences can be private or public.

Portal has a collection of thousands of programs and files of public domain software and SIGs (Special Interest Groups) for many popular computers including IBM and Macintosh. They also have extensive libraries of online publications from many sources.

Using the meetings feature, you can converse in real time with other people using Portal meetings. When you are in a meeting, the messages you type are displayed immediately to others in the same conversation.

Portal is easy to navigate with its friendly user interface. They have complete online documentation, good tools, and nationwide local access phone numbers. And they offer worldwide communication with your fellow professionals.

In the next chapter, we'll take a look at the key technology databases that serve engineering and scientific professionals.

# Exercises

1. What databases or services that CompuServe provides will be of use to you in your profession?
2. What databases or services that Prodigy provides will be of use to you in your profession?
3. What databases or services that GEnie provides will be of use to you in your profession?
4. How could you use E-mail in your profession?

# 7
# Navigating consumer databases

*If a man will begin with certainties, he shall end in doubts;*
*but if he will be content to begin with doubts, he shall end in certainties.*
Francis Bacon

Scientists and engineers must perform with precision to implement their designs or to prove their theses. So also must database searchers function with precision to access the records they need that are located somewhere deep down inside a mountain of information. An enormous amount of data is available, and it's important to electronically peel through the peripheral layers to reach the core of the databases where the precise knowledge you need is stored. This chapter is dedicated to helping you achieve that necessary precision so you can efficiently and quickly maneuver inside consumer databases.

## Who should perform the search?

There are many reasons why the end user—engineer, scientist, manager, executive, technician—should conduct his or her own searches:

- You are the only person who knows precisely what you need.
- You can apply your expertise to conduct a thorough and efficient search.
- You can obtain the information when you need it, instead of waiting for someone else to do it at some later time.
- Searching is a learning process. Often as you search, you'll make new discoveries, devise alternate approaches to problems, and find answers to new questions.

To illustrate searching techniques, I'll access representative consumer databases in this chapter and extract information from them.

## Using CompuServe

You can logon to CompuServe using either your telecomm program or the excellent CompuServe Information Manager (CIM) front-end software. I strongly recommend the CIM. It stores both your account number and password, inputs them, and automatically logs you on to CompuServe. And if you use CIM, you can use the GO command to jump directly to your desired destination—skipping all of the intermediate menus—and save time. Another advantage of using the CIM is that you can plan and prepare much of your search strategy and compose messages and replies when you are offline, saving connect time and costs.

Also available are other software programs that allow you to set up and basically automate your online access and search. ATOSIG is one of the automated programs that can be downloaded from the IBM Communications Forum, and it's free. ATOSIG allows you to prepare much of your search strategy offline by selecting options from a menu to tell the telecomm program which tasks to perform, such as checking news in designated forums and retrieving CompuServe messages. Another program, TAPCIS, is available as Shareware and can be downloaded. TAPCIS accomplishes similar tasks.

The automated programs automatically log you on with your User ID and password and carry out your assignments, using expert commands, and saving new messages in disk files as it goes. Later, you can read the saved files at your leisure. You can also logoff, compose your replies offline, and instruct the program to logon again and post them.

Here's a summary of the automated programs available from CompuServe:

- ATOSIG, for IBM and its compatibles
- TAPCIS, for IBM and its compatibles
- Compuserve Navigator, for the Macintosh
- ST/Forum, for the Atari ST
- QuickCIS, for the Atari ST
- Whap!, for the Amiga

All of these can be downloaded except for the CompuServe Navigator, which must be ordered.

```
1.  Member Assistance (FREE)

2.  Find a Topic (FREE)

3.  Communications/Bulletin Boards

4.  News/Weather/Sports

5.  Travel

6.  The Electronic MALL/Shopping

7.  Money Matters/Markets

8.  Entertainment/Games

9.  Hobbies/Lifestyles/Education

10.  Reference

11.  Computers/Technology

12.  Business/Other Interests

Enter choice number!
```

**7-1** Typical CompuServe Main menu.

## Logging on to CompuServe

To demonstrate the use of CompuServe, I'll search for articles covering the popular tele-comm software program, Procomm Plus, and for articles that also describe MNP5 as used with Procomm Plus.

After you logon CompuServe, you'll be greeted by some input screens and finally the TOP menu of Fig. 7-1.

Let's choose Selection 10, Reference, from this menu, which then gives us the sub-menu of Fig. 7-2.

From the submenu of Fig. 7-2, choose Selection 6, Computer Library. We then receive the submenu of Fig. 7-3.

```
 1 IQuest

 2 Academic American Encyclopedia

 3 Business Database Plus

 4 Demographics & Government Information

 5 Consumer Reports

 6 Computer Library

 7 Magill's Survey of Cinema

 8 Magazine Database Plus

 9 Name/Address/Phone Directories

10 Books in Print

11 Health Database Plus

12 Newspaper Library

Enter choice!
```

**7-2** Reference submenu.

```
Computer Database Plus

1 What Is Computer Database Plus

2 Instructions for Use (W)

3 Pricing

4 Publication List

5 ** Now with Downloading **

6 Feedback

7 Access Computer Database Plus ($W)

  Enter choice !
```

**7-3** Computer DataBase Plus menu.

Let's choose 1 to learn a little about the Computer DataBase Plus to see if we selected the right menu choice. We then receive this description:

WHAT IS COMPUTER DATABASE PLUS
Computer Database Plus is a service that lets you search for and retrieve computer-related articles from more than 130 magazines, newspapers, and journals. You'll find news, reviews, product introductions and more, in areas such as hardware, software, electronics, engineering, communications, and the application of technology.
    Comprehensive coverage includes popular titles such as PC Magazine, Byte, and MacUser, as well as trade and professional titles such as PC Week and Communications of the ACM. Coverage for most publications starts with January 1, 1987. The database is updated whenever a significant amount of new material is available, often weekly. Every article contains either a summary or full text; many have both. See option 4 (Publication List) for a list of publications in the database.
    Computer Database Plus gives you nine methods to locate articles. These methods can be used either singly or in any combination to find just what you are looking for. Computer Database Plus has been structured to permit menu searching or, if you are experienced with information retrieval services, you may shortcut some of the menus by entering complex search expressions. The result is the same: an almost instantaneous response with the number of articles that meet your search criteria. To help you get the most out of the service, there is an extensive on-line manual available (see option 2, Instructions for Use).
    Computer Database Plus contains both a connect surcharge and charges for article summaries and full text. Please review option 3 (Pricing) for full details. To search for listings of computer and communications products with specifications, try Computer Directory (GO COMPDIR). If you're interested in coverage of health-related topics, try Health Database Plus (GO HLTDB). And if you want a comprehensive look at business and trade, try Business Database Plus (GO BUSDB). Last page !

After reviewing this background, this looks like the right area, so let's backup to the menu of Fig. 7-3 and access the Computer DataBase Plus by selecting item 7. We receive some greetings, then this submenu:

Copyright 1991 Information Access Company
Copyright 1991 Ziff Communications Company
        1 Search Computer Database Plus
        2 Quick Reference
        3 Exit
Last page, enter choice !

Let's select 1 to start our search.

Computer Database Plus
Search Methods
START a Search for Articles by Specifying:
        1 Key Words (words occurring in article titles, subject headings,
        company names, or product names)
        2 Any Words (words occurring anywhere in articles)
Enter choice (<CR> for more) !
Enter word or phrase  (? for help):

Let's select 2 to see if our keywords—Procomm plus—appear in the text of the article. We receive these presentations:

Searching ...

Computer Database Plus
Search Summary

```
Search Method
Search Terms
Articles
Words Anywhere:               procomm plus                    185

Full-text or abstracted articles matching ALL search methods: 185
        1  Display a Menu of Matching Articles
        2  Match Only Full-text Articles
        3  Narrow the Search
        4  Replace (Erase) an Existing Search Method
        5  Widen the Search Using an Existing Search Method
        6  Start Over
        7  Display Connect and Retrieval Charges
Last page, enter choice !
```

Let's select 3 to narrow our search and receive this display:

```
Computer Database Plus
Search Methods
NARROW the Search for Articles by Specifying:
        1  Key Words (words occurring in article titles, subject headings,
           company names, or product names)
        2  Any Words (words occurring anywhere in articles)
Enter choice (<CR> for more) !
```

Because the number of articles is too large, let's narrow the search by inputting 2 and receive this presentation:

```
Narrowing the Search. Enter word or phrase
(<CR> no change, ? for help):
```

At this point, let's add MNP5 as an additional search term, so our search will be made for procomm plus AND MNP5. We then receive this display:

```
Searching ...

Computer Database Plus              Search Summary
Search Method                       Search Terms
Articles
Words Anywhere:                     procomm plus & mnp5         3
Full-text or abstracted articles matching ALL search methods: 3
           1  Display a Menu of Matching Articles
Enter choice (<CR> for more) !
```

The number of articles has been reduced to a reasonable number, so let's input 1 to display abstracts of the three articles:

```
Computer Database Plus              Article Citations
        1 COMDEX: laptop communication trend picks up. (modems and
          facsimile equipment) (product announcement), Newsbytes, Nov 16,
          1990 pNEW11160001. Article # 09624005  -- Full Text
          (3206 characters) --
```

```
2 Putting it on the line. (Software Review) (review of five
    communications packages) (evaluation), PC User, Nov 22, 1989
    n120 pS57(6). Article # 07967290 -- Full Text (17626 characters) --
3 Putting it on the line. (communication software) (evaluation),
    PC User, Nov 1989 n120 p57(4). Article # 08231495  -- Full
    Text (19464 characters) --
Last page, enter as many as 3 choices (? for help) !
```

If you choose to view or download the articles, you could do that at this point. The result we obtained is adequate for our demonstration, so let's logoff by inputting TOP to return to the TOP menu, then input BYE to logoff and receive this signoff tally:

```
Thanks for using Computer Database Plus!
Summary of Charges:
Item                      Number   Unit Charge   Total Charge
Minutes Connected (est.)    3        $ 0.25         $ 0.75
Article Retrieved           0        $ 2.50         $ 0.00
Text (No Summ.) Retrieved   0        $ 1.50         $ 0.00
Summary Retrieved           0        $ 1.00         $ 0.00
Total Charges                                       $ 0.75
Press <CR> to exit:
Thank you for using CompuServe!
Off at 17:48 PDT 8-Sep-91
Connect time = 0:07
```

So, for a cost of less than one dollar, we have located three articles that meet our search strategy.

Next we'll take a look at Prodigy, another of the popular consumer databases.

# Prodigy

To access the Prodigy system, you must have their front-end software program installed. Assuming that is accomplished, we'll illustrate the ease of accessing and using this consumer database by checking on an encyclopedic entry on MODEMS.

When you activate the program, you're greeted at first by a signon menu that asks for your ID number and your password, both of which you obtained when you signed up for the service. After you've input this data, hit the Return (or Enter—I'll use <CR>) key. Instantly, a large WORKING announcement appears on the upper right corner of the screen to let you know that you are in the process of accessing Prodigy.

Next you are greeted by a very colorful and complex graphic screen entitled HIGH-LIGHTS, with an ad displayed along the bottom portion of the screen. Along the very bottom of the screen are a series of boxed commands, MENU, PATH, JUMP, and EXIT. (These commands were explained in Chapter 6.) You can select these commands either by using the cursor keys, or you can position your mouse arrow on the box and double click the left button to activate the command.

Two basic methods of navigating around Prodigy are MENUs and JUMP. If you select the menu mode, the initial MENU leads you through a series of submenus that will eventually bring you to the database of your choice. When you are unfamiliar with precisely how to get where you want to go and if you don't know the names of the various databases, the menu mode is the best approach to use.

The JUMP command, however, provides a quick leap over Prodigy's intermediate menus, much as the GO command does in CompuServe. When you choose JUMP, you're also given other choices, including the FIND command if you need to use it. The JUMP command takes you directly to where you want to go. Refer to Prodigy's JUMPWORD LISTINGS book that came with your software for a detailed list of the JUMP words you can use to access the specific database of your choice. Input this JUMP word (it can be up to thirteen characters) and hit <CR>.

The FIND command is a subset of the JUMP command and is used to show you what is available by topic. You can use a FINDword of up to 20 characters. If you have not chosen a precise FINDword, you will be presented with an index of FINDwords that are close alphabetically to what you entered. You can choose a precise one from that list.

To reach the encyclopedia via the menu route, you select LIVING from the first menu, INFORMATION from the next submenu, and ENCYCLOPEDIA from the final menu.

However, to make a quick leap, type ENCYCLOPEDIA at the JUMP command. We are soon greeted with an introductory screen for the Academic American Encyclopedia and with a blank to fill in to search for our word. So, input MODEM in the blank and hit <CR>. In a few seconds the beginning page of the article is displayed:

"A modem is a device that converts digital data into analog signals for transmission over telephone lines, and that converts the received analog signals back into digital data. Its name is derived from these two functions of modulation and demodulation. Modems are used to connect COMPUTERS and COMPUTER TERMINALS to telephone lines, which cannot carry digital signals, so they can transmit data to one another at a distance. Modems are also able to carry out a number of control functions for coordinating the transmitted data . . . ."

The article continued, but I've only included the first paragraph of the encyclopedia article to illustrate the ease with which information can be readily obtained, whether the information is from a scientific reference book or periodical, a computer club, a news wire, or a travel service.

That accomplished, select EXIT at the bottom of the screen to leave Prodigy and be presented with a signoff screen. Select END THIS SESSION to be disconnected from the service.

This is but a simple example of the power and ease of using this versatile database. Many other services and databases are also available from Prodigy. The best way to find out how this low-cost, easy-to-use database vendor can serve you is to try it.

# GEnie

Another easy-to-use consumer database vendor is GEnie. They have a plethora of databases, not only of general interest, but also of specific interest to engineers and scientists.

To illustrate its use, we'll plan an airline trip from Los Angeles, CA to an American Chemical Society Convention in Philadelphia, PA.

GEnie's front-end software, Aladdin, is available from most bulletin boards, software libraries, etc. Before you logon using Aladdin, make sure you have CAPTURE on (accessed by pressing F4 A and by listing a directory in which you want to capture the file). With CAPTURE on, you can record all of the two-way conversations and review them, or print them out after you logoff.

Before we logon, however, let's pause a moment and review some of the key commands so we have them available for quick reference. They are:

| | |
|---|---|
| KEYWORD or M PAGE# | Moves you to a specific GEnie menu. Check the GEnie booklets for these KEYWORDs or PAGE#s. |
| Ctrl-S | Stops GEnie from scrolling, so you can pause and read what's on the screen. |
| Ctrl-Q | Tells GEnie to resume scrolling. |
| BREAK | Hitting your Break key (check your telecomm program to see which key is the break key) interrupts the display of text or the execution of menu selections and commands. |
| BYE | Tells GEnie you want to end your session. To stay within GEnie's low-cost GEnie*Basic Services, always use keywords that start with an asterisk (e.g., *NEWS) or navigate using the four-digit numbers starting with 8 that are listed in GEnie's booklets. For example, Page 8010 jumps you to the EDUCATION submenu. |

```
┌─────────────────────────────────────────────┐
│  1. [*] GEnie*Basic Services                 │
│                                              │
│  2. [*] GEnie News, Index, & Information      │
│                                              │
│  3. [*] User Settings/Billing Info. Services  │
│                                              │
│  4.     Communications (GE Mail and Chat)     │
│                                              │
│  5.     Computing Services                    │
│                                              │
│  6.     Travel Services                       │
│                                              │
│  7.     Finance/Business Services             │
│                                              │
│  8.     Online Shopping Services              │
│                                              │
│  9.     News, Sports & Weather                │
│                                              │
│ 10.     Multi-Player Games                    │
│                                              │
│ 11.     Professional Services                 │
│                                              │
│ 12.     Leisure Services                      │
│                                              │
│ 13.     Educational Services                  │
│                                              │
│ 14.     Leave GEnie (Logoff)                  │
└─────────────────────────────────────────────┘
```

7-4 GEnie's Top menu.

When you've completed your logon procedure, you'll be greeted by GEnie's Top Menu of Fig. 7-4:

To make a quick jump to Travel, type *SABRE and you'll receive this presentation:

```
GEnie*Basic
*SABRE
Page 8760

        American Airlines' EAASY SABRE
1.  About EAASY SABRE
2.  EAASY SABRE Rates
3.  Enter EAASY SABRE Gateway
4.  Feedback to EAASY SABRE
Enter #, <P>revious, or <H>elp?
```

To find out more about EAASY SABRE, type 1 and receive this information:

```
GEnie is pleased to offer this gateway to the American Airlines
EAASY SABRE system, with no surcharges.  You can browse through
the system, and retrieve flight, hotel, and weather information.
All this at normal GEnie rates. (See Selection 2 for rates details.)
You can set up an account on the EAASY SABRE system, and
actually book flights, and make hotel reservations on-line!  Choose
selection 3 to logon to EAASY SABRE.
```

There was also a lengthy dissertation on the rules and regulations about using EAASY SABRE that you should read, but I won't repeat it here.

Also, as part of accessing Selection 2, the following presentation is displayed:

```
EAASY SABRE Rates: American Airlines offers EAASY SABRE to
GEnie members with no subscription fee, or additional surcharges.
Charges for tickets and reservations will be billed directly by
American Airlines, and will not appear on your GEnie bill.
```

With some more bookkeeping out of the way, input /R to go right to the Reservations Menu and receive this presentation:

```
        RESERVATIONS MENU
1   Flight Reservations and Availability
2   Flight Arrival/Departure Information
3   Hotels
4   Rental Cars
5   Airline Fares
6   Itinerary Review and Change
7   Sign On for Reservations
8   Flight Schedules
9   Specific Flight Details
To select one of the options above, enter the number:
```

To go directly to the Flight Reservations and Availability, type a 1 and receive this series of questions:

```
From what city will you be departing?
```

Example:  LOS ANGELES or LAX
>

Input lax

To what city will you be traveling
Example:  LOS ANGELES or LAX
Feel free to enter the entire city name (up to 20 characters),
or you may type the city code for fewer keystrokes.
>

Input Philadelphia at the > prompt. You are then asked to input a specific code: Most
common codes are

PHILADELPHIA
1   PHL   PHILADELPHIA, PA
2   QPH   PHILADELPHIA, PA
3   PNE   PHILADELPHIA, PA
Enter selection, or another city/airport name
or press Enter to continue.
>

Input PHL at the > prompt and receive this query:

What date will you be traveling?
Example:  JAN 01
(EAASY SABRE can display flight availability information
for up to 330 days from today.)
>

Input July 16 at the > prompt and receive these directions:

You may customize the display of available flights by selecting one or more options:
1   Show only flights with a specific class of service available
2   Show only flights for a specific airline
3   Show availability for a specific airline and flight number
4   Show only flights connecting via a specific city
5   Schedules displayed based on arrival time
Example:  2  or  1,3
Or press Enter to view all available flights.
>

Hit Enter to view all available flights and receive this next question:

What is your desired DEPARTURE time?
Example: 630A
>

Leave about 9 in the morning, so input 900 am at the > prompt. This chart is then presented:

FLIGHT AVAILABILITY
From:  (LAX) LOS ANGELES, CA
To: (PHL) PHILADELPHIA, PA                              TUESDAY   JUL-16-91

```
----------------------------------------------------------------------------------
Flight       Leave       Arrive      Meal  Stop  Aircraft  OnTime  Classes of Service**
1 US1060  LAX 745A   PHL 344P    B     0     767       N       F  Y  B  H  Q  M  K  V
2 UA 48   LAX 745A   PHL 349P    BS    0     757       7       F  Y  B  M  Q  H  V
3 UA 98   LAX 1010P  PHL 613A    S     0     757       8       F  YN B  M  Q  H  V
4 US 648  LAX 1100P  PHL 704A    S     0     767       N       FN YN BN HN QN MN KN VN
5 TW 756  LAX 700A   PHL 447P    BS    1     767       5       F  C  Y  B  Q  M  V  K
6 AA1222  LAX 1256P  PHL 1036P   LD    1     S80       8       F  Y  B
----------------------------------------------------------------------------------
```

**To SELECT a flight, enter the line number, or**
      8   View MORE flights
      9   CHANGE flight request
     10  View FIRST flight display
     11  View all FARES
     12  Translate CODES
     13  View LOWest one-way fares
**\*\* Quick Tip: Select your flight, then choose Bargain Finder when prompted**
**and EAASY SABRE will select the class of service for the lowest available fare.**
**>**

To take the second listed flight, input 2 at the > prompt:

**Please indicate the number of passengers, up to 4, or press Enter for 1:**
**>**

Travel alone, so input 1:

**Please select a class of service preference.**
**Flight: UNITED AIRLINES  48 JUL16**
**From: LOS ANGELES, CA  (LAX) 745A**
**To: PHILADELPHIA, PA (PHL) 349P**
**1   F Class       5  Q Class**
**2   Y Class       6  H Class**
**3   B Class       7  V Class**
**4   M Class**
**13  Use Bargain Finder to locate lowest discounted fare available**
**14  None acceptable**
**>**

Opt for first class, option 1, and receive this notice:

**The following reservation is reserved:**
**UNITED AIRLINES    48 CLASS F**
**LAX 745A  PHL 349P TUES**
**Seat(s): On request   Jul-16-91**

This is as far as we need to go to demonstrate this example. You can also request to see their SEAT MAP and select the specific seat you want. Your next step is to confirm and accept this reservation. To continue with the process, you can check on the cost of the flight, have the tickets charged to your charge account, and either have them delivered to you or else you can pick them up at a local travel agency or at the airport.

    EASSY SABRE can also be used to reserve a car and a hotel room for your trip to Philadelphia, as well as help you locate restaurants and information on local entertainment and sightseeing.

# My recommendations for consumer databases

If you initially decide to signup for and access only one database, I strongly recommend that you first choose CompuServe. Their front-end software is excellent, making navigating easy. The costs are very reasonable, and it has an extensive variety of databases. I am particularly enamored of CompuServe's IQuest, the excellent gateway that has been provided for searching a number of databases from one logon. IQuest is everything front-end software should be. IQuest

- is easy to use.
- has enormous depth and scope.
- is fast.
- has a wide variety of databases available.
- is comprehensive.
- is up to date.

However, because various professionals' interests and tastes differ, I recommend that you also join up with and sample both Prodigy and GEnie. These vendors have many similar databases to CompuServe, and some of their databases are less costly than CompuServe's. Also, they have different methods of access and navigation that you should explore to see if they have the information you need and if you enjoy working with their menus and commands.

If for no other reason, by sampling all three, you will be obtaining excellent training in navigating and searching databases. There's no better way to learn the art and science of searching databases than to go online and do the searching yourself.

In the next chapter, we'll take a look at database vendors that supply high technology information, providing a world of engineering and science knowledge at your fingertips.

# Exercises

1. Create a different topic to search on CompuServe's Computer Database Plus using the Boolean AND function.
2. Construct a PATH for Prodigy that meets your requirements.
3. Which of the services listed in GEnie's Top Menu will be of assistance to you in your profession, and how will you use them?
4. Which of the three major consumer databases would be of interest to you for your personal and/or home life?

# 8

# Technology databases

*There is only one good, knowledge, and one evil, ignorance.*
Socrates

This chapter will introduce you to the major vendors of technology and specialty databases and cover the basic topics contained in those databases. Some vendors offer the identical databases as their competitors do, others have exclusive distribution rights for certain databases.

However, before you use any of the technology databases, I strongly recommend that you take advantage of the services of a gateway system so you can explore a variety of databases to see which one(s) suit you best. One of the easiest and best gateways to use, and the one with the most databases, is EasyNet.

## EasyNet

There are some good reasons for you to use EasyNet:

- It can be accessed via SprintNet, CompuServe, EPIC, and Tymnet.
- EasyNet requires no training or experience with computers nor with online searching, yet EasyNet is powerful enough for experienced users.
- You gain a one-stop access to 12 major database vendors and over 850 databases.
- You can scan and pinpoint the right database before you begin your search.
- 300, 1200, and 2400 baud speeds are available.
- You don't have to go through the bother and expense of signing up and experimenting with many different database vendors to locate what you need.
- A common set of easy-to-use menus or commands is used to search all 850 databases, so you won't have to learn the new and different commands used by other database vendors.
- It's available 24 hours a day, 365 days a year.
- Both menu and command modes of searching can be used.

The EasyNet gateway has a powerful search and retrieval capability so you can search databases from many different vendors without having to purchase separate subscriptions to each. EasyNet is a surcharged service, with the basic search fee being $11 per search. No special equipment or software is required to access the service.

Here are the major database vendors you can access with the EasyNet gateway:

- BRS Information Technologies
- Data-Star
- Dialog Information Services, Inc.
- L'EUROPEENNE DE DONNEES
- NewsNet
- ORBIT Search Service
- Pergamon Financial Data Services
- Profile Information
- Questel, Inc.
- Telescan, Ind.
- VU/TEXT Information Services, Inc.
- The H.W. Wilson Company

EasyNet comes with a group of online information specialists. At any prompt, if you have a question or problem, just type SOS and an EasyNet expert will come to your aid in real-time.

## Menus

The opening menu for EasyNet is depicted in Fig. 8-1.

```
1. EasyNet chooses the database ....... Menu searching

2. EasyNet scans a group of databases...Menu searching

3. User enters a database name ........Menu searching

4. User enters a database name.........Command searching

5. NEW! This Month: Database Updates

6. Instructions, Database Directory

 H for Help, C for Commands
```

**8-1** EasyNet Opening menu.

Use the first option if you're not sure which database has the information you are seeking, you want EasyNet to choose the database for you, and you want to use menu searching. This option selects a database on the basis of the choices you make using a series of menus and submenus that EasyNet presents. It also provides a list of related databases and gives you menu-access to the various scans. The cost of each search and scan is fixed. Once the database is selected, you are prompted to make choices from the menus, and then you enter your keywords and begin your search.

Option 2 leads into the scan feature that allows one search string to be searched in several databases at once. You are then provided with a chart of the scan categories listing groups of databases. Here, for example, are the scan categories listed under SCIENCE and TECHNOLOGY:

- Aerospace
- Agriculture

- Biology
- Chem-engn
- Chemistry
- Civil
- Computer
- Earth-science
- Electrical
- Energy-science
- Materials
- Mathematics
- Mechanical
- Metals
- Physics
- Telecom
- Transportation

From this list, you select a group of databases by subject area to be scanned for your search string. Then you input your keywords. You can use the Boolean AND plus the OR functions to expand or narrow your search at this point. For an EasyNet search, a slash (/) is used as a wild card.

EasyNet then scans groups of databases relevant to the subject areas you have specified. The scan produces a menu that shows you the number of records in each database that satisfy your search. The cost of each scan is fixed.

For the third option to the menu, you are prompted to enter a database name. You then go directly to the menus for that database, or in some cases, directly to a prompt for your search topic. Also, you can use the database directory, Option 6 in the previously shown menu, to help you select a specific database. The cost of each search in this specific mode is fixed. This option can make your searches considerably more efficient, quicker, and more economical by narrowing your search down to a specific database that is most likely to contain relevant information.

For the fourth option, you enter a database name. You can then search using Easy-Net's Common Command Language, which allows you to search on six database hosts using just one search language. This option is for the more experienced searchers. The cost of each search varies, depending on the database searched.

For Option 5, you receive current announcements of all types, database updates. Option 6 provides Instructions and a directory of the databases available. Option 6 also provides terms and conditions for specific databases.

H for Help and C for Commands appear on the bottom of the main menu and all other submenus. Selecting H provides Help relating to the specific menu or submenu being displayed. Selection C lists the commands used to view data on your screen, as well as the commands needed to navigate in and out of EasyNet's menu driven system.

## Submenus

For our example, assume you have chosen Option 1: EasyNet chooses a database. This process eliminates and helps make selections that narrow down subject categories through a series of subsequent menus. When Option 1 is chosen, the next menu is illustrated in Fig. 8-2.

The categories listed in Fig. 8-2 are pretty much self-explanatory. However, if you do have trouble at this point, you can call up the Help function to find out what each category covers.

```
1. Business

2. Science and Technology

3. Medicine & Allied Health

4. Law, Patents, Trademarks

5. Social Sciences & Education

6. Arts, Literature, Religion

7. Entertainment & Travel

8. Persons

9. News

H for Help, C for Commands
```

**8-2**  EasyNet search categories.

From this menu, assume you choose Option 2, Science and Technology. You would then be greeted with the menu of Fig. 8-3.

Note that at this point both the /H (Help) and /C (Commands) selections are still available to expand on and—if necessary—elucidate the menu selections, or are available to provide a quick reference to the navigational commands. If you change your mind at any point, simply input B to back up one menu.

Once you've made these selections, EasyNet will take this information, along with your keywords, and present you with a menu that enables you to search a specific database. Alternatively, it will present you with a list of potential databases, or it will scan a group of related databases.

When your search is completed, you will receive a message similar to this:

Search completed...
There are 29 item(s) which satisfy your
search phrase. We will show you the most
recent 10. You may wish to PRINT or CAPTURE
this data if possible.

Now you can either print out your results, or capture them on your disk for later review.

An example of using EasyNet to access and navigate the Science & Technology database of H.W. Wilson's is included in Chapter 9.

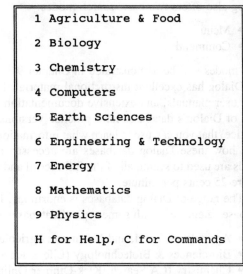

```
1 Agriculture & Food

2 Biology

3 Chemistry

4 Computers

5 Earth Sciences

6 Engineering & Technology

7 Energy

8 Mathematics

9 Physics

H for Help, C for Commands
```

**8-3**  Science & Technology menu.

# The big five technology databases

The big five major technology vendors offering significant engineering and scientific databases are

- Dialog
- BRS
- Mead Data Central
- STN
- Orbit

### Dialog

The world's largest and most comprehensive database vendor, Dialog Information Services, Inc., is especially strong on business, science, and technology. It has over 425 databases, with more than 330 million references to over 100,000 publications, including the complete text of over 1600 periodicals and listings of all the millions of books in the Library of Congress. Here are the basic facts about this megamountain database:

- Owned by Knight-Ridder, Inc.
- Initial fee of $45 per password and an annual service fee of $35. There are no monthly minimums.
- Available 24 hours a day from 1PM EST Sunday to 5AM the following Sunday, 160 hours a week.
- Can be accessed through the major public telecomm networks as well as through DIALNET, Dialog's private network.
- Costs range from 25 cents to $5.00 per minute, depending on the database accessed, with the average cost being about $1.50 per minute. Typical search costs range from $5 to $25, discounts are available for extensive usage.

Dialog also offers two basic search modes:

- Menu
- Command

Both modes will be demonstrated in Chapter 9.

Dialog has excellent instructional material. Handbooks, tutorials, videotapes, seminars, user manuals, and extensive documentation for each database are available. Thirty-eight of Dialog's databases have practice versions called ONTAP (ONline Training And Practice) that you can use to learn what information they contain, as well as to practice and learn how these Dialog databases are accessed and searched. The same English commands are used to search all of the full-record and ONTAP databases. The ONTAP cost is a mere 25 cents per minute.

The range of Dialog databases is enormous. Here's a summary listing of their major database categories, with some typical databases listed in parentheses:

- Agriculture, Food, and Nutrition (Agricola)
- Biosciences & Biotechnology (Life Sciences Collection)
- Chemistry (CA Search, Kirk-Othmer Online)
- Company Information (Dun's Electronic Business Directory)
- Computers & Software (Computer Database)
- Energy & Environment (Energyline)
- Engineering (INSPEC and COMPENDEX*PLUS)
- Government & Public Affairs (Federal Register, Tax Notes Today)
- Industry Analysis (Investext)
- Law (Legal Resource Index)
- Medicine & Drug Information (Embase, Medline, Cancerlit, Smoking & Health)
- News & Full Text Publications (Chicago Tribune, Los Angeles Times, Washington Post)
- OAG: Official Airline Guide (Airline Reservations)
- Patents, Trademarks, Copyrights (World Patents Index, Trademarkscan, U.S. Copyrights)
- People, Books, & Consumer News (Consumer Reports, Book Review Index, Magill's Survey of Cinema)
- Physical Science & Technology (NTIS, Compendex)
- Social Sciences and Humanities (ERIC, PsycINFO)

## Engineering and scientific databases

Of special interest to engineers and scientists, Dialog provides a number of high-quality and diverse technology databases. Here's a list of their engineering and science databases which are divided into the following reference libraries (the content of the individual databases is summarized in Appendix B):

- ABI/Inform
- Academic Index
- Aerospace Database
- Agricola

- American Men and Women of Science
- Analytical Abstracts
- Arab Information Bank
- Architecture Database
- Avery Architecture Index
- Beilstein Online
- Biosis Previews
- Biotechnology Abstracts
- Book Review Index
- Business Dateline
- CA Search
- Ceramics Abstracts
- Chapman & Hall Chemical Database (formerly Heilbron)
- Chemical Engineering and Biotechnology Abstracts
- Claims/U.S. Patents
- Commerce Business Daily
- Compendex*Plus
- Computer ASAP
- Computer Database
- Computer News Fulltext
- Conference Papers Index
- Consumer Reports
- Current Biotechnology Abstracts
- DMS/FI Contract Awards
- Electric Power Database
- Embase
- Encyclopedia of Associations
- Energy Science & Technology
- Energyline
- Engineered Materials Abstracts
- ERIC
- Everyman's Encyclopedia
- Federal Research in Progress
- Fluidex
- Geoarchive
- Geobase
- Georef
- Harvard Business Review
- IHS International Standards and Specifications
- Information Science Abstracts
- Inspec
- Investext
- Ismec
- Jane's Defense & Aerospace News/Analysis
- Kirk-Othmer Online
- Life Sciences Collection

- McGraw Hill Publications Online
- Magazine Index
- Marquis Who's Who
- Materials Business File
- MathSci
- Medline
- Metadex
- Meteorological & Geo/Astrophysical Abstracts
- Microcomputer Index
- Microcomputer Software Guide
- National Newspaper Index
- Newsearch
- Nonferrous Metals Abstracts
- NTIS
- PaperChem
- P/E News
- Petroleum Exploration & Production
- Polymer Online
- PTS Aerospace/Defense Markets & Technology
- PTS PROMT
- Research Centers and Services Directory
- SciSearch
- Soviet Science and Technology
- SPIN
- Standard and Poor's Register—Biographical
- Standards & Specifications
- SuperTech
- Textile Technology Digest
- Trade and Industry ASAP
- TRIS
- World Aluminum Abstracts
- World Patents Index
- World Textiles
- Zoological Record Online

Dialog offers its own line of personal computer communications software for accessing Dialog services with an IBM or an IBM compatible. The "Communications Manager" offers a one step logon to all of the Dialog services, including DIALOG, KNOWLEDGE INDEX and DIALMAIL, as well as other online services. It also allows searchers to display, print, and save images received on DIALOG.

For Macintosh users, Dialog offers "ImageCatcher," a desk accessory that works in conjunction with Macintosh telecomm software that allows searchers to display, print, and save images. Images include design images from the TRADEMARKSCAN-FEDERAL database and chemical images from CHAPMAN AND HALL CHEMICAL DATABASE.

Dialog provides both menu-driven and command search modes. The menu mode offers step-by-step searching through tailored menus that greatly simplify database selection, search formulation, and refinement of your retrieval topic. The command mode features a simplified version of Dialog commands.

If you're searching for a particular journal and want to know which database carries it, try Dialog's Journal Name Finder. This database tells you which database carries the journal and how many records each one contains for the title. This will tell you how comprehensively the publication is covered in each database that carries it.

## Knowledge Index

Knowledge Index (KI) is a low cost, after-hours version of DIALOG. It provides access at reduced rates to over 100 of DIALOG's most popular databases. KI contains over sixty million items from thousands of publications.

Here are the basic facts about the Knowledge Index:

- A service of Dialog Information Services
- Availability: Mon–Thurs, 6PM–5AM the next morning, local time. Weekends, 6PM Fri–5AM Mon (local time), but not available from Midnight, Sat to 11AM Sun, Pacific Time.
- One-time subscription fee is $35
- Cost $24 per hour (40 cents per minute), no monthly minimum
- 300, 1200, and 2400 baud

You can use either the menu or the command search modes. If you can't find the complete article you need in your own library, you can order it online from Knowledge Index. A printed copy will be mailed to you promptly and charged to your credit card.

DIALMAIL, an electronic mail service offered by Knowledge Index, allows you to send messages, post announcements on bulletin boards, and join conferences with other Knowledge Index users.

Here are the major categories of databases offered by KI, with some representative databases listed in parentheses:

- Agriculture (Agricola)
- Arts (Art Literature International)
- Biology, Biosciences, and Biotechnology (Life Sciences Collection)
- Books (Books in Print)
- Business Information (ABI/Inform, Chemical Business Newsbase, Harvard Business Review, Trade & Industry Index)
- Chemistry (Agrochemicals Handbook, Analytical Abstracts, Chapman & Hall Chemical Database, Kirk-Othmer Online)
- Computers & Electronics (Business Software Database, Computer Database, Computer Index, Computer News Fulltext, Inspec, Microcomputer Software Guide, Micro Software Directory)
- Corporate News (Standard & Poor's News)
- Drugs (Drug Information Fulltext)
- Economics (Economic Literature Index)
- Education (ERIC, Peterson's College Database)
- Engineering (Aerospace Database, Chemical Engineering Abstracts, Compendex-*Plus)

- Environment (Pollution Abstracts)
- Food (Food Science and Technology Abstracts)
- Government Publications (NTIS)
- History (America: History and Life)
- Legal Information (Legal Resource Index)
- Literature and Language (MLA Bibliography)
- Magazines (Magazine Index)
- Mathematics (MathSci)
- Medicine (Medline)
- News (National Newspaper Index, Newsearch)
- Psychology (PsycINFO)
- Reference (Consumer Reports)
- Religion (The Bible)
- Social Sciences (Ageline, Sociological Abstracts)
- Travel (The Official Airline Guides Electronic Edition)

## KI technology databases

Here are some of the specific technology databases that KI offers. All are described in Appendix B:

- ABI/Inform
- Academic Index
- Aerospace Database
- Agricola
- Analytical Abstracts
- Books in Print
- Business Software Database
- Chemical Business Newsbase
- Chemical Engineering Abstracts
- Compendex*Plus
- Computer News Fulltext
- Current Biotechnology Abstracts
- Dissertation Abstracts Online
- ERIC
- Everyman's Encyclopedia
- GPO Publications Reference File
- Harvard Business Review
- Inspec
- Kirk-Othmer Online
- Life Sciences Collection
- Magazine Index
- Marquis Who's Who
- MathSci
- Microcomputer Index
- Microsoftware Directory

- National Newspaper Index
- Newsearch
- NTIS
- Peterson's College Database
- Trade and Industry Index

With over 100 of Dialog's most popular databases, Knowledge Index is an excellent bargain. Except for the inconvenience of the access hours for some searchers, KI provides access to a wide variety of high technology databases, many of them in comprehensive scientific and engineering related topics.

Knowledge Index will be accessed and searched in Chapter 9.

# BRS

Bibliographical Reference Service (BRS) is a major online search service that provides access to major databases in all areas of the life, physical, social, and engineering sciences, as well as business, economics and news. Their databases provide analytical, biographical, historical and how-to information covering science and medicine, business and finance, and education and reference. BRS has three basic services:

- BRS/SEARCH
- BRS COLLEAGUE
- BRS AFTER DARK

Here are the basic facts about BRS:

- BRS is a division of Maxwell Online
- BRS/Search: Annual renewable fee: $80, with a choice of payment options. No monthly minimum. Connect rates range from $28 to $139 per hour. Various money saving plans are also available.
- Availability (all times Eastern) Mon – Fri 6AM to 4AM; Sat 6AM to 2AM; Sun 9AM to 4AM.
- BRS Colleague: Individual accounts: $95 one-time subscription fee, $20 per month minimum, and connect charges ranging from $22 per hour to $125 per hour. Group accounts: $175 for the first two passwords and $15 for each additional password, $50 per month minimum, and connect charges ranging from $22 per hour to $125 per hour.
- Operating hours (all Eastern Time): Mon – Fri – 6AM to 4AM; Sat – 6AM to 2AM; Sun – 9AM to 4AM.
- Prime-time – Mon – Fri 6AM to 6PM, local time.
- Non-prime-time – Mon – Fri, after 6PM local time, weekends; and holidays.
- BRS After Dark: One-time subscription fee of $75. Monthly minimum of $12. Connect time charges average from $8 per hour to $25 per hour (evenings only) Operating hours (all times Eastern, except where noted): Mon – Fri 6PM (local time) to 4AM, Sat 8AM to 5AM, Sun 9AM to 5PM.

## Services offered

BRS three major subdivisions offer these services:

- BRS SEARCH, the prime service, delivers a complete electronic library with databases covering virtually every major discipline: health, medicine, pharmacology, the biosciences, science and technology, education, business and finance, the social sciences and humanities.

- BRS COLLEAGUE is a medical literature and information service designed for physicians. The menu-driven system offers more than 40 databases in the areas of medicine. Colleague accepts search terms in plain English, making it a powerful clinical and academic research tool for both novice and experienced computer users.

- BRS AFTER DARK offers an easy-to-use, menu-driven system that accesses some of the biggest and most popular databases (about 112) contained in the BRS Search Service. AFTER DARK is available at reduced rates for evening and weekend users (6PM local time to 4AM Eastern Time).

## Databases

Few vendors offer the quantity and variety of BRS's business, medical, scientific, and technical information. BRS has a menu-driven system which, according to BRS, "requires no computer expertise and no more keying proficiency than a pocket calculator." And they offer you a full hour to get comfortable with the system at no cost when you first join.

Retrieved documents usually contain document citations or full-text. Requested portions of retrieved records can be printed or displayed on your terminal, or the document can be printed by BRS and mailed to you within 24 hours.

You can search all or a specified number of selected databases simultaneously with the CROSS command. This is particularly important when you are conducting interdisciplinary or elusive searches.

User education and training courses are available throughout the U.S. and Canada. BRS also has available a video training course that provides a thorough basic training in BRS search and display features. A BRS Bulletin keeps subscribers updated on new databases, developments, and features.

Here are some of the major databases of interest to engineers and scientists. The databases designated by an asterisk are also available on the low cost BRS After Dark:

- ABI/Inform*
- Academic Index*
- Agricola*
- Applied Science and Technology Index*
- Biosis Previews*
- Books In Print*
- Book Review Digest
- Bowker's International Serials Database (Ulrich's)
- BRS/CROS
- Business Software Database*

- Buyer's Guide to Micro Software*
- CAB Abstracts*
- CA Search*
- Compendex
- Computer and Mathematics Search*
- Computer Database*
- Computer Retrieval of Information on Scientific Projects, Backfile and Merged File*
- Cumulative Book Index
- Current Contents Search
- Diogenes
- Dissertation Abstracts Online
- Embase
- Encyclopedia of Polymer Science & Engineering*
- ERIC*
- Fairbase*
- Federal Register Abstracts*
- General Science Index
- GPO Monthly Catalog*
- Harvard Business Review
- Investor's Daily*
- Kirk-Othmer Online
- Magazine ASAP*
- Magazine Index*
- Medline*
- National Newspaper Index*
- Newsearch*
- NTIS Bibliographic Database*
- Patdata*
- PTS PROMT
- UMI Article Clearinghouse*

BRS provides access to many additional databases covering the following fields:

- Life Sciences (e.g., Agricola, Biobusiness, Fairbase)
- Physical/Applied Sciences (e.g., Business Software, Patdata, Compendex)
- Social Sciences/Humanities (e.g., Arts and Humanities Search Family Resources, Legal Resource Index, Religion Index)
- Business (e.g., ABI/Inform, Business Software, Harvard Business Review, PTS/ PROMT)
- Education (e.g., ERIC, National College Databank, Resources in Vocational Education)
- Reference/Multidisciplinary (e.g., Academic Index, Books in Print, GPO Monthly Catalog)
- Plus some practice databases (ABI/INFORM, Arts and Humanities, CA Search, Embase, Medline, Practice Complete Text Journals, and Social SciSearch).

BRS sponsors training sessions throughout the U.S. and Canada geared towards beginning, experienced, and specialized users. The BRS Bulletin keeps subscribers updated on the new databases, developments and features. And they provide a user's manual illustrating the features of the search system in one volume. One-page summaries are also available for each database.

# Mead Data Central, Inc.

Here are the basic facts about another of the database giants, Mead Data Central, Inc.:

- Subsidiary of Mead Corporation, located in Dayton, OH.
- Hours of operation 24 hours a day, 7 days a week, except for the period 2AM to 10AM, EST, Sun.
- Subscription fee of $50 per month.
- Extra charges for searches, with typical charges being around $35 per hour, calculated to the nearest second. A typical search ranges from $6 to $50.

Mead provides LEXIS and NEXIS, the world's largest full-text, online legal, news, and business information sources. Its vast electronic library covers more than 350 news, business, and trade sources, like The New York Times, the Los Angeles Times, the Chicago Tribune, and the Associated Press. There are 3264 databases between LEXIS and NEXIS and more than 315 billion characters. About 350,000 documents are added each week to the more than 120 million documents alone.

LEXIS-NEXIS Turbo Software is Mead's menu-driven, interactive software that simplifies access to their databases. You don't need any special training to use this excellent software and you aren't required to "speak" computer jargon either. All you need to know is what you want to find. Searches can be as broad or as narrow as you choose, from single files to global searches of an entire library.

Also available is a GUIDE library, an online resource that provides detailed descriptions of all NEXIS and related libraries and selected LEXIS libraries. This is a good place to start with on Mead. There are no search or connect charges for any information accessed through the GUIDE library, only telecommunications and print charges apply.

Mead also has a Practice Library (PRACT) for new users that contains portions of LEXIS/NEXIS files available for practice purposes at special rates. These files are not updated but still are excellent for honing your practice skills.

An Electronic Clipping Service (ECLIPSE) is also available. For a search request you have made and saved, ECLIPSE automatically updates it at daily, business day, weekly, or monthly intervals on related topics that interest you.

Mead Data Central has the following basic information services:

- Lexis Service, the world's leading computer-assisted legal research service, with extensive files of federal and state case law, codes, regulations, and other authoritative legal materials.

- Medis Service is a medical information service with clinical, biomedical, and pharmaceutical information, including Medline. It offers the full-text of over 40 current medical journals and textbooks.

- Nexis Service is the world's leading full-text, news and business information service and provides access to more than 800 news, business, government, trade/technology, financial, and publications, including leading newspapers, magazines, professional journals, consumer and trade publications, newsletters, and international newspapers and wire services, plus more than 2,000 sources of abstracts.

Some of the other services available from Mead are:

- Trade/Technology Files is a collection of publications covering a trade, science, or technology. Includes such periodicals as Chemical Engineering, Datamation, and Platt's Oilgram News.

- Lexpat Library in the Nexis Service has more than one million patents issued by the U.S. Patent Office since 1975, about 75,000 patents are added each year, usually within four days of issue.

- The Lexis Financial Information Service has an extensive library containing more than 150 files of business and financial information, including thousands of in-depth company and industry research reports from leading national and international investment banks and brokerage houses. The Disclosure Online Database is also included.

Here are some libraries of specific interest to engineers and scientists:

- Computers and Communications Library includes Communication News, Computer News, Electronic News, and Technology News.
- Energy News Library provides industry-specific sources and major regulatory decisions from more than 40 full-text sources.
- Transportation Library combines respected industry publications with major federal regulatory decisions and information.

Although the recurring cost of using Mead is high, they have a large variety and depth of archival and current information of interest to engineers and scientists.

Mead will be accessed and searched in Chapter 10.

# STN International

STN International (The Scientific & Technical Information Network) lives up to its claim, "Opens the door to the world's scientific information." STN provides information (in many cases, including abstracts) covering a variety of areas including chemistry, engineering, math, physics, geology, biotechnology, thermodynamics, energy, patents, and materials science. Here are the basic facts about this outstanding international database vendor:

- STN is operated in North America by Chemical Abstracts Service, a division of the American Chemical Society; in Europe by FIZ Karlsruhe, Germany; in Japan by JICST (The Japan Center for Science and Technology)
- Hours of availability: 24 hours a day, 7 days a week, except for the periods of Fri, 10PM – Sat 3AM, and Sat, 6PM – Sun 6PM.

- Costs: $25 to open an account, online costs vary from about $50 to $200 per hour; average is about $110 per hour.
- STN Mentor LAB practice disks available.
- STN Express—its advanced front-end software—is available for both the IBM (with a Hercules or better graphics card) and the Macintosh.

STN provides a broad spectrum of information choices: bibliographic, full-text, chemical structure, and numeric files. You can choose the search technique that is most efficient and with which you feel the most comfortable.

Their databases range from small, specialized databases, such as a 1000-record file of German university research projects, to a 12-million-record file of bibliographic references and a 12-million-entry dictionary of chemical substances.

Here are their basic categories of databases, with some representative databases (they have over 120 databases) listed in parentheses:

- Biotechnology/Medicine (BIOSIS Previews, Medline, Phar)
- Business (Bioquip, CSCorp, CIN)
- Chemistry (Beilstein, CA, GMELIN, REGISTRY)
- Engineering (Ceramics Abstracts, CompuScience, GeoRef, INSPEC, NBSFluids, COMPENDEX)
- Environment/Energy (APILIT, Chemlist, Energy, MSDS)
- Materials/Construction (EMA, Iconda, MatBus, METADEX, Plaspec, Silica)
- Math/Physics (Math, MATHDI, Phys)
- Patents (APIPAT, INPADOC, PATDPA, MARPAT)
- Social Sciences (SOLIS, Foris, TA)
- Training Files (LBeilstein, LBiblio, LCA, LMedline, LPHYS)

Using STN Express, you can automatically logon to STN (via a telecom network), build your text or structure queries offline, construct simple guided searches, and enjoy extra search and display graphics, along with help features.

Scientists around the world use the system to access STN databases. STN software also has a feature that allows a user who does not know the name of a chemical substance to input a drawing of its molecular structure. The search software performs a pattern search and match, in somewhat the same way that fingerprints are identified.

STN will be accessed and queried in Chapter 10.

# ORBIT

ORBIT Search Service provides instant access to more than 100 computerized databases with more than 75 million citations that are heavily concentrated in the areas of science, technology, and patents. A number of their databases are exclusive.

Here are the basics about ORBIT:

- Division of Maxwell Online.
- Availability: EST, Mon−Fri, all day except 9:45PM−10:15PM; Sat, all day until 9:45PM; Sun, 10AM−Midnight.
- Annual service charge for one user password is $45 per year.
- $15 per month minimum for any month you're logged on.

- Hourly rates range from $45 to $300 per hour.
- Operates on a mnemonic command language.
- Selective Dissemination of Information Service available.

Here are the databases they offer (all are described in Appendix B):

- ABI/INFORM
- American Men and Women of Science
- Analytical Abstracts
- API Energy Business News Index (APIBIZ) (formerly P/E News)
- APILIT
- APIPAT
- Aqualine
- Beilstein Online
- Biotechnology Abstracts
- Ceramic Abstracts
- Chemical Abstracts, Chemical Abstracts Service Source Index, Chemical Dictionary, Chemical Economics Handbook, Chemical Engineering and Biotechnology Abstracts, Chemical Industry Notes, Chemical Reactions Documentation Service, Chemical Safety NewsBase, and ChemQuest.
- Chinapats.
- CLAIMS, CLAIMS Classification, CLAIMS Compound Registry, and CLAIMS Reassignments.
- COLD
- COMPENDEX*PLUS
- CorpTech
- CORROSION
- Cuadra Directory of Databases
- Current Patents Evaluations & Current Patents Fast Alerts
- Directory of American Research & Technology
- Electric Power Industry Abstracts
- Energy Bibliography and ENERGYLINE
- Engineered Materials Abstracts
- ENVIRONLINE
- Food Science and Technology Abstracts
- GEOBASE, GeoMechanics Abstracts, and GEOREF
- Health and Safety Executive
- ICONDA - The CIB International Construction Database
- Imaging Abstracts
- INPADOC/INPANEW
- INSPEC
- IPABASE
- ISTP SEARCH
- Japan Technology and JAPIO
- Library and Information Science Abstracts
- LitAlert
- Materials Business File

- METADEX and Metals Data File
- MICROSEARCH
- National Institute for Occupational Safety and Health Technical Information Center (NIOSHTIC)
- National Union Catalog Codes
- NTIS
- ORBCHEM/ORBPAT
- ORBIT
- PIRA—Paper, Printing, and Publishing, Packaging, and Nonwovens Abstract
- Patent Status File
- PESTDOC
- Power
- RAPRA Abstracts, RAPRA Trade Names
- RINGDOC
- Remote Sensing
- SAE Global Mobility Database
- Safety Science Abstracts
- Scientific & Technical Books & Serials in Print
- SciSearch
- Supertech
- TULSA (Petroleum Abstracts)
- UK Trademarks
- US Classification and US Patents
- WasteInfo
- Weldasearch
- Who's Who in Technology
- World Ceramics Abstracts
- World Patents Index
- WPIA /WPILA
- World Surface Coatings Abstracts

ORBIT will be accessed and searched in Chapter 9.

# DataTimes

DataTimes provides coverage from over 640 information sources and the full text of hundreds of newspaper and magazines, including national publications, regional publications, newswires, business and economic magazines, industry magazines and newsletters, plus news from Europe, Asia, and The Middle East.

Here are the basic facts about DataTimes:

- Subscriber initiation fee: $85.00 (one time)
- Costs range from $1.21 to $1.65 per minute at 2400 baud (lower for lower baud rates) and a $75 per month service fee; or $1.94 to $2.60 per minute at 2400 baud (lower for lower baud rates) and a $15 per month service fee

- Coverage for over 250 regional publications from 42 states and the District of Columbia
- Seven News and Press Releases services, including Dow Jones News Service and Business Wire, can be searched simultaneously

DataTimes provides coverage of 10 wire services including The Associated Press and U.S. Newswire. Their national publication coverage includes Barron's, Forbes, Fortune, and The Wall Street Journal. Dow Jones quotes are available, as is considerable company and industry information, including Standard and Poors. Regional publications include the Tucson Citizen, The Orange County Register, and The Dallas Morning News.

Coverage in the Science and Technology section of DataTimes includes:

- The Daily and Sunday Telegraph
- The Economist
- Financial Times Business Reports: Technology
- New Scientist Coverage in the General Services section includes:
- Academic American Encyclopedia
- Magill Book Reviews
- Official Airline Guide
- Peterson's College Selection Service
- Sports Report
- Weather Report.

All of these sources may be searched by company, individual, date, or keyword combinations. Several databases can be searched simultaneously using their global search technique.

# Dow Jones news retrieval

News Retrieval was begun in 1974 to provide news and stock market data. It has expanded considerably since its start and now offers access to business and financial information, real-time news, sports, weather, and movie reviews. It remains especially strong in financial affairs, but also supplies business and technical information in many areas, including personal computing.

Basic facts about the service:

- Owned by Dow Jones & Company, Inc.
- $29.95 start-up fee per account.
- Three free hours to be used within 30 days of signing on.
- $18 annual service fee waived the first year
- Hours of customer service operation: Mon–Fri, 8AM to midnight (EST); Sat, 9AM–6PM (EST)

Here's the master menu that lists the major services available. Some typical databases are listed in parentheses:

- Business and World Newswires (Dow Jones News, Dow Jones International News)

- Dow Jones Text Library (The Wall Street Journal, Business Week, McGraw Hill Library of 25 trade publications, and more than 1000 national, regional, local, and industry publications)
- Company/Industry Information (Dun & Bradstreet, SEC filings, earnings forecasts, analysts' reports)
- Quotes, Statistics, & Commentary (Current quotes, real-time and historical quotes, Wall Street Week transcripts)
- General Services (Book Reviews, Academic American Encyclopedia, Peterson's College Guide, Electronic Mail and Communications, OAG travel services, Sports, Shopping and Weather)
- Customized Information (Clipping service searches hundreds of publications and seven newswire services and retrieves pertinent articles on your topic for forwarding to your personal letter folder for later viewing)

## DowQuest

News Retrieval offers an excellent and innovative service called DowQuest. This unique idea utilizes 32,000 processors to simultaneously search their DowQuest databases. Each processor is responsible for searching only eight or nine articles of the hundreds of thousands of articles written in recent months. The result is lightning speed in your retrievals.

Information in this service comes from more than 350 sources of current business information including The Wall Street Journal, Barron's, Fortune, Forbes, Business Week, Money, The Washington Post and other influential national and regional publications.

Not only is speed a major feature of this service, DowQuest has been designed to respond to search words entered in plain English, such as "Which disposal methods approved by Department of Something?" or a string of words such as COMPUTER SOFTWARE REGULATION GOVERNMENT LEGISLATION. (Note that Boolean operators are not required). DowQuest will quickly search the databases and return with the headlines of articles with the highest incidence of hits from the phrase you entered listed first, then the other headlines in decreasing order. By reviewing and analyzing these headlines, you can then narrow your search down to the one or more articles that pertain to your specific topic, or you can choose to read an article that looks promising.

DowQuest is very easy to use and doesn't require that you learn complex commands. As long as you phrase your question clearly and with a minimum of surplus words (don't use "and," "the," "on," etc.), your search will be thorough, efficient, and quick. DowQuest is updated at 6AM (EST) Monday through Friday. Articles from most publications date back about six months.

## Dow Jones News/Retrieval after hours

Dow Jones News/Retrieval also offers a low-cost After Hours/Flat Fee Plan that provides unlimited access to six of their more popular databases during off-peak hours. The cost for this service is $25 per month. The off-peak hours are:

- 9:01 PM your local time to 6 AM EST, Mon–Fri
- All day Saturday and Sunday and on the six holidays observed by Dow Jones.

Access is provided to the following databases:

- //DJNEWS-Dow Jones News-Stories from Dow Jones News Service, The Wall Street Journal, Barron's, and the Canadian Dow Jones News Service available within seconds of distribution and back as far as 90 days.
- //CQ, //CQE, and //HQ (Current and historical quotes)
- //DJA-Historical Dow Jones Averages
- //SYMBOL-Dow Jones News/Retrieval Symbols Directory—A comprehensive online listing of the symbols and used with Dow Jones/Retrieval databases, updated daily.
- //FUTURES—includes commodities and financial futures quotes as well as the Dow Jones Equity Market and Industry Group Indexes.

# The EPIC Service

The EPIC Service is provided by OCLC (Online Computer Library Center, Inc.). EPIC provides subject access and Boolean searching of a variety of online databases. Here are the basic facts about the service:

- Located in Dublin, Ohio.
- System hours are 6AM to 11PM ET Monday through Friday, 8AM to 8PM Saturday, and 8AM to 12 Noon Sunday.
- Annual fee is $75 or $37.50 for OCLC members (An OCLC member is an institution that contributes to the Online Union Catalog.)
- Hourly rate is $95 per hour, or $24 for OCLC members
- Support is available at (800) 848-5800
- Computer-based training course available for $6
- Practice database available at a low cost

Their Online Union Catalog, EPIC's premier database, contains an incredible 23 million bibliographic records dating back to 2150 B.C. It is updated daily and contains records for the following types of materials: books, serials, sound recordings, musical scores, audiovisual media, maps, archives and manuscripts, and computer files.

EPIC also provides access to the ERIC (Educational Resources Information Center) database. ERIC consists of annotated references to nonjournal material issued in the monthly Resources in Education (RIE) and to journal articles issued in the monthly Current Index to Journals in Education (CIJE). This database contains references to unpublished technical reports, research reports, educational material and library science. It is updated monthly.

The Book Data database is a bibliographic database covering the publication status of British and an increasing number of North American published books. Records contain bibliographic citations, publication status, availability, short and long abstracts, and subject headings.

The Dissertation Abstracts database covers the complete range of academic subjects appearing in dissertations accepted at accredited institutions since 1861. In addition, master theses, British dissertations, Canadian dissertations and other European dissertations have been indexed selectively. Abstracts are included for doctoral dissertation records beginning July 1980 and for masters theses beginning in the Spring of 1988. It is updated monthly.

The Business Dateline database focuses on regional information vital to business. It contains the full text of selected articles from regional business publications, press releases from Business Wire, and articles from major newspapers. It is updated weekly.

ABI/Inform, the GPO Monthly Catalog, Consumers Index, BIOSIS Previews, GeoRef, Newspaper Abstracts, and Reader's Guide to Periodicals are some of the databases currently available. You can also connect to the EasyNet Gateway Service, which provides access to more than 450 databases offered by five major vendors through EPIC. The costs of EasyNet searches vary by database and the type of command/menu access used. (The average price of a menu interface search is $3).

EPIC will be accessed and searched in Chapter 10.

# NewsNet

NewsNet's technology is business news. They deliver timely, in-depth inside information from over 550 industry newsletters and wire services (such as Reuters and UPI) on companies, products, technologies, and trends covering over 35 industries and professions. About half of their databases are not available elsewhere online.

Here are the basics about NewsNet:

- Annual subscription $120, Monthly $15.
- Connect rates—300 and 1200 baud, $60 per hour. 2400 baud—$90 per hour
- Access available to Dun & Bradstreet Business Credit Services Database
- TRW credit reports are available online

News topics specifically of interest to the engineering and scientific professions are located in the following categories (some typical databases are listed in parentheses):

- Aerospace and Aviation (Aerospace Electronics Business, Space Business News)
- Biotechnology (Applied Genetic News)
- Building and Construction (Energy Design Update)
- Chemical (The Chemical Monitor)
- Defense (Advanced Military Computing)
- Electronics and Computing (Electronic Engineering Times)
- Energy (Coal Outlook)
- General Business (Corporate Jobs Outlook!)
- Management (Management Matters)
- Manufacturing (Advanced Manufacturing Technology)
- Research and Development (Inside R&D)
- Telecommunications (Fiber Optic News)

They also cover a wide spectrum of related news ranging from Advertising and Marketing, to Investex, to Taxation, to Transport and Shipping, to Investments, to Telecommunications.

Newsnet will be accessed in Chapter 10.

# VU/TEXT

The largest U.S. online newspaper collection is VU/TEXT. This source offers the full-text of more than 70 U.S. newspapers, 9 major magazine databases, over 320 regional business journals and magazines, and five worldwide news and business wires.

Here are the basic facts about VU/TEXT:

- It is a division of DIALOG Information Services, Inc., and a Knight-Ridder Company.
- Complete, full text stories are available
- More than half of the newspapers are exclusive, not available anywhere else.
- The full text of most newspapers and all newswires is available within 24 hours.
- One-time fee of $50 is charged for accessing VU/TEXT, it often has special sign-up offers. Different options are available, depending on how much you use the service.
- Hourly rates range from $1.90 to $2.60 per minute.
- Training databases are available for 9 cents per minute.

You can restrict your search to locate exactly what you want. You can search for a particular newspaper section, date, or reporter. You can search databases individually, by region, by state, or even by year.

VU/TEXT stores the text from almost every major U.S. city and many medium-sized towns. You can usually download issues going back two to four years. Some go back as far as ten years.

VU/TEXT coverage is extensive. They have the full text of such national newspapers as the Christian Science Monitor, regional newspapers such as the Chicago Tribune and the Philadelphia Inquirer, and others in the U.S. and Canada. Magazine databases include Fortune, Life, and Time. The newspapers are usually updated within 24−48 hours, while the magazines are updated within seven to ten days.

# Clip-art databases

A unique type of database is available that provides a variety of clip-art images. If you use clip art in your work, Adonis Corporation offers a Clip Art Window Shopper that has a library of 20,000 "thumbnails" or low-resolution, postage-stamp-size versions of the original clip art. This Window Shopper is essentially a catalog depicting samples of the full-size art. This provides access to a large variety of clip art images from 16 different publishers, and you only have to pay for the few images that you choose to use.

Keyword searching is available to help zero in on the catalog and to locate the category of clip art you're interested in. For example, you could input "cat" and be shown the thumbnails that fall under that category. After selecting the specific clip art you want, you can go online and download the clip art at rates of up to 9600 bps. Individual images range in size from 3K for silhouettes to 50K for complex images. The average time to download at 2400 bps is between two and four minutes.

The one-time signup fee is $49.95 and the annual fee is $35. Individual images range in cost from $1 to $18 each, with an average image download of $6.50. For additional information, contact

The Adonis Corporation
12310 NE 8th St.
Bellevue, WA 98005
(206) 451-4742.

The next two chapters will access and search some of the more popular and useful technology and technology-related databases.

# Exercises

1. Of the database vendors that EasyNet can access, which will be useful to you in your profession?
2. Which Dialog databases are of the most application in your profession?
3. Of all the database vendors in this chapter, which one has the most databases that are useful for your purposes?
4. What type of information do you expect to receive from these databases?
5. What types of newstories—of the type offered by Dow Jones, NewsNet and VU/TEXT—would you need to search for and access for your profession?

# 9

# Navigating technology databases

*Knowledge is power.*
Francis Bacon

For much of your scientific and engineering assignments, you will be accessing and searching technology databases. Because of continuing advances in technology, there is perhaps no other profession in which having access to the latest information can result in the success or failure of a project than it is for science and engineering. And the best sources of up-to-date, comprehensive, and accurate information are the online technology databases.

However, there is so much information available that some scientists maintain that it takes less time to perform an experiment than it would take to manually search the mountains of available literature to see if it has been done before. But modern databases are resolving this problem, eliminating the need for manual searches, providing the needed data in minutes.

This chapter covers typical technology database searches to illustrate the accuracy, variety, and depth of coverage, along with the speed and low cost of retrieving the latest information for virtually any branch of technology.

The following technology databases will be accessed and searched in this chapter:

- H.W. Wilson via EasyNet
- Dialog
- Knowledge Index
- Orbit

## Telebase EasyNet

EasyNet, with its access to over 850 databases, is an easy system to use and gives you the opportunity to query twelve major database vendors without having to sign up with any of the twelve.

Before logging on to EasyNet, here's some of the basic commands to keep handy:

| | |
|---|---|
| B | Backup one menu |
| M | Return to the Main Menu |
| L | Logoff |

^S/^Q    Stop/Start (^S is Ctrl-S and ^Q is Ctrl-Q)

H        Help

SOS      This is a special command you can input to receive online human assistance.
         An expert will come online and help you with your search, an excellent fea-
         ture.

To illustrate the use of EasyNet, let's search the Applied Science and Technology
database of H.W. Wilson on the topic of conducting polymers. Let's assume we want to
locate a specific article authored by F. Gauterin.

One very effective technique to keep in mind when creating search terms for EasyNet
is the use of / (forward slash) as a wild character. So let's use the root search terms conduct / and polymer/ so our search will cover both the singular and plural of these search
terms, plus any other derivative forms.

After logging on to EasyNet, we receive this Main Menu. (To save space, I've left out
some of the greetings and front matter that appear when you logon):

```
+ ------------------------------------------------------------- +
|                                                               |
|       WELCOME TO EASYNET                                      |
|                                                               |
|    (c) 1991 Telebase Systems, Inc.                           |
|        U.S. Patent No. 4,774,655                             |
|    The Knowledge Gateway (sm) Company                        |
|                                                               |
|        Customer Service                                      |
|         1-800-421-7616                                       |
|        (in PA 215-526-2835)                                  |
|                                                               |
+ ------------------------------------------------------------- +


  Logon XXXXXXX 19Sep91 17:56 EST

  PRESS    TO SELECT * Main Menu *

  1 EasyNet chooses a database .........................Menu searching
  2 EasyNet scans a group of databases................Menu searching
  3 Enter a database name ...................................Menu searching
  4 Enter a database name .............. Common Command searching
  5 Investment ANALY$T................. Stock quotes, reports & news
  6 Instructions, Database directory
  7 NEW! This Month: OmniNews; Database Updates
  H for Help,  C for Commands
  Total charges thus far:   $0.25
  ->
```

Because we already know the name of the database, input 3 at the arrow prompt. We then
receive this query:

```
  Please enter the database name as you know it. (Use B to back up.)
  ->
```

Let's input Applied Science and Technology Index at the arrow prompt. We then receive these displays as the search is conducted:

Searching.....................................................

* APPLIED SCIENCE AND TECHNOLOGY INDEX *

PRESS TO SELECT
    1     By subject words
    2     By author name
    3     By publication year
H for Help, C for Commands
Total charges thus far:  $0.25
->

Because we're going to make a subject search, let's input 1. This display will appear:

* ENTER SUBJECT WORDS *

SEARCH TIPS:  Omit punctuation except the hyphen (-) and small
              common words  (examples: the, of, for, on, in, to, a, an).
SEARCH EXAMPLES:  laser/ fault-toleran/ and network/
Type H for more help and examples.
ENTER SUBJECT WORDS
->

Let's input conduct/ polymer/ as our search terms. We get this query:

Is:  CONDUCT/ POLYMER/
Correct ? (Yes/No) ->

Note that you are given an opportunity to double-check your input to make sure you didn't make any errors before you begin your search—an excellent feature. Input Y to verify that the search terms are correct. We then see this menu:

PRESS TO SELECT
    1     Narrow your search  (add more fields)
    2     Begin your search now
H for Help, C for Commands
Total charges thus far:  $1.25
->

To further narrow the search, input 1. We get this information:

* APPLIED SCIENCE AND TECHNOLOGY INDEX *

PRESS TO SELECT
    1     By subject words
    2     By author name
    3     By publication year
H for Help, C for Commands
Total charges thus far:  $1.25
->

To narrow the search still further, input 2 so we can limit the search by author name:

* ENTER AUTHOR NAME *

SEARCH TIPS: Enter the last name, a comma and a space, then the
            first initial and the WILD LETTER slash (/); include punctuation.
SEARCH EXAMPLES: Gianelli, J/
                          Smith-Magowan, D/
Type H for more help and examples.
ENTER AN AUTHOR NAME
->

Let's input Gauterin, F/ as the author:

Is:  GAUTERIN, F/
Correct ? (Yes/No) ->

Input y to verify that the author's name is correct.

PRESS  TO SELECT
    1     Narrow your search  (add more fields)
    2     Begin your search now
H for Help,  C  for Commands
Total charges thus far:  $1.50
->

Because we are now ready to begin the search, input 2 to begin the search. We receive this display:

System is searching the Applied Science & Technology Index database,
copyrighted 1991  by H.W. Wilson Company, New York, NY and available
through Wilsonline.

        Accessing Network.............................. Completed.
        Accessing Database Host ...................... Completed.
        Logging on ........................................ Completed.
        Selecting Database ............................ Completed.
        Submitting Search .............................. Completed.
        There are 1 item(s) that satisfy your search phrase.
        You may want to PRINT or CAPTURE this data if possible
        Heading # 1          Searched: 09-19-1991  18:03
        ^S/^Q: stop/start; ^T: Paging OFF; ^C/(esc): interrupt
        (^ = CTRL/CONTROL key)
        Poled polymers for optical testing of electrical circuits
        Gauterin, F.
        Jager, D.
        bibl diags
        Journal of Applied Physics 70:1656-9 Ag 1 '91
        Language: English
        Subject heading: Conductive polymers
        Subject heading: Electrooptics
        Subject heading: Electric fields
        Subject heading: Refractive index/Measurement
        BAST91044026

```
910917
Article   Press (return) to continue...
->
```

Hit Return (Enter) to continue. We then see this display:

```
PRESS TO SELECT
    1     Review results again
    5     Start a new search
    6     Leave System
Total charges thus far:  $11.75
->
```

At this point, the sample search has been completed, so we select 6 to logoff, receive a listing of the charges incurred, plus a final greeting:

```
Charges:
System Access:  $1.75
Database Charges:
       1 Searches:  $10.00
Total Charges:  $11.75
Logoff XXXXXXX 19Sep91 18:03 EST
Thank you for using EasyNet KGC-4
```

# Dialog

The giant of the online technology vendors, Dialog has an awesome and varied selection of databases. They have both a menu and a command search mode of operation. The menu system is much easier to use but is slower.

The command mode provides a large number of sophisticated search techniques that are difficult to learn, but once learned they enable you to quickly zero in on any specific topic in a short amount of time and for a minimum cost.

To illustrate the difference between the two modes, a typical search will be made first using the Menu Mode to search one of the ONTAP databases that Dialog has available for training. Then the Command Mode will be used. The cost of using the ONTAP databases is low, 25 cents a minute, and they have a wide variety of records in these practice databases. The ONTAP databases contain a limited range and number of records from the larger files bearing the same name. However, they are searched in precisely the same manner as are the up-to-date files on Dialog.

For example, the ONTAP CA SEARCH database has information only from September 1 through December 5, 1977. But, when learning how to search, the fact that the information is outdated is not important. What is important is the opportunity to apply all of the various techniques that are available to search for information. The basic search techniques do not change, no matter how old or new the data is.

So, let's search the ONTAP CA SEARCH database. This time let's look into a topic dealing with paper chromatography. Let's search to find out what information this database has on this topic.

## Menu search on DIALOG

After logging on, you will be given HOMEBASE automatically. You will receive this starting menu:

```
SYSTEM:HOME
*** DIALOG HOMEBASE Main Menu ***

Enter an option number and press ENTER to view information on any item
listed below; enter a BEGIN command to search in a different database.

     1     Announcements (new databases, price changes, etc.)
     2     DIALOG HOMEBASE Features
     3     DIALOG Free File of the Month
     4     DIALOG Database Information and Rates
     5     Database Selection (DIALINDEX/OneSearch Categories)
     6     DIALOG Command Descriptions
     7     DIALOG Training Schedules and Seminar Descriptions
     8     DIALOG Services
     9     Begin DIALOG Menus (sm)
     10    Begin DIALOG Business Connection (r)
     Enter an option number or a BEGIN command and press ENTER.
     /H = Help      /L = Logoff      /NOMENU = Command Mode
     ?
```

Note that some of the key commands are listed at the bottom of the menu for ready reference, which is an excellent feature. Input 9 at the ? prompt to select the Begin DIALOG Menus. We receive this presentation, listing the various subject categories available:

```
SYSTEM:MENUS
DIALOG MENUS (sm) Main Menu

Choose a subject CATEGORY by entering an option NUMBER. Select a
DATABASE by entering its acronym (e.g. PROMT), or #file number (#16).

     1     Agriculture, Food & Nutrition
     2     Biosciences & Biotechnology
     3     DIALOG Business Connection (SM)
     4     Business Information
     5     Chemistry
     6     Company Information
     7     Computers & Software
     8     Energy & Environment
     9     Engineering
     10    Government & Public Affairs
     11    Industry Analysis
     12    Law
     13    Medicine & Drug Information
     14    News & Full Text Publications
     15    OAG: Official Airline Guide
     16    Patents, Trademarks, Copyrights
     17    People, Books, & Consumer News
     18    Physical Science & Technology
     19    Social Sciences & Humanities
     20    DIALMAIL
```

21  Help in Database Selection
22  DIALOG News, Help & Practice (ONTAPS)

Output Review/Cancel Options

/H = Help  /L = Logoff   /B <Dialog File no. > = Command mode
?

To search an ONTAP database, input 22 at the ? prompt to get this presentation:

DIALOG News, Help, & Practice (ONTAPS)

1.  DIALOG News
    NOTE: New DIALOG files may not be in MENUS yet.
2.  Review or Cancel current output request
3.  Help in constructing a search
4.  General DIALOG information (services, hours etc)
5.  DIALOG ONTAP Databases (Online Training and Practice)
    ($.25 per minute; offline Prints not available)
6.  Return to Main Menu

Enter option NUMBER and press ENTER to continue.
/H = Help   /L = Logoff   /M- = Previous Menu   /MM = Main Menu
?

Enter 5 to obtain a listing of all the available ONTAP databases:

DIALOG Ontaps

1. ONTAP ABI/Inform Business Management
2. ONTAP Aerospace
3. ONTAP Agricola (Agriculture)
4. ONTAP Analytical Abstracts (Chemistry)
5. ONTAP Art Literature International
6. ONTAP BIOSIS (Biology)
7. ONTAP Boston Globe
8. ONTAP CA Search (Chemistry)
9. ONTAP CAB Abstracts (Agriculture)
10. ONTAP Chemname (Chemical Substances)
11. ONTAP Claims (Patents)
12. ONTAP Compendex* Plus (Engineering)
13. ONTAP Computer Database
14. ONTAP D&B--Dun's Market Identifiers (Companies)
15. ONTAP DMS Contract Awards (Government contracts)
16. ONTAP Embase (Medicine)
17. ONTAP Energy Science & Technology (DOE)
18. ONTAP ERIC (Education)
19. ONTAP Food Science & Technology Abstracts
20. ONTAP Inpadoc (Patents)
21. ONTAP Inspec (Technology)
22. ONTAP Investext (Financial Research)
23. ONTAP Kirk-Othmer Online (Chemistry)
24. ONTAP Magazine Index (General Interest)
25. ONTAP Medline (Medicine)

26. ONTAP Metadex (Metals)
27. ONTAP NTIS (Technology)
28. ONTAP PsycINFO (Psychology)
29. ONTAP PTS Marketing & Advertising Service
30. ONTAP PTS Promt (Markets & Technology)
31. ONTAP Scisearch (Science & Technology)
32. ONTAP Social Scisearch (Social Science)
33. ONTAP Sociological Abstracts
34. ONTAP Trademarkscan--Federal
35. ONTAP World Patents Index

Choose a file by entering the option NUMBER.  Enter D<option number>
(e.g., D30) for a description of a specific database.
Press ENTER to return to first page.
?

Input 8 to access the ONTAP CA SEARCH database and receive these search mode
options:

ONTAP CA Search (Chemistry)
Search Mode Options

Select one of the following options:
    1. Subject Search
    2. Author Search
    3. Journal Search
    4. CAS Registry Number Search
    5. Author's Organization Search

Enter option NUMBER and press ENTER to continue.
/H = Help    /L = Logoff   /M- = Previous Menu   /MM = Main Menu
?

Enter 1 because we are going to perform a subject search and get this presentation:

ONTAP CA Search (Chemistry)
Enter your subject terms. If you saved a CAS Registry number, your terms
will be linked to your saved search with a logical AND. Search terms may
be separated with AND, OR or NOT (INSULAT? OR ASBESTO?).
?

Enter the search terms, paper AND chromatography, and receive this presentation:

Your search is being processed
        ONTAP CA Search (Chemistry)
        Continuation Options
** 23 ** records were found.
Concept 1:PAPER AND CHROMATOGRAPHY
    1.    Modify your search
    2.    Display records at your terminal
    3.    Print records and receive them by U.S. Mail, DIALMAIL or EMAIL
    4.    Order source documents (DIALORDER)
    5.    Review or Cancel current output request

6.   SAVE CAS registry number--use DIFFERENT database
7.   Start a new search

Enter option NUMBER and press ENTER to continue.
/H = Help     /L = Logoff     /MM = Main Menu
?

At this point, 23 hits are too many, so let's modify the search to limit the number of hits. Input 1 and receive this Modify Search menu:

ONTAP CA Search (Chemistry)
Modify Search
** 23 ** records were found.
Concept 1:PAPER AND CHROMATOGRAPHY
1.   Narrow subject concepts (logical AND)
2.   Widen subject concepts (logical OR)
3.   Replace subject concepts
4.   Select limits (e.g., publication year)
5.   Select author (logical AND)
6.   Select journal (logical AND)

Enter option NUMBER and press ENTER to continue.
/H = Help     /L = Logoff     /MM = Main Menu
?

Because we don't know a specific author or journal or any other pertinent information, let's input 4 to see which other ways we can use to limit the search. We then receive this display:

ONTAP CA Search (Chemistry)
Limit Options
** 23 ** records were found.
Concept 1:PAPER AND CHROMATOGRAPHY
1:   Limit by Publication Year
2:   Limit to Patent Records
3:   Limit to Non-Patent Records
4:   Limit to English Language

Enter option NUMBER(s), (e.g., 1,2) to add limit(s) to the search.
Press ENTER to continue.
?

Let's try by limiting it to the English language and input 4 at the ? prompt. We receive the results of the next search:

Your search is being processed
ONTAP CA Search (Chemistry)
Continuation Options
** 7 ** records were found.
Concept 1:PAPER AND CHROMATOGRAPHY   Limit to English Language
1.   Modify your search
2.   Display records at your terminal
3.   Print records and receive them by U.S. Mail, DIALMAIL or EMAIL
4.   Order source documents (DIALORDER)

5.      Review or Cancel current output request
6.      SAVE CAS registry number--use DIFFERENT database
7.      Start a new search

Enter option NUMBER and press ENTER to continue.
/H = Help    /L = Logoff    /MM = Main Menu
?

That reduced our number of hits to 7, so let's take a look at one of them by hitting 2 to receive this menu:

ONTAP CA Search (Chemistry)
Display Options

1.  Title and Journal Reference
2.  Bibliographic Citation and Keyword Phrase(s)
3.  Full Record
4.  Start a new search

Enter option NUMBER and press ENTER to continue.
/H = Help    /L = Logoff    /MM = Main Menu
?

Let's input 2 to obtain a look at Bibliographic Citation and Keyword Phrases and receive this next query:

Enter range of records to be displayed (e.g., 1-5, or ALL):
?

Let's just look at the first one by inputting 1. We receive this display:

4/2/1
87173488   CA: 87(22)173488q   JOURNAL
Cation chromatography on tin(II) hexacyanoferrate(II) papers in
hydrochloric acid and hydrochloric acid + ammonium chloride systems.
Prediction of Ksp values from Ri values
        AUTHOR(S): Varshney, K. G.; Varshney, S. S.
        LOCATION: Z. H. Coll. Eng. Technol., Aligarh Muslim Univ., Aligarh, India
        JOURNAL: Chromatographia DATE: 1977 VOLUME: 10 NUMBER: 9
PAGES: 542-4
        CODEN: CHRGB7 LANGUAGE: English
        SECTION:
CA068001 Phase Equilibriums, Chemical Equilibriums, and Solutions
CA066XXX Surface Chemistry and Colloids
        IDENTIFIERS: soly product calcn ferrocyanide chromatog, tin ferrocyanide
paper chromatog
        Copyright 1991 by the American Chemical Society
        ?

At this point our menu mode search has been completed, so input LOGOFF to leave DIA-LOG and get this summary of our search:

Menu system 5.32G ends.
        16sep91 20:01:49 User XXXXX Session B23.5

```
    $1.15    0.077 Hrs File MENUS
    $0.00    2 Types
    $0.92    TYMNET
    $2.56    Estimated total session cost   0.096 Hrs.
Logoff: level 28.01.01 B  20:01:49
```

Next let's try the command mode.

## Command mode on Dialog

This time we'll make the same search, but use the faster and more direct command mode, skipping all of the intermediate menus. However, before going online, let's keep handy the basic four key commands needed to navigate:

BEGIN    Used to access a database directly or to move from one database to another. For example, BEGIN 204 for ONTAP CA Search.

SELECT    Used to request a search of the occurrences of the topic words in the database(s). For example, SELECT paper AND chromatography.

TYPE    Shows the first record in a set. For example, TYPE S1 shows the first record in set S1.

LOGOFF    Ends the search and displays the cost estimate.

Dialog can be accessed via the local access numbers of DIALNET and INWATS, TYMNET, and TELENET. Most telecommunication programs can provide this access. Once logged on, you receive this presentation:

```
    File 201:ONTAP ERIC
        Set  Items  Description
        ---  -----  -----------
    ?
```

The default database is ONTAP ERIC. To jump to the ONTAP CA SEARCH database, number 204, input BEGIN 204 at the ? prompt. We immediately receive this display:

```
16sep91 20:43:55 User XXXXXXX Session B26.1
    $0.03    0.002 Hrs File 201
    $0.03    Estimated cost File 201
    $0.02    TYMNET
    $0.05    Estimated cost this search
    $0.05    Estimated total session cost   0.002 Hrs.
```

File 204:ONTAP CA SEARCH (99,122 documents)
    (Copr. 1990 by the Amer. Chem. Soc)

**FILE204: Use is subject to the terms of your user/customer agreement.

Use display code TI for Title only.  Formats 9 and 5 are now the same.

```
        Set  Items  Description
        ---  -----  -----------
    ?
```

Let's input SELECT paper AND chromatography at the ? prompt as the search criteria. We receive this presentation after a short wait:

```
        980    PAPER
       1067    CHROMATOGRAPHY  (SEE ?GENERAL)
  S1    23     PAPER AND CHROMATOGRAPHY
  ?
```

The search results show the number of hits for paper (980) and chromatography (1067) separately and 23 hits for both terms ANDed together.

Let's limit this search to English documents by inputting Select S1/Eng at the ? prompt. We receive this display:

```
  S2   7  S1/ENG
```

Our search has now resulted in 7 documents in the English language for our search topic, the same result as we obtained in the menu search mode. Let's take a look at the first one by inputting TYPE S2 at the ? prompt:

```
   2/2/1   87173488   CA: 87(22)173488q   JOURNAL
      Cation chromatography on tin(II) hexacyanoferrate(II) papers in
hydrochloric acid and hydrochloric acid + ammonium chloride systems.
Prediction of Ksp values from Ri values
      AUTHOR(S): Varshney, K. G.; Varshney, S. S.
      LOCATION: Z. H. Coll. Eng. Technol., Aligarh Muslim Univ., Aligarh, India
      JOURNAL: Chromatographia  DATE: 1977  VOLUME: 10  NUMBER: 9
PAGES: 542-4
      CODEN: CHRGB7  LANGUAGE: English
      SECTION:
CA068001 Phase Equilibriums, Chemical Equilibriums, and Solutions
CA066XXX Surface Chemistry and Colloids
      IDENTIFIERS: soly product calcn ferrocyanide chromatog, tin ferrocyanide
paper chromatog
Copyright 1991 by the American Chemical Society
```

At this point we have retrieved the first reference, the same one that was retrieved for the menu search. We can continue to have as many references displayed as desired. For our purposes, however, the demonstration has been completed, so type LOGOFF to leave the system and receive this presentation:

```
  17sep91 15:15:58 UserXXXXXXX Session B31.2
      $0.50    0.033 Hrs File 204
      $0.00    2 Type(s) in Format  2
      $0.00    2 Types
      $0.50    Estimated cost File 204
      $0.40    TYMNET
      $0.90    Estimated cost this search
      $0.99    Estimated total session cost   0.036 Hrs.
```

That was indeed a quick search for a very low cost—the principal advantages of a command search mode. Here's a quick summary comparing the two modes:

| | | |
|---|---|---|
| **Menu mode** | $2.56 | 0.096 hours |
| **Command mode** | $0.99 | 0.036 hours |

This illustrates the importance of being properly prepared before going online to minimize online time, frustration, and costs.

## Knowledge Index

When you sign up for Knowledge Index, you receive a huge notebook full of directions and documentation about using the service, plus additional booklets and brochures. Overall, their documentation is excellent, comprehensive, and easy to use.

The method of logging on to Knowledge Index depends on the data communication network you choose. You have three options:

- Dialog's DIALNET
- Tymnet, Inc.'s TYMNET
- U.S. Sprint's SprintNet.

Review the documentation that came with your signup kit to obtain a local phone number from one of these services that lets you access KI without incurring long distance phone charges.

A few reminders when logging on and navigating:

- Use the Enter (or Return) key to send your commands to KI.
- Do not backspace when you're logging on; it switches you into a half duplex mode. However, backspacing (or Ctrl-H) is acceptable when you are inside KI.
- Don't worry about capitalization, all alphabetical input is treated as capital letters.
- Have your ID and your password handy when you logon.

Here are the most important KI commands to keep handy:

| | |
|---|---|
| /L | Logoff |
| /H | Help |
| - | Display previous page |
| /MM | Return to the Main menu |
| /M | Redisplay current menu |
| /M- | Back up one menu |
| /COST | (Lists your running charges) |

After you logon to Knowledge Index, you are presented with this Main Menu:

Welcome to KNOWLEDGE INDEX

Main Menu

Select one of the following options:

1. Menu Mode
2. Command Mode
3. DIALMAIL

4. Help in formulating a search
5. Knowledge Index Bulletin
6. General Information

Enter option NUMBER and press ENTER to continue
/H = Help  /L = Logoff
?

Your two basic choices are a search mode (1 through 3) or help options (4 through 6). The help options give you assistance in formulating a search, the KNOWLEDGE INDEX Bulletin (which provides the latest news about system features and/or changes), or General Information (which includes a series of help messages on such topics as hours of system availability, rates, etc).

When you logon for the first time, select the last two options to learn about the system. After you've done that and are prepared to start a specific search, select Option 4 to see what help you can get in formulating an efficient and effective search.

Once you've accomplished that and you're ready to do some serious searching, select the Menu mode. Although navigation is slower than for the Command mode, the Menu mode is a lot easier to use until you become acquainted with the commands. It also gives you a good picture of the basic topics available and how they are accessed.

For this example, let's see what is happening in the important area of Open Systems Interconnection, a vital topic that aims to establish the interconnection standards needed to tie together systems from different manufacturers.

Assuming we select the Menu mode by inputting a 1 at the ? prompt, we receive this screen listing the basic topics available (I've edited and rearranged some of the presentations):

Knowledge Index
Sections

1 Agriculture & Nutrition
2 Bibliography--Books & Monographs
   & Drugs
3 Business Information
4 Chemistry
5 Computers & Electronics
6 Directories & Reference

7 Education

8 Law & Government
9 Medicine, Biosciences,

10 News & Current Affairs
11 Popular Information
12 Science & Technology
13 Social Sciences
   & Humanities
14 Travel--Official
   Airline Guide

Enter option NUMBER and press Enter to continue. Enter D for a list of databases in each subject category or D<option number> (e.g., D2) for specific section descriptions.

/H = Help       /L = Logoff       /Nomenu = Command Mode
?

Let's input 12 to obtain the Science and Technology databases and receive this breakdown of subtopics:

Environment
1 CAB Abstracts 84-
2 CAB Abstracts 72-83
3 Chemical Engineering Abstracts
4 Compendex PLUS
5 Pollution Abstracts
Science & Technology
6 Aerospace Database
7 Analytical Abstracts
8 Compendex PLUS
9 The Computer Database
10 INSPEC
11 MathSci
12 NTIS

Choose a file by entering the option NUMBER. Enter D for a section description or D<option number> (e.g., D2) for a specific database description.

/H = Help   /L = Logoff   /M- = Previous Menu   /MM = Main Menu
?

After having reviewed Knowledge Index's literature before logging on, it appears that the Compendex Plus database should have a number of articles on this topic. So input 4 to access the Compendex Plus database. We receive this display:

Compendex PLUS
Search Options
Select one of the following options:
1. Subject Search
2. Author Search
3. Journal Search
Enter option NUMBER and press ENTER to continue.
/H = Help    /L = Logoff   /M- = Previous Menu   /MM = Main Menu
?

Opting for a subject search, input 1 at the ? prompt and receive this information:

Enter subject concept(s). Logical OR, AND, or NOT may be used
to separate concepts (e.g., MICROCOMPUTER? OR PERSONAL COMPUTER?).
?

At this point, input Open AND Systems AND Interconnection at the question mark prompt to start the search and receive this presentation:

Your search is being processed
Compendex PLUS
Continuation Options
** 885 ** records were found.
Concept 1:OPEN AND SYSTEMS AND INTERCONNECTION
1 Modify your search
2 Display records at your terminal (maximum is 980 records)
You may /SET SCROLL ON or /SET SCROLL OFF
3 Order source documents

```
        4   Start a new search
Enter option NUMBER and press ENTER to continue.
/H = Help   /L = Logoff  /M- = Previous Menu   /MM = Main Menu
?
```

Because 885 records is much too large a group to review, let's modify the search by inputting 1 at the ? prompt and receive this data:

```
        Compendex PLUS
        Modify Search
**  885  ** records were found.
Concept 1:OPEN AND SYSTEMS AND INTERCONNECTION
        1.  Narrow subject concepts (logical AND)
        2.  Widen subject concepts (logical OR)
        3.  Replace subject concepts
        4.  Select limits
        5.  Select author(s) (logical AND)
        6.  Select journal(s) (logical AND)
Enter option NUMBER and press ENTER to continue.
/H = Help   /L = Logoff /M- = Previous Menu   /MM = Main Menu
?
```

Let's input 4 to select limits and receive this presentation of the limit options:

```
        Compendex PLUS
        Limit Options
**  885  ** records were found.
Concept 1:OPEN AND SYSTEMS AND INTERCONNECTION
        1.  Limit by Publication Year
        2.  Limit to Specific Approaches (treatment codes)
        3.  Limit to English Language
Enter option NUMBER(s), (e.g., 1,2) to add limit(s) to the search.
Press ENTER to continue.
?
```

Let's first of all limit the search to the English Language to try to reduce the number of hits and receive this information:

```
Your search is being processed
        Compendex PLUS
        Continuation Options
**  851  ** records were found.
Concept 1:OPEN AND SYSTEMS AND INTERCONNECTION
Limit to English Language
        1   Modify your search
        2   Display records at your terminal (maximum is 980 records)
            You may /SET SCROLL ON or /SET SCROLL OFF
        3   Order source documents
        4   Start a new search
Enter option NUMBER and press ENTER to continue.
/H = Help  /L = Logoff /M- = Previous Menu    /MM = Main Menu
?
```

That wasn't too great a reduction, so let's look at another possible method of limiting the hits. Input 1 again at the prompt and receive this menu:

Compendex PLUS
Modify Search
** 851 ** records were found.
Concept 1:OPEN AND SYSTEMS AND INTERCONNECTION
Limit to English Language
    1. Narrow subject concepts (logical AND)
    2. Widen subject concepts (logical OR)
    3. Replace subject concepts
    4. Select limits
    5. Select author(s) (logical AND)
    6. Select journal(s) (logical AND)
Enter option NUMBER and press ENTER to continue.
/H = Help  /L = Logoff  /M- = Previous Menu  /MM = Main Menu
?

Again select 4 to determine other possible methods of setting limits and receive this menu:

Compendex PLUS
Limit Options
** 851 ** records were found.
Concept 1:OPEN AND SYSTEMS AND INTERCONNECTION
Limit to English Language
    1:    Limit by Publication Year
    2:    Limit to Specific Approaches (treatment codes)
  *3:    Limit to English Language
Limits currently selected are marked with a "*".
Enter option NUMBER to add another limit, or D<option NUMBER>,
(e.g., D1)   to delete an existing limit.
Press Enter to process search.
?

Note that our search is progressive and is still being limited to English only. We are going to add another limitation, limit by publication year, so input 1 at the prompt and receive this display:

Compendex PLUS
Limit by Publication year
Select one of the following options:
    1. Limit to current publication year (1991)
    2. Limit to current and last publication year (1990-91)
    3. Limit to last five publication years (1987-91)
    4. Limit to your own publication year(s)
Enter option NUMBER and press Enter to continue.
/H = Help  /L = Logoff  /M- = Previous Menu  /MM = Main Menu
?

Because our interest is in the latest developments in the field, let's input 1 to limit the search to the current publication year and receive this information:

Your search is being processed
Compendex PLUS
Continuation Options
** 13 ** records were found.
Concept 1:OPEN AND SYSTEMS AND INTERCONNECTION
Limit to current publication year (1991)

Limit to English Language
```
    1    Modify your search
    2    Display records at your terminal (maximum is 980 records)
         You may /SET SCROLL ON or /SET SCROLL OFF
    3    Order source documents
    4    Start a new search
```
Enter option NUMBER and press ENTER to continue.
/H = Help   /L = Logoff   /M- = Previous Menu   /MM = Main Menu
?

Because we have narrowed the number of hits down to a reasonable number, input 2 to display the records and receive this presentation (note that the first 10 are presented at one time):

```
Compendex PLUS
** 13 ** records for DISPLAY
Enter HALT to exit DISPLAY
        Option     TITLE
        No.  ------------------------------------------------------------------------------
        1    Integrated network management for real-time operations.
        2    Distributed operation of the X.500 directory.
        3    Technology 1991: Data communications.
        4    Emerging high speed transfer protocols.
        5    Tool for the modelling of network architectures based upon the OSI/RM.
        6    Open systems co-operation.
        7    Knowledge based fault management for OSI networks.
        8    Third IEE Conference on Telecommunications.
        9    A protocol structure for high-speed communication over broadband ISDN.
        10   High-speed transport components.
Enter option number(s), HALT, /H for help, or press ENTER for next screen:
?
```

To see an abstract of the first article, input 1 at the question mark prompt and receive this presentation:

```
        selection 1 of 1
        03101045   E.I. Monthly No: EI9108090181
        Title: Integrated network management for real-time operations.
        Author: Tjaden, Gary; Wall, Mark; Goldman, Jerry; Jeromnimon, Constantine N.
        Corporate Source: NYNEX, USA
        Source: IEEE Network v 5 n 2 Mar 1991 p 10-15
        Publication Year: 1991
        CODEN: IENEET   ISSN: 0890-8044
        Language: English
        Document Type: JA; (Journal Article)   Treatment: T; (Theoretical);
A; (Applications)
        Journal Announcement: 9108
        Abstract: An approach to integrated network management that eliminates the
need for interface protocol conformance and provides applications that seamlessly
isolate and resolve faults in the entire network is described. The approach uses
off-the-shelf artificial intelligence tools and open-architecture client/server
workstation technology. A sophisticated tool similar to a fourth-generation
language, called the Universal Device Interface Generator, is used to develop and
support agent interface modules very quickly and easily. This tool is used to
provide a manager of managers, called the ALLINK Operations Coordinator (AOC),
that can interface to virtually any existing element management system. With the
AOC, information from all of the subnetwork managers is gathered and correlated,
the results of this correlation are presented to the human operators in a uniform
```

fashion, and any other interactions between the subnetwork managers and the human operators are also performed in a uniform fashion. 2 Refs.

Descriptors: *COMPUTER NETWORKS--*Management; TELEPHONE EXCHANGES, PRIVATE; COMPUTER SYSTEMS, DIGITAL--Real Time Operation

Identifiers: OPEN SYSTEMS INTERCONNECTION (OSI); CORPORATE NETWORKS

Classification Codes: 718 (Telephone & Line Communications); 723 (Computer Software); 912 (Industrial Engineering & Management)

71 (ELECTRONICS & COMMUNICATIONS); 72 (COMPUTERS & DATA PROCESSING); 91 (ENGINEERING MANAGEMENT)

Copyright 1991 Engineering Information, Inc
**************************************************************

Press ENTER to return to list of items for display
?

At this point any or all of the abstracts can be displayed and reviewed. However, for our purposes the search has been successfully completed, so input /L to logoff and leave Knowledge Index and receive this final tally:

17sep91 20:48:51 UserXXXXXXX Session B3.16
$1.55     0.062 Hrs FileKI
$1.55     Estimated total session cost     0.062 Hrs.

You searched thousands of records and quickly obtained results for a minimum cost. You could have also done this search in command mode, which would have cost even less.

# ORBIT

Orbit is heavily endowed with engineering and scientific databases, many of which are exclusive with Orbit. To illustrate a typical search, let's check for articles on the magnetic properties of semiconductors with temperature.

Before logging on, let's review some of the key commands and operations:

|  |  |
|---|---|
|  | Used as a wild card for any number of suffix or prefix characters (e.g., Çhlor: will pick up any words with the chlor root). |
| FILE PLUS | Will begin to search the COMPENDEX*PLUS database. |
| TFILE | Checks information in another file without losing search results in current file. |
| RETURN | Returns to original file from a TFILE (temporary file) after using the TFILE command. |
| RESTART Y | Begins a new terminal session without having to logout/login again to the system. |
| STOP Y | Ends a session. Orbit defaults to the search mode. |
| USER: | The prompt after which you enter your search term(s). |
| PROG: | Gives the results of the search, in essence the number of hits for the term(s) entered. |

Most of the basic database methods can be used to search, including the Boolean AND, OR, NOT, plus proximity operators, truncation, dates and update codes, retrieval using search qualifiers, retrieval of strings of characters, etc.

After logging on, you'll see the following screen (again I have abbreviated the presentation to conserve space):

```
WELCOME TO ORBIT SEARCH SERVICE, A DIVISION OF MAXWELL ONLINE.

PROG:
YOU ARE NOW CONNECTED TO THE ORBIT DATABASE.
FOR A TUTORIAL, ENTER A QUESTION MARK. OTHERWISE,
ENTER A COMMAND.
    USER:
```

From reviewing Orbit's database descriptions before going online, it seems that the best database for this topic would be INSPEC, so input FILE INSC (the code name for INSPEC for records from 1977 to the present) at the USER: prompt and receive this information.

```
PROG:
ELAPSED TIME ON ORBIT: 0.03 HRS.
$0.00 ESTIMATED COST CONNECT TIME.
$0.39 ESTIMATED COST TELECOMMUNICATIONS, IF APPLICABLE.
$0.00 ESTIMATED COST OFFLINE PRINTS: 0
$0.00 ESTIMATED COST ONLINE PRINTS: 0
$0.39 ESTIMATED TOTAL COST THIS ORBIT SESSION.
YOU ARE NOW CONNECTED TO THE INSPEC DATABASE.
COVERS FROM 1977 THRU BIWEEKLY UPDATE (9116)
SEE FILE INSP6976 FOR COVERAGE FROM 1969 THROUGH 1976.
    USER:
```

At this point let's pause and see how to obtain help in case we need it, so input ? at the USER: prompt and receive these screens:

```
THE FOLLOWING GROUPS OF EXPLANATIONS ARE AVAILABLE:
EXPLAIN EXPLAINCOMPLETE    LIST OF EXPLANATIONS
EXPLAIN COMMANDS           LIST OF COMMANDS AND ABBREVIATIONS
EXPLAIN PROGRAM MESSAGES   LISTS PROGRAM MESSAGES IN SHORT AND
                           LONG FORMATS
EXPLAIN ORBIT              LISTS SEARCH-RELATED EXPLANATIONS
    IF YOU ENCOUNTER PROBLEMS, DISCONNECT PHONE FROM TERMINAL AND CALL
AN ACTION DESK FOR HELP:
    USER:
```

At the USER: prompt, input MAGNETIC PROPERTIES, the first term we want to search for (again I've rearranged the format for clarity), and we receive the results of the first search:

```
SS 1 /C?
USER:  magnetic properties
PROG:
SS 1 PSTG (7161)
```

There are 7161 hits (PSTG-postings) on magnetic properties. The computer is now asking for the second search:

```
SS 2 /C?
USER:
```

Input SUPERCONDUCTORS at the USER: prompt and receive the results of this second search:

```
PROG:
SS 2 PSTG (37610)


SS 3 /C?
USER:
```

The SS2 search resulted in 37,610 hits, so next input TEMPERATURE at the prompt:

```
PROG:
SS 3 PSTG (346158)
SS 4 /C?
USER:
```

To further limit the search, let's use the year 1991 as another limiter and enter 91 at the USER: prompt:

```
PROG:
SS 4 PSTG (4777)
SS 5 /C?
USER:
```

That resulted in 4777 hits, so for a final search, input magnetic properties AND superconductors AND temperature AND 91 and receive this search summary:

```
PROG:
OCCURS      TERM
7161        MAGNETIC PROPERTIES
37610       SUPERCONDUCTORS
346158      TEMPERATURE
4777        91
SS 5 PSTG (6)
SS 6 /C?
USER:
```

When the terms are all ANDed, the topic is finally reduced in the fifth search to 6 hits. To see the abstracts, input PRT 5 to "print" or display the first five abstracts (I've included only one for illustration):

```
PROG:
CITATIONS SELECTED FROM SEARCH STATEMENT 5.
-1-
AN - A90047935
TI - Effect of intergranular flux pinning on the magnetic properties of
YBa/sub 2/Cu/sub 3/O/sub 7- delta / and (Bi/sub 0.9/Pb/sub 0.1/)Sr/sub
1/Ca/sub 1/Cu/sub 1.8/O/sub x/ {IN Physica C (Netherlands), International
Conference on Materials and Mechanisms of Superconductivity: High-Temperature
Superconductors II, Stanford, CA, USA, 23-28 July 1989}
   AU - Russell, G.J.; Taylor, K.N.R.; Matthews, D.N.; Bailey, A.; Vaile, R.A.
   OS - Sch. of Phys., New South Wales Univ., Kensington, NSW, Australia;
   SO - Physica C (Netherlands), vol.162-164, pt.1, PP.327-8, Dec. 1989, 2 REF.
   SS 7 /C?
   USER:
```

Because the search was completed, input STOP Y at the prompt to logoff and receive this final tally:

```
PROG:
TERMINAL SESSION FINISHED 08/01/91  6:58 P.M.  (CENTRAL TIME)
ELAPSED TIME ON INSPEC: 0.07 HRS.
$0.00 ESTIMATED COST CONNECT TIME.
$0.91 ESTIMATED COST TELECOMMUNICATIONS, IF APPLICABLE.
$0.00 ESTIMATED COST OFFLINE PRINTS: 0
$0.00 ESTIMATED COST ONLINE PRINTS: 5
$0.91 ESTIMATED TOTAL COST THIS INSPEC SESSION.
ELAPSED TIME THIS TERMINAL SESSION: 0.10 HOURS.
$0.00 ESTIMATED COST CONNECT TIME.
$1.30 ESTIMATED COST TELECOMMUNICATIONS, IF APPLICABLE.
$0.00 ESTIMATED COST OFFLINE PRINTS: 0
$0.00 ESTIMATED COST ONLINE PRINTS: 5
$1.30 ESTIMATED TOTAL COST THIS TERMINAL SESSION.
ORBIT SEARCH SESSION COMPLETED.  THANKS FOR USING ORBIT!
```

This is a low cost tally for searching some 3.7 million records for the topic. That's why proper preparation before going online is so important.

Next we'll look into some more technology and technology-related databases.

# Exercises

1. Outline a search for a topic via EasyNet using one of the database vendors Easy-Net can access.
2. Outline a search for a topic on Dialog using the Command Mode.
3. Outline a search for a topic on the Knowledge Index using the Menu Mode.
4. Outline a search for a topic on Orbit using their command mode.

# ───────10───────
# Navigating technology &
# technology-related databases

*Knowledge must come through action; you can have no test
which is not fanciful, save by trial.*

Sophocles

Vendors supplying both technology and technology-related databases will be covered in this chapter, with examples of their use. Technology-related databases will be of importance to you in many phases of your profession dealing with news, finances, travel, and your personal interests and hobbies. The following databases will be accessed and searched in this chapter:

- BRS
- Dow Jones News Retrieval
- EPIC
- Mead
- NewsNet
- STN

## BRS

For this example, we'll search BRS After Dark, the low-cost service that is available during non-prime-time. Let's demonstrate the use of the menu mode and search for information on "packet switching," a technique that is used in telecommunications. But before logging on, let's review some of the key BRS commands:

| For help with | Enter |
|---|---|
| Help | H |
| Search | S |
| Display Documents | D |
| Print Documents Continuously | PC |
| Review Search | R |
| Change Databases | C |
| Return to Main Menu | M |
| Change Libraries | L |
| Sign Off | O |
| Sign Off Continue | OC |

After logging on and receiving some general information about the service, the following main menu is presented:

```
              BRS/AFTER DARK
              MAIN MENU
SERVICE                              NUMBER
Search Service                          1
BRS/After Dark Update (8/23/91)        11
How To Use BRS/After Dark              12
Customer Services                      13
ENTER SERVICE NUMBER OR H FOR HELP-->
```

To access the Search Service, input 1 at the arrow prompt and receive this presentation:

```
BRS/AFTER DARK SEARCH SERVICE LIBRARIES
         LABEL LIBRARY NAME
         SCME Science and Medicine
         BUSI Business and Finance
         REFE Reference
         EDUC Education
         SOCS Social Science and Humanities
         PRAC Practice Databases
ENTER LIBRARY OR DATABASE LABEL-->
```

By referring to BRS's literature before logging on, we can skip the Science and Medicine menu and jump directly to the Computer and Mathematics Search database by inputting CMCI at the arrow prompt. We then receive this display:

```
CMCI  1980-AUG 1991 (9135)
ENTER Y TO DISPLAY DATABASE DESCRIPTION OR
PRESS ENTER TO BEGIN SEARCHING-->
```

To begin searching, hit the <CR> (Enter) key and receive this information:

```
ENTER SEARCH TERMS, COMMAND, OR H FOR HELP
```

At this point we can enter our search terms, packet AND switching, and receive these results:

```
ANSWER 1 195 DOCUMENTS FOUND
ENTER SEARCH TERMS, COMMAND, OR H FOR HELP
```

This is obviously too large a number of hits to explore, so let's further limit the search by adding another restricting term, telecom. Enter packet AND switching AND telecom at the arrow prompt and receive these results:

```
ANSWER 2 12 DOCUMENTS FOUND
ENTER SEARCH TERMS, COMMAND, OR H FOR HELP
SEARCH  3-->
```

At this point we have reduced the number of hits to a manageable number, so let's input

PC (Print Documents Continuously) at the Search 3—> prompt to display the documents and receive this query:

ENTER ANSWER NUMBER-->

We want to display the results of search 2, so input 2 at the Enter Answer Number prompt and receive these choices of presentations:

ENTER TI (TITLE ONLY), S (SHORT FORMAT), M (MEDIUM FORMAT),
L (LONG FORMAT), TD (TAILORED DISPLAY) -->

Let's take a look at the short format by entering S at the prompt and receive this query:

ENTER DOCUMENT NUMBERS-->

To view one of the results of the second search, enter 2 at the above prompt and receive this presentation:

```
AN 0506370. 9112.
AU COOPER-CS.
TI HIGH-SPEED NETWORKS - THE EMERGENCE OF TECHNOLOGIES FOR
MULTISERVICE SUPPORT.
SO COMPUTER COMMUNICATIONS. 1991, V14 N1. P27-43.
RF 0116.
GA FB081.
LG ENGLISH (EN).
PT REVIEW (R).
KW HIGH-SPEED-NETWORKS. MULTISERVICE-SUPPORT. INTEGRATED-SERVICES.
KP BROAD-BAND-ISDN. KNOCKOUT-SWITCH. COMMUNICATION-NETWORK.
INTEGRATED-SERVICES. LIGHTWAVE-SYSTEMS. OPTICAL-NETWORK. PACKET-
SWITCH.
HIGH-CAPACITY. TRANSMISSION. ATM.
  AI (AA) Abstract Available.
  -END OF DISPLAY REQUEST-
  RETURNING TO SEARCH
  ENTER SEARCH TERMS, COMMAND, OR H FOR HELP
  SEARCH 3-->
```

You can now back up and review any of the other entries, or receive a long format or other type of display of the results of the search. However, for the purposes of this example, the search has been completed, so input the letter O at the prompt to logoff and receive this wrapup of the search:

```
*CONNECT TIME   0:01:38 HH:MM:SS   0.027 DEC HRS   SESSION 24
*SIGN OFF   21:41:00   09/18/91
```

# Dow Jones

In addition to having comprehensive and up-to-date stock and financial information, News/Retrieval also has an outstanding coverage of news. To see how it functions, let's try DowQuest, the excellent service that searches articles from more than 350 sources of current business information, including The Wall Street Journal, Barron's, Business Week, Fortune, and Forbes.

DowQuest can search for topics based on combinations of common and/or scientific terms (lasers excimer) or even a statement in a sentence.

And they can locate almost anyone who is in the news. Let's check News/Retrieval and see whatever happened to Fran Tarkenton, one of the greatest football quarterbacks of all time.

Here are some of the key commands to keep handy after you're logged on:

DISC   Logoff at any point except when you're in //TEXT
..OFF   Followed by DISC to logoff from //TEXT
/T   Go to top screen
/M   Go to previous menu
PRINT   Display one or more articles in full
HELP   View relevant instructions

After logging on to News/Retrieval and to skip past all of the intermediate menus, type //dowquest at the prompt and receive this information (I've shortened it a little to conserve space):

**TO BEGIN A SEARCH:** Enter several words that are relevant to the subject you are interested in and press (Return).
**ENTER QUERY:**

To find Fran Tarkenton, type FRAN TARKENTON after the **ENTER QUERY** prompt and receive this information:

```
\DOWQUEST          STARTER LIST          HEADLINE
PAGE
1 of 4
   1 Cover Story: KNOWLEDGEWARE: FRAN TARKENTON SCORES . . .   BUSINESS
WEEK, 05/27/91   (501 words)
   2 FMR Corp. - Knowledgeware, Inc.   DOW JONES NEWS SERVICE, 05/20/91
(98 words)
   3 KnowledgeWare Unveils Updated Version of DOS-Based Software DOW JONES
NEWS SERVICE, 12/19/90 (143 words)
   4 CASE power for OS/2. (computer-aided software engineering) ...
DATAMATION, 11/15/90 (2,632 words)

   TO IMPROVE A SEARCH: Type SEARCH and the numbers of up to three articles that
are examples of your subject.
   TO VIEW AN ARTICLE:      Enter article number and press (Return)
                           Enter BEST and article number to see "best" section
   TO PRINT ARTICLES: Type PRINT and the article numbers.
   PRESS (RETURN) FOR MORE HEADLINES. TYPE HELP FOR MORE INFORMATION.
```

So you have the choice of viewing, or printing the full text of the article, or seeing listings of more articles. To find out a little more about Fran, input PRINT 1 at the prompt:

```
\YOU HAVE ASKED TO DISPLAY ARTICLE(S) 1
   PRESS TO
         1 Display text in a continuous stream
         2 Display text page by page
         3 Return to headlines
   NOTE: BE SURE YOUR PRINTER IS ON IF YOU WANT TO PRINT ARTICLES
```

Input 1 and receive this information (I've truncated the article):

Cover Story: KNOWLEDGEWARE:
FRAN TARKENTON SCORES IN SOFTWARE
BUSINESS WEEK, 05/27/91
Copyright 1991 McGraw-Hill, Inc.
By Stephanie Anderson Forest in Atlanta
As a pro football quarterback, Fran Tarkenton habitually zig-zagged
around opposing linemen to score touchdowns. He retired from the sport
in 1978, but Tarkenton is still scrambling into the end zone. Since 1986,
the Hall of Famer has built Atlanta- based KnowledgeWare Inc. into the
dominant player in the nascent market for automated products that help
businesses develop their own software...

That completed the search, so let's logoff, wishing Fran Tarkenton luck in his ventures.

# EPIC

To illustrate the procedures and ease of access and navigation in the GPO Monthly Catalog
database, let's see what information is available on oil for energy purposes that was dis-
cussed during a Senate hearing in Oklahoma. Before logging on, let's first review some of
the key commands:

F       Find. Used to start searches (e.g., F surgery).
C       Choose. Used to select a specific database to search.
D       Display. D 1-10 displays references 1 through 10.
STOP    Logoff.

You can also use the Boolean AND, OR, and NOT operators.

After logging on with a telecomm program, we are presented with this screen (again
I've abbreviated and edited the response):

You are connected to OCLC Online Reference Services.
W E L C O M E   T O   E P I C
E P I C   S E R V I C E   N E W S
Page: 1 of 2
The current database is OCLC Online Union Catalog
Updated 08/03/91.
Last record in database 24172481.
Copyright 1991 OCLC
DATABASES AVAILABLE:
1 - ERIC                          30 - ABI
10 - GPO Monthly Catalog          31 - Business Dateline
20 - Dissertation Abstracts       40 - PNI
22 - Book Data                    23 - OCLC Online Union Catalog
For PRACTICE DATABASES add "9" to the number; e.g., "930" for PABI.
For EASYNET access enter "easynet" instead of "epic" at logon. For
complete EPIC service NEWS, enter EXPLAIN MORENEWS
1 = >

Because we want to navigate in the GPO Monthly Catalog database, input CHOOSE 10 at the 1 = > prompt and receive this presentation:

> By choosing a new database your current searches will be deleted. Are you sure you want to choose "GPO"? <y/n>

Input Y because we have no current searches recorded and receive this information:

```
E S T I M A T E D   T I M E  &  C O S T
Page: 1 of 1
Database 23 - OCLC Online Union Catalog
Sat Aug 03 16:34:10 1991
```

| Item | Quantity | This Database | Session Total |
|------|----------|---------------|---------------|
| Displays | 0 | $ 0.00 | $ 0.00 |
| Offline Prints | 0 | $ 0.00 | $ 0.00 |
| Database Charge | 0.02 (00:01) | $ 0.40 | $ 0.40 |
| Communications | 0.02 (00:01) | | $ 0.16 |
| | Totals $ | 0.40 | $ 0.56 |
| | Credits $ | 0.00 | $ 0.00 |

```
Welcome to database GPO Monthly Catalog.  Updated 07/15/91.
Last record in database 336092.  Not copyright protected
1 = >
```

For our first search, enter F ENERGY at the prompt:

```
Searching ...
S E A R C H  R E S U L T S
```

| Search ID | Records Found | Search Term |
|-----------|---------------|-------------|
| S1 | 11613 | energy |

```
2 = >
```

For the next search, enter F OIL at the prompt:

```
Searching ...
S E A R C H  R E S U L T S
```

| Search ID | Records Found | Search Term |
|-----------|---------------|-------------|
| S2 | 2475 | oil |

```
3 = >
```

For the final search, enter F OKLAHOMA at the prompt:

```
Searching ...
S E A R C H  R E S U L T S
```

| Search ID | Records Found | Search Term |
|-----------|---------------|-------------|
| S3 | 1388 | oklahoma |

```
4 = >
```

Next, let's combine the three terms F S1 AND S2 AND S3:

```
Searching ...
S E A R C H   R E S U L T S
Search      Records      Search Term
ID          Found
------      -------      -----------
S4          1            s1 and s2 and s3
5 = >
```

We've narrowed the search down to one record, so input D to display the one record:

```
R e c o r d   1   o f   1
Not copyright protected
GN:  Y 4.En 2:S.hrg.99-10
AU:  United States. Congress. Senate. Committee on Energy and
Natural Resources.
TI:  Impact of Treasury Department's tax reform proposal on oil
and gas industry: hearing before the Committee on Energy and Natural
Resources, United States Senate, Ninety-ninth Congress, first session
.... Oklahoma City, OK, February 15, 1985.
YR:  1985
```

This listing gives the GN—the government document classification number, which might help you locate the items in a library—AUthority, the TItle, and the YeaR of the hearings, and completes the search, so input STOP at the prompt to logoff:

```
E S T I M A T E D   T I M E   &   C O S T
Page: 1 of 1
Database 10 - GPO Monthly Catalog
Sat Aug 03 16:35:16 1991
Item              Quantity       This Database      Session Total
------------      ------------   -------------      -------------
Displays          1              $      0.00        $      0.00
Offline Prints    0              $      0.00        $      0.00
Database Charge   0.02 (00:01)   $      0.25        $      0.65
Communications    0.02 (00:01)                      $      0.16
                                 -----------        -------------
                     Totals      $      0.25        $      0.81
                     Credits     $      0.00        $      0.00
5 = >  Are you sure you want to log off?  <y/n>
```

Because we have located our information, input Y and receive:

```
Thank you for searching EPIC.
You are disconnected
CONNECT TIME = 00:02:22
```

This search was accomplished for less than one dollar and took a little over two minutes of online time. This is a powerful method to obtain information and illustrates the importance of preplanning your search strategy before going online.

# MEAD

Next let's search MEAD LEXIS/NEXIS to see the type of information they have of interest to scientists and engineers. Because MEAD has considerable information about patents and law, let's check into the topic of "thermoluminescence" as used in dating methods to see what has been recorded at LEXIS/NEXIS on that aspect of the topic.

Before logging on, let's review some of the basic commands required to operate LEXIS/NEXIS:

| | |
|---|---|
| Alt-Q | Quit and logoff |
| Alt-H | Help |
| F5 | KWIC. Display file with Key Words In Context |
| F1 | Next page |
| F2 | Previous page |
| Alt-F8 | Modify search terms |
| F8 | New search |
| F10 | Change library |

Logging on to LEXIS/NEXIS has been completely automated by their excellent front-end software. After logging on, we are presented with a listing of all the basic libraries available. Because we want to search the PATENT library, input PATENT and hit Enter. We are then presented with the following display (I've rearranged the presentations to make them more readable):

```
Please TRANSMIT the NAME of the file you want to search. To see a
description of a file, type its page number and press the TRANSMIT key.
            FILES - PAGE 1 of 5 (NEXT PAGE for additional files)
NAME       PG DESCRIP
 ----- CASES, CODES & PRIOR ART
PTOMNI      1 Patent cases from Fedl Cts, COMMR, PATAPP, ITC & ALLREG
CASES       1 Patent cases from Federal Cts
FEDCTS      1 Ct Customs & Patent Appeals
CAFC        1 Patent cases from Fed Circuit
IPOMNI      2 All Int Prop cases & Reg Matl
ALLREG      3 Fed register & CFR Titl 19,37
USCS        3 U.S.C.S. title 35, Patents
FCRUL       3 Fedl Circuit Rules, eff 5/89
BILLS       7 House & Senate Bills, Tracking
PUBS        7 Trade and Technical Journals
 - - - - - FULL TEXT PATENTS - - - - - - -
ALL         4 Utility, Design & Plant
UTIL        4 Utility patents from 1975
DESIGN      4 Design patents from 1976
PLANT       4 Plant patents from 1976
 - - - - - PATENT CLASSIFICATIONS - - - - - -
CLASS       4 All Patent Nos. by Class
CLMNL       4 Manual of Classifications
INDEX       4 Index to Manual of Classif.
 - - - - - PATENT ADMINISTRATIVE DECISIONS - -
PTO         2 Comb PATAPP & COMMR
PATAPP      2 Bd Pat Interf & Appeals
```

COMMR      2 Commissioner of Patents
Enter LEXDOC to order patents and file wrappers. Find trademark
information in the new TRDMRK library. Find copyright information
in the new COPYRT library.
Press Alt-H for Help or Alt-Q to Quit

Let's input PUBS to see what the seven Trade and Technical Journals have recorded about this topic and we receive this presentation:

Please type your search request, then press the TRANSMIT key. What you
transmit will be Search Level 1.
     For further explanation, press the H key (for HELP) and then the
TRANSMIT key. Press Alt-H for Help or Alt-Q to Quit.

Let's input thermoluminescence to see what the 7 Trade and Technical Journals have recorded about this topic and we receive this presentation:

Your search request has found 20 STORIES through Level 1.
     To DISPLAY these STORIES press either the KWIC, FULL, CITE or
SEGMTS key.
     To MODIFY your search request, press either the M key (for MODFY)
and then the TRANSMIT key.
     For further explanation, press the H key (for HELP) and then the
TRANSMIT key. Press Alt-H for Help or Alt-Q to Quit.

Because 20 stories are more than anticipated, let's reduce the total by adding another qualifier, the year 1991. To accomplish this, we first hit the Alt-F8 key for Modify and receive this screen:

Your search request is:
THERMOLUMINESCENCE
Number of STORIES found with your search request through:
          LEVEL 1...          20
Please transmit the modification to your search request (Level 2).
REMEMBER to start your modification with a CONNECTOR.
     For further explanation, press the H key (for HELP) and then the
TRANSMIT key. Press Alt-H for Help or Alt-Q to Quit.

At this point, let's input AND 1991 to limit our search to STORIES that are current to 1991 and receive this presentation:

Your search request has found 3 STORIES through Level 2.
     To DISPLAY these STORIES press either the KWIC, FULL, CITE
or SEGMTS key.
     To MODIFY your search request, press either the M key (for MODFY)
and then the TRANSMIT key.
     For further explanation, press the H key (for HELP) and then the
TRANSMIT key. Press Alt-H for Help or Alt-Q to Quit.

Because this is a reasonable number, let's take a look at one of the representative STORIES to see the format and the type of information they contain. Let's try the KWIC or Key Words In Context presentation, a display that shows all of the keywords we have searched for with some of the information before and after our keywords. I've included only one sample of the three:

```
              LEVEL 2 - 2 OF 3 STORIES
Scientific American Copyright (c) 1990 Information Access Company;
              Scientific American Inc. 1990
LENGTH: 4350 words
HEADLINE: The emergence of modern humans
BYLINE: Stringer, Christopher B.
...40,000 years. Now this impediment is slowly being overcome by
the development and wider application of the uranium series (U-S),
thermoluminescence (TL) and electron-spin resonance (ESR) techniques.
The first method can be used on cave sediments such as stalagmites;
the second ...
LOAD-DATE-MDC: March 07, 1991
Press Alt-H for Help or Alt-Q to Quit
```

By reviewing the KWIC presentation, you can quickly evaluate whether you are interested in the full length version of the STORY. If so, you can request it and print it out.

For purpose of our demonstration, the search has been completed, so we can input Alt-Q and logoff LEXIS/NEXIS and we receive this final presentation:

```
Session with LEXIS/NEXIS Services Terminated
You have terminated this session.
```

Any cases you selected for printing will be saved for 24 hours . . .. Please allow a few moments for your connection to LEXIS/NEXIS services to be terminated.

```
THIS MESSAGE IS GENERATED BY YOUR COMPUTER
```

LEXIS/NEXIS is more complicated to learn to navigate, but the front-end software and the excellent help along the way ease the burden of searching.

# NewsNet

NewsNet lives up to its claim of "The daily news the night before." Their coverage of up-to-the-minute news is excellent, and they encompass a wide swath of subjects. To illustrate its use, let's check on the subject of "ceramic microwave processing," a topic growing now and one that will continue to grow in importance in the future. Let's check the RD or Research and Development section of NewsNet's coverage.

After logon, we receive a few announcements and soon are presented with the NewsNet main command prompt:

```
Enter command or <RETURN>
-->
```

Before we start navigating, hit <CR> to display and review a menu of the main commands used by NewsNet:

```
SCAN .................... Display headlines      DNB ........... Dun & Bradstreet reports
SEARCH............ Search for keywords          TRW ...... TRW business credit profiles
READ....................... Display full text     QUOTE .... Stock & commodity quotes
OAG ............... Official Airline Guides      FLASH ....... Update NewsFlash profile
NOTICES........ Display NewsFlash hits          $................. Display session estimate
HELP .................Detailed instructions      BACK ............ Return to prior prompt
LIST ...........Display services by code        STOP............... Stop current activity
PRICES ................ Complete price list      QUIT .............Return to main prompt
OFF....................... Sign off NewsNet       PAGING ........ Display text by screens
$OFF ........... Display costs at signoff       PROJECT ......Track sessions by tasks
MAIL ......... To NewsNet or publishers         <CONTROL>S........... Freeze display
ORDER.......... Order print subscription        <CONTROL>Q ........ Resume display
INVOICE.............. Recent billing detail      <CONTROL>P...........Break function
PASSWORD.... Change your password
At any time, enter ? for assistance or HELP for detailed instructions.
Enter command or <RETURN>
-->
```

Enter SEARCH at the arrow prompt to begin the search and receive this information:

```
Enter service or industry code(s)
-->
```

Enter the service RD at the arrow prompt and receive this information:

```
Enter Latest for latest issue, or other date options in MM/DD/YY format
```

To receive up-to-date information, let's enter LATEST and receive this request:

```
Enter keyword phrase
-->
```

Now it's time to enter the keyword phrase that we want to search for. Enter microwave ceramic processing and receive this presentation as the search is made:

```
...........!.....
        1 Occurrences
Enter HEAd for headlines; TExt for full text; Analyze for occurrences
in each service; or Back for new keyword(s)
-->
```

There is only one occurrence of the topic. First let's take a look at the headline to make sure it's what we are looking for by entering HEAD at the prompt and receive this display:

| Head # | Date | Service Code and Title | Words /Lines |
|--------|------|------------------------|--------------|
| 1) | 09/01/91 | EY12 - UTILITY REPORTER--FUELS ENERG. CERAMIC TECHNOLOGY FOR ADVANCED HEAT ENGINES | 103/24 |

```
Enter headline number(s) or ALL to read; PREview; AGain to redisplay
headlines
-->
```

The topic has 103 words and is 24 lines long. It looks interesting, so let's enter ALL to read the details of the article and receive this presentation:

```
Headline #1
Copyright
UTILITY REPORTER--FUELS ENERGY & POWER [EY12] via NewsNet
September 1991
CERAMIC TECHNOLOGY FOR ADVANCED HEAT ENGINES
This report (from Oak Ridge National Laboratory) presents progress
on the development of ceramic technology to meet the needs of
advanced heat engines for automotive technology programs.
Research is presented and discussed covering:
          - turbomilling of SiC whiskers;
          - microwave sintering of SiN;
          - milling characteristics;
          - processing of monolithics;
          - matrices of SiN, oxides, and silicate;
          - thermal and wear coatings;
          - joining and contact interfaces;
          - time-dependent behavior;
          - fracture mechanics;
          - nondestructive evaluation (NDE);
          - environmental effects; and
          - much more.
(Order from InfoTeam Inc., P.O. Box 15640, Plantation, FL 33318-
5640; Phone (305) 473-9560, Fax (305) 473-0544: Report No. UD114QC;
Sep. 1990, 517 pp. Price; $479.00, prepaid.)
Enter headline number(s) or ALL to read; PREview; AGain to
redisplay headlines
-->
```

The search completed, input OFF at the prompt and be logged off from Newsnet and receive this tally:

```
XXXX (user YY) logged out Sunday, 15 Sep 91 16:38:28.
Time used: 00 hour(s), 03 minute(s).
```

So, in only three minutes we have searched all the pertinent documents and are able to read an abstract of a research and development report discussing the latest developments on ceramic technology for advanced heat engines.

# STN

Before we search this excellent database vendor, let's review some of the key commands:

| | |
|---|---|
| FILE | Gets you into a specific database. For example, FILE PHYS selects the PHYS database to be searched. |
| EXPAND | Expands a search by showing you a variety of ways in which a search term appears in the database |
| SEARCH | Sets your search in motion (e.g., SEARCH superconductivity). |

DISPLAY    Provides a number of methods of displaying the hits resulting from the searches.

LOGOFF    Ends your session. You can also use LOG Y.

Wild Cards    The question mark ? is used as a wild card to represent any number of characters to the right of the search term. The # symbol can also be used to represent one or zero additional characters.

For a search example using an STN database, let's look for documents in the PHYS database on the fascinating and quickly developing topic of "superconductivity." Because this will probably result in a large number of hits, let's also restrict the search to documents relating to the developments reported in the U.S. Finally, let's add another restrictor by adding temperature as another search term so we can see what specific temperatures are involved with this technology.

After logging on, giving STN a LOGINID and a PASSWORD, we then receive some greeting screens with announcements and then this display with the STN prompt:

```
= >
```

Because we want to access the PHYS database, let's input FILE PHYS and receive this information:

```
= > file phys
COST IN U.S. DOLLARS
SINCE FILE          TOTAL
ENTRY               SESSION
FULL ESTIMATED COST
        0.36        0.36
FILE 'PHYS' ENTERED AT 21:54:40 ON 09 OCT 91
COPYRIGHT 1991 (c) FACHINFORMATIONSZENTRUM  KARLSRUHE
FILE LAST UPDATED: 28 SEP 91      <910928/UP>
FILE COVERS 1979 TO DATE.
= >
```

To begin the search, let's input superconduct? as the first search term, using the wild card ? to capture all versions of the root search term:

```
= > search superconduct?
```

Quickly we receive a not unexpected result, nearly 52,000 references to this search term:

```
L1        51697 SUPERCONDUCT?
```

Next let's search for temperature:

```
= > search temperature
```

This time we also receive over a huge third of a million citations to the word temperature:

```
L2        343502 TEMPERATURE
```

For the final search, let's limit our search to topics that are concerned with developments in the United States:

> => search united states

We then receive this tally:

|      | 2285   | UNITED                          |
|------|--------|---------------------------------|
|      | 181292 | STATES                          |
| L3   | 1283   | UNITED STATES (UNITED(W)STATES) |

Note that the search has been broken down into the individual and collective terms we searched for, and it even suggested another search variation (UNITED(W)STATES) where the two words could be within W words of each other in the database. But for our purposes, let's try to AND the three search terms together to see how many hits we receive:

> => search L1 AND L2 AND L3

With this combined search, we then receive this tally:

> L4      9 L1 AND L2 AND L3

We now have reduced the search to a reasonable number, 9 hits, so let's take a look at the first three to see what information we can learn from them. To do this, let's input D 1-3 to display the first three citations.

> => D 1-3

We then receive these displays:

```
L4    ANSWER 1 OF 9
AN    90(6):26644  PHYS
TI    Potential benefits of superconductivity to transportation in
the United States.
AU    Rote, D.M.; Johnson, L.R. (Energy and Environmental Systems
Div., Argonne National Lab., IL (USA))
SO    Advances in superconductivity. Proceedings.
      Kitazawa, Koichi (Tokyo Univ. (Japan). Dept. of Industrial
      Chemistry); Ishiguro, Takehiko (Kyoto Univ. (Japan). Dept.
      of Physics) (eds.)
      Tokyo (Japan): Springer 1989 p. 65-70 of 943 p.
      Conference: 1. International Symposium on Superconductivity
(ISS-1),
      Nagoya (Japan), 29-31 Aug 1988
      ISBN 4-431-70039-0
CY    JAPAN
DT    Book Article; Conference
TC    Apparatus
LA    English

L4    ANSWER 2 OF 9
AN    89(20):93710  PHYS
```

TI    Research briefing on high-temperature superconductivity.
CS    National Research Council, Washington, DC (USA)
NR    PB--88-133004/XAB
      Oct 1987 32 p.
      Available: NTIS, PC A03/MF A01.
CY    UNITED STATES
DT    Report
TC    Experimental
LA    English


L4    ANSWER 3 OF 9
AN    89(4):17265  PHYS
TI    International large coil task. Testing of the largest
superconducting toroidal magnet system.
AU    Lubell, M.S.; Fietz, W.A.; Haubenreich, P.N.; Lue, J.W.; Luton,
J.N.; Shen, S.S. (Oak Ridge National Lab., TN (USA)); Okuno, K.
(Atomic Research Inst., Tokyo (Japan)); Ulbricht, A.R.
(Kernforschungszentrum
      Karlsruhe GmbH (Germany, F.R.)); Zichy, J.A. (Schweizerisches
Inst. fuer Nuklearforschung, Villigen (Switzerland))
CS    Oak Ridge National Lab., TN (USA)
SO    Plasma physics and controlled nuclear fusion research 1986.
Vol. 3.Proceedings.
      International Atomic Energy Agency, Vienna (Austria)
      Vienna (Austria): IAEA 1987 p. 279-291 of 629 p.
      Nuclear fusion, supplement.
      Conference: 11. International Conference on Plasma Physics and
Controlled Nuclear Fusion Research, Kyoto (Japan), 13-20 Nov
      1986 ISBN 92-0-130287-8
CY    INT. AT. ENERGY AGENCY (IAEA)
DT    Book Article; Conference
TC    Experimental
LA    English


These are merely bibliographic citations. If you see some you are interested in exploring further, you can ask for other display formats until you locate what you need.

Because the search has been successful for the purposes of this example, let's input logoff to leave the system and receive this information:

= > logoff

You are then given an opportunity to delete or save your answer sets at logoff. Let's input Y to delete them and receive this display:


ALL L# QUERIES AND ANSWER SETS ARE DELETED AT LOGOFF
LOGOFF? (Y)/N/HOLD:N


We then receive this final tally and signoff:


COST IN U.S. DOLLARS
SINCE FILE TOTAL

```
ENTRY  SESSION
FULL ESTIMATED COST
12.24     12.60
STN INTERNATIONAL LOGOFF AT 21:56:51 ON 09 OCT 91
```

The search was conducted for less than $13 and enormous numbers of records were searched. This search easily demonstrates the futility of manual searches and the efficacy of this excellent service.

# My recommendations

First of all, and most importantly, whenever you go online, I recommend that you make sure your telecomm program capture mode is turned on. A capture mode saves your two-way conversation with the computer and stores it on your disk. Most telecomm programs have a capture mode, the program I use and recommend, Procomm Plus, defaults to record all of my two-way conversations. Once recorded, you can input them into your word processor and print these conversations out for reference, or simply erase them if you have no need for them. But if you've failed to record your online conversation, all of the questions and answers have been lost forever.

EasyNet is my overwhelming choice for initially accessing and evaluating some of the major technology database vendors. If you don't use EasyNet, you not only have to sign up with one or more different vendors, you also have to learn the vendor's different and more difficult commands. EasyNet is easy to use, the menus and commands are pretty much self-explanatory, and they have an outstanding crew of experts standing by to answer your SOS's if you need instant online help.

The cost for using EasyNet might be a little higher than if you access the vendor's database directly, but the speed with which you can navigate and receive comprehensive results with EasyNet might end up costing you much less than if you had to learn to circu-itously navigate with each vendor's different set of commands.

In any event, you should use EasyNet when you first start accessing its technology database vendors. When you have gained some experience and have discovered one or two of the major specialist database vendors that you intend to use a lot and that have most of the information you are going to search for, then you should consider signing up with the individual specialist's database vendor(s) and invest the time needed to learn to efficiently navigate and search those databases.

Knowledge Index is my second preference. Although their hours might be inconvenient for some, their excellent instruction manuals, low cost, and their relative ease of operation make it a service worth trying. You might consider KI to be a junior partner of the more complex and comprehensive Dialog. So KI can serve not only as a source of prime informa-tion, it can also serve as an excellent training ground for the largest, most comprehensive, and perhaps most versatile and diversified set of databases in the entire world: Dialog.

If you are going to be doing considerable database searching, and after you have had some experience navigating both EasyNet and Knowledge Index, you should sign up with and begin to use one or more of the technology databases. Which one you choose depends on your specialty in engineering and science.

At first, use the menu mode to become familiar with the databases you are going to work with. Access and store the many helpful suggestions that most of them display on some of their introductory screens. You can print them out and study them at your leisure.

Once you have acquired some familiarity with the menu mode, try the command modes. Your searches will be accomplished much faster, be more thorough, and will cost considerably less.

If you need the latest engineering, scientific or related news business information, or stock quotes, you should also check into the services offered by Dow Jones, DataTimes, NewsNet, and VU/Text. They have the information on all of the latest developments in engineering and science and the business aspects of the professions, plus other news of interest to all engineering and scientific professionals. NewsNet and VU/TEXT can be accessed through IQuest.

ERIC is a comprehensive database but is more suited to professional searchers, engineering and science librarians, scientific researchers, or professionals involved in education.

## Exercises

1. Which of the BRS databases are of most interest to you in your profession?
2. What type of information would you be able to access from Dow Jones and utilize in your professional pursuits?
3. Outline a search for Mead that will provide data for your profession.
4. Which STN databases will be useful for your profession?
5. What type of news does NewsNet carry that would be of interest to you in your professional and/or personal life?

# Appendix A
# Online database vendors

America Online
8619 Westwood Center Dr.
Vienna, VA 22182-2285
(800) 227-6364
(703) 448-8700

BRS (Bibliographic Retrieval Services, Inc.) Information Technologies
Division of Maxwell Online
8000 Westpark Dr.
McLean, VA 22102
(800) 955-0906
(703) 442-0900

CompuServe Information Services
5000 Arlington Centre Blvd.
P.O. Box 20212
Columbus, OH 43220
(800) 848-8199
(614) 457-8600

Data-Star
485 Devon Park Dr., #110
Wayne, PA 19087
(800) 221-7754
(215) 687-6777

DataTimes
14000 Quail Springs Pkwy Suite 450
Oklahoma City, OK 73134
(800) 642-2525
(405) 751-6400

DELPHI
1030 Massachusetts Ave.
Cambridge, MA 02138-5302
(800) 544-4005
(617) 491-3342
(617) 491-6642 (fax)

Dialog Information Services, Inc.
3460 Hillview Av.
Palo Alto, CA 94304
(800) 3-DIALOG
(415) 858-2700
(415) 858-7069 (fax)

Dow Jones News Co., Inc.
Information Services Group
P.O. Box 300
Princeton, NJ 08543-0300
(800) 522-3567
(609) 520-4000
(609) 520-4660 (fax)

Dun's Marketing Services
Three Sylvan Way
Parsippany, NJ 07054-3896
(800) 223-1026
(201) 605-6000

EASYNET
*(see Telebase Systems)*

EPIC
Online Computer Library Center
6565 Frantz Rd.
Dublin, OH 43017-3395
(800) 848-5800
(614) 764-6000

Gale Research, Inc.
835 Penobscot Bldg.
Detroit, MI 48277-0748
(800) 877-GALE
(313) 961-2242

GEnie
General Electric Information Services
401 N. Washington St.
Rockville, MD 20850
(800) 638-9636
(301) 340-4000

Knowledge Index
Dialog Information Services, Inc.
3460 Hillview Av.
Palo Alto, CA 94304
(800) 334-2564
(415) 858-3785

MCI International, Inc.
Two International Drive
Rye Brook, NY 10573-1098
(914) 937-3444
666-101 (telex)

MEAD Data Central, Inc.
9393 Springboro Pike
P.O. Box 933
Dayton, OH 45401
(800) 227-9597
(513) 865-6800

NewsNet
945 Haverford Rd.
Bryn Mawr, PA 19010
(800) 345-1301
(215) 527-8030

Pergamon ORBIT Infoline, Inc.
8000 Westpark Dr.
McLean, VA 22102
(800) 955-0906
(703) 442-0900

Portal Communications, Co.
20863 Stevens Creek Blvd., Suite 260
Cupertino, CA 95014
(408) 973-9111 (voice)
(408) 725-0561 (data)
(408) 725-1580 (fax)

Prodigy Interactive Services, Co.
445 Hamilton Av.
White Plains, NY 10601
(800) PRODIGY
(914) 993-8000

R.R. Bowker Company
205 E. 42nd St.
New York, NY 10017
(212) 916-1600

STN International
c/o Chemical Abstracts Service
2540 Olentangy River Rd.
P.O. Box 3012
Columbus, OH 43210
(800) 848-6533 (in continental U.S.A. except Ohio)
(800) 848-6538 (in Ohio and Canada)
(614) 447-3600 (worldwide)

Telebase Systems
435 Devon Park Dr., Suite 600
Wayne, PA 19087
(215) 293-4700
(215) 341-9660 (fax)

VU/TEXT Information Services, Inc.
325 Chestnut St., Suite 1300
Philadelphia, PA 19106
(800) 323-2940
(215) 574-4400

WilsonLine
The H.W. Wilson Co.
950 University Av.
Bronx, NY 10452
(800) 462-6060
(800) 367-6770 (In New York State)
(212) 588-8400

# Appendix B
## Databases

Included in this appendix is an alphabetical listing of technology and technology-related databases with their title listed first (e.g., ABI/INFORM), generally followed by the organization that created and updates the database (e.g., UMI/Data Courier). Next comes the years that the database covers (e.g., "1984 +" indicates that records are available from 1984 and are still being updated). A brief summary of the database contents follows, along with the frequency at which the database is updated. The final listing is of the database vendors that market access to each specific database (e.g., Dialog.)

**ABI/Inform**, UMI/Data Courier (1971 +). Covers over 800 international periodicals that publish articles on general business, data processing, management, personnel, advertising, and administration. Over 100 of the journals have full text. Updated weekly. BRS, Data-Star, Dialog, EPIC, KI, Orbit.

**Academic American Encyclopedia**, Grolier Electronic Publishing, Inc. (Current). Full-text database of the entire 20-volume encyclopedia on a variety of subjects. Ten-million-word current and comprehensive encyclopedia with over 30,000 entries. Updated quarterly. BRS, CompuServe, Dow Jones, GEnie, VU/TEXT.

**Academic Index**, Information Access Co. (1976 +). Indexes more than 400 scholarly and general interest publications. Coverage represents the most commonly held titles in over 120 university and college libraries. Updated twice a month. BRS, Dialog, KI.

**Aerospace Database**, American Institute of Aeronautics and Astronautics, Technical Information Service (1962 +). Online version of two printed publications: *International Aerospace Abstracts* and *Scientific and Technical Aerospace Reports (STAR)*. Covers aerospace research and development in over 40 countries. Updated twice a month. Dialog, KI.

**Agricola (CAIN)** (1980 +) and **Backfile (CAIB)** (1970–1979), both created and updated by the National Agricultural Library (NAL). CAIN contains citations to journal articles, government reports, serials, monographs, pamphlets and other material as acquired by the National Agricultural Library (NAL) and contributed by cooperating agencies. CAIB Thesaurus is used as source for descriptors for all indexing records. Updated monthly. BRS, Dialog, KI.

**American Library Directory**, R.R. Bowker (Current). Information on public, academic, special, and government libraries, as well as library facilities, personnel, and programs. Updated annually. Dialog.

**American Men and Women of Science**, Bowker Electronic Publishing (Current). Active register of U.S. and Canadian scientists in the physical and biological sciences. Public health scientists, engineers, mathematicians and computer scientists are also included. Updated every three years. Dialog, Orbit.

**American Statistics Index**, Congressional Information Service (1973 +). Guide to all statistical publications of more than 500 U.S. federal offices or regional issuing agencies but does not contain the statistics. Updated monthly. Dialog.

**Analytical Abstracts**, The Royal Society of Chemistry, Cambridge, England (1980 +). Corresponds to the printed publication of the Royal Society of Chemistry, the world's most comprehensive abstracting service dealing solely with analytical chemistry in all its aspects. Updated monthly. Dialog, KI, Orbit.

**API Energy Business News Index (APIBIZ)** (formerly P/E News), The American Petroleum Institute; Central Abstracting and Information Services (1975 +). Worldwide coverage of commercial, financial, marketing and regulatory information concerning the petroleum and energy industries. Updated weekly. Dialog, Orbit.

**APILIT**, American Petroleum Institute (1964 +). Covers worldwide petroleum literature back to 1964, including petroleum processes, fuels, lubricants, petro-chemicals, pipelines, tankers, storage, health, safety and environmental matters, synthetic fuels, etc. Updated monthly. Dialog, Orbit, STN.

**APIPAT**, American Petroleum Institute (1964 +). Contains more than 200,000 patents on petroleum processes, fuels, lubricants, petrochemicals, pipelines, tankers, storage, pollution control, synthetic fuels, synthesis gas, and Chemistry for the U.S. and eight other countries. Updated monthly. Dialog, Orbit, STN.

**Applied Science and Technology Index**, Wilsonline (Nov 83 +). Indexes 335 of the key English-language periodicals in applied science and technology. Updated periodically. BRS, H.W. Wilson.

**Aqualine**, Aqualine Abstracts (1960 +). Covers world's literature on water and wastewater technology and environmental protection. Updated biweekly. Orbit.

**Arab Information Bank**, Al Bayan Press (1983 +). Provides information on all aspects of political, economic, and social life in the Arab world. Updated weekly. Dialog.

**Architecture Database**, Royal Institute of British Architects (1978 +). Online version of the print publication *The Architectural Periodicals Index* and is supplemented with catalog records for other materials. Updated monthly. Dialog.

**Avery Architecture Index**, Avery Architectural and Fine Arts Library, Columbia University (1979). Indexes periodicals, covering all aspects of architecture, including technical and aesthetic material. Updated twice a year. Dialog.

**Beilstein**, The Beilstein Institute (1779–1979). Access to approximately 3.5 million records from the Beilstein Handbook of Organic Chemistry. Updated periodically. Dialog, Orbit, STN.

**BioBusiness**, BIOSIS (1985 +). Information on business applications of biological and medical research, particularly in areas of agriculture and forestry, genetic engineering, biotechnology, pharmaceuticals, medical technology, energy and the environment and food technology. Updated weekly. BRS, Dialog.

**Biography Index**, Wilsonline (Current). Indexes biographical material from 2700 periodicals of all kinds, as well as current books of individual and collective biography. Updated periodically. BRS, H.W. Wilson.

**Biography Master Index**, Gale (Predominantly current). Biographical information on people whose biographies have been listed in more than 1500 volumes from nearly 700 biographical sources. Covers more than 3 million people with more than 7 million citations. All occupations from all areas of the world. Can be searched by name, biographical source indexed, year of birth and year of death. Updated annually with nearly half a million new entries. Dialog.

**BIOSIS Previews**, BIOSIS (1969 +). Contains citations from publications that constitute the major English-language service providing comprehensive worldwide coverage of research in the biological and biomedical sciences. Updated twice a month. BRS, Dialog, STN.

**Biotechnology Abstracts**, Derwent Publications (1982 +). Covers all technical aspects of biotechnology, from genetic manipulation and biochemical engineering to fermentation and downstream processing. Updated monthly. Dialog, Orbit.

**Book Review Index**, Gale (1965 +). Gives location of nearly two million reviews of books and periodicals, approximately 990,000 titles that appear in over 470 publications. Searches can be made by title, author, reviewing journal, book type, and publication year of review. Updated every four months with about 40,000 new entries recorded with each update. Dialog.

**Books in Print**, R. R. Bowker (Current). All books in print and scheduled to be published as far as six months in advance. Includes titles declared out of print from 1980 and on. Comprehensive and continually updated source of information on virtually the entire U.S. book publishing output. Also has special volume Scientific and Technical Books & Serials in Print. Updated monthly. BRS, CompuServe, Dialog, KI.

**Bowker's International Serials Database (Ulrich's)**, R.R. Bowker (Current serials). Comprehensive and continuously updated source of information on selected periodicals and serials published in the United States and throughout the world. Updated monthly. BRS.

**BRS/CROS**, BRS Information Technologies (Current). Automatic cross-database search capability, includes Physical and Applied Sciences database. Updated periodically. BRS.

**BRS/FILE**, BRS Information Technologies (Current). Current information about BRS/Search Service. Updated twice a month. BRS.

**Business Dateline**, UMI/Data Courier (Jan 1985 +). Full text. Contains over 58,000 news and feature stories from more than 170 regional business publications. Updated weekly. BRS, Dialog, EPIC.

**Business Periodicals Index**, Wilsonline (Current). Indexes 304 international English-language periodicals, including trade and business research journals. Updated periodically. BRS, H.W. Wilson.

**Business Software Database**, Information Sources, Inc. (Current). Descriptions of software products available for business users of micro- and mini-computers. Updated quarterly. BRS, Dialog, KI.

**Buyer's Guide to Micro Software (SOFT)**, Online, Inc. (Current). Directory of business and professional microcomputer software available in the U.S. Updated monthly. BRS, Dialog.

**CA Search**, Chemical Abstracts Service (1967 +). Worldwide coverage of literature published in all fields of chemistry. Offers citations of millions of journal articles, patents, reviews, technical reports, monographs, conference and symposium proceedings, dissertations and books so that researchers can track the most active applications in their fields. Updated biweekly. BRS, Dialog, KI, Orbit, STN.

**Ceramic Abstracts**, American Ceramic Society (1976 +). Covers world's technical literature on scientific, engineering, and commercial literature pertaining to ceramics and related materials, including processing and manufacturing aspects. Updated bimonthly. Dialog, Orbit, STN.

**Chemical Abstracts**, Chemical Abstracts Service, American Chemical Society (1977 +). Worldwide coverage of the chemical sciences literature from over 9000 journals, patents from 27 countries and 2 industrial property organizations, new books, conference proceedings, and government research reports. Includes 80 main subject sections, over 7 million records. Updated bimonthly. Dialog, Orbit.

**Chemical Abstracts Service Source Index**, Chemical Abstracts Service, American Chemical Society (1907 +). Listing of bibliographic and library holdings information for scientific and technical primary literature relevant to the chemical sciences. Updated quarterly. Orbit.

**Chemical Business Newsbase**, Royal Society of Chemistry, England (1981 +). Contains facts about the chemical and allied industries with a particular emphasis on European News. Updated weekly. Dialog, KI.

**Chemical Dictionary**, Chemical Abstracts Service, American Chemical Society (1972 +). Companion files to Chemical Abstracts databases. Each of the over 7 million records contains a CAS Registry Number, the molecular formula, CAS nomenclature for a specific compound, and many common synonyms. Updated monthly. Orbit.

**Chemical Economics Handbook**, SRI International (1955–1965 +). Provides more than 12,000 records containing international supply/demand data for the chemical industry. Updated monthly. Orbit.

**Chemical Engineering and Biotechnology Abstracts**, The Royal Society of Chemistry (1970 +). Covers theoretical, practical, and commercial material on all aspects of chemical engineering as well as articles covering chemically-related aspects of processing, safety, and the environment. Updated monthly. Dialog, KI, Orbit.

**Chemical Industry Notes**, Chemical Abstracts Service, American Chemical Society (1974 +). Citations to worldwide chemical business news related to production, pricing, sales, facilities, products and processes, corporate activities, government activities, and people. Updated weekly. Dialog, Orbit, STN.

**Chemical Reactions Documentation Service**, Derwent Publications, Ltd. (1942 +). Provides up-to-date information on new developments in the field of synthetic organic chemistry. Updated monthly. Orbit.

**Chemical Regulations & Guidelines**, CRC Systems, Inc. (1981–1983). Authoritative index to U.S. federal regulatory material relating to the control of chemical substances. Closed file. Dialog.

**Chemical Safety Newsbase**, The Royal Society of Chemistry (1981 +). Covers a wide range of information on the health and safety effects of hazardous chemicals encountered by employees in industry and laboratories. Updated monthly. Dialog, Orbit.

**Chemlist**, Chemical Abstracts Service (1979 +). Information about chemical substances listed on the EPA TSCA (Environmental Protection Agency Toxic Substances Control Act) Inventory or those subject to regulations. STN.

**ChemQuest**, Molecular Design Ltd. (Current). Comprehensive, automated catalog of commercially available research chemicals and where they can be obtained. Updated semi-annually. Orbit.

**ChinaPats**, International Patent Documentation Centre (1985 +). Covers all patent applications published under the patent law of the People's Republic of China. English language abstracts. Updated monthly. Orbit.

**CJACS**, American Chemical Society (1982 +). Complete English-language text of 18 ACS Primary Journals. Updated biweekly. STN.

**CJWILEY**, Chemical Abstracts Service (1987 +). Documents published in five polymer journals of John Wiley & Sons, Inc. Updated biweekly. STN.

**Claims**, IFI/Plenum Data Corporation (1950 +). Provides access to over 2 million U.S. patents issued by the U.S. Patent and Trademark Office. Chemical patents are covered from 1950 on; mechanical and electrical patents from 1963 on; design patents from 1980 on. Updated weekly. Orbit.

**Claims Classification**, IFI/Plenum Data Corporation (1790 +). Provides a dictionary index to the U.S. Patent Office's classification code system containing more than 115,000 subclasses. Updated biannually. Dialog, Orbit.

**Claims Compound Registry**, IFI/Plenum Data Corporation (1950 +). Contains uniterms for specific compounds that have been referenced in five or more patents contained in the CLAIMS/U database. Updated quarterly. Dialog, Orbit.

**Claims Reassignments**, IFI/Plenum Data Corporation (1980 +). Provides information about more than 145,000 patents that have been reassigned since 1980, or reexamined since 1981. Updated bimonthly. Dialog, Orbit.

**Claims/U.S. Patents Abstracts**, IFI/Plenum Data Corporation (1950 +). Contains patents listed in the general, chemical, electrical, and mechanical sections of the Official Gazette of the U.S. Patent Office. Updated monthly. Dialog.

**Cold**, Cold Regions Research and Engineering Laboratory of the U.S. Army Corps of Engineers and the National Science Foundation (1951 +). Covers all disciplines dealing with the Arctic, Antarctica, the Antarctic Ocean and sub-Antarctic islands. Updated quarterly. Orbit.

**Commerce Business Daily**, Commerce Business Daily, U.S. Dept. of Commerce (1982 +). Full-text online of printed Commerce Business Daily that announces products or services wanted or offered by the U.S. Government. Available by 9PM the day before the print publication is distributed. Some daily updates, some weekly. CompuServe, Dialog, NewsNet.

**Compendex\*Plus (Computer Engineering Index)**, Engineering Information, Inc. (1970 +). Online equivalent of Engineering Index, which covers the world's literature in engineering and technology.

Compendex covers the following subject areas: Aeronautical and Aerospace Engineering; Applied Physics (High Energy, Plasma, Nuclear and Solid State); Bioengineering and Medical Equipment; Chemical Engineering, Ceramics, Plastics and Polymers, Food Technology; Civil and Structural Engineering, Environmental Technology; Electrical Instrumentation, Control Engineering, Power Engineering; Electronics, Computers, Communications; Energy Technology and Petroleum Engineering; Engineering Management and Industrial Engineering; Light and Optical Technology; Marine Engineering, Naval Architecture, Ocean and Underwater Technology; Mechanical Engineering, Automotive Engineering and Transportation; Mining and Metallurgical Engineering, Materials Science. Updated monthly. BRS, Dialog, KI, Orbit, STN.

**Computer and Mathematics Search**, Institute for Scientific Information (1980 +). Full-text. Articles from journals and multi-authored books on general and applied mathematics, computer science, statistics, operations research, and management science. Updated weekly. BRS.

**Computer ASAP**, Information Access Corp. (1988 +). Contains abstracts and indexing from journals covering almost every aspect of computers, telecommunications, and electronics. Updated weekly. Dialog.

**Computer Database Plus**, Information Access Company (1983 +). Comprehensive index to and abstracts of 144 major computer industry journals. CompuServe has full-text records from over 60 journals. Information on hardware, software, peripherals, and services as well as information on high-tech fields. Updated weekly. BRS, CompuServe, Dialog, KI.

**Computer News Fulltext**, IDG Communications (1989 +). Contains full-text articles from Computer World and Network World, publications of IDG Communications, Inc., a leading publisher of nearly 120 computer related magazines. Updated weekly. Dialog, KI.

**Computer Readable Databases**, Gale (Current). Contains detailed descriptions of over 5000 publicly available databases in the U.S. and international, including databases available online, through batch access, on CD-ROM, magnetic tape, diskette, or other magnetic media. All types of databases are listed: bibliographical, numerical, bulletin board, directory, full-text, dictionary, audio, time-savers, graphical, statistical, and transactional. Databases can be located on the basis of topic, form, geographical location, vendor, producers, and search fields. Updated semiannually. Dialog.

**Conference Papers Index**, Cambridge Scientific Abstracts (1973 +). Covers over 50,000 papers of approximately 150 scientific and technical meetings worldwide each year. Updated bimonthly. Dialog.

**Computer Retrieval of Information on Scientific Projects, Backfile and Merged File**, National Institutes of Health (1986 +). A major scientific information system covering the largest single organization supporting biomedical research in the world. Updated monthly. BRS.

**Consumer Reports**, Consumers Union (1982 +). Complete text of the 11 regular monthly issues of the Consumer Reports and the 12 monthly issues of Consumer Reports Travel Letter and the Consumer Reports Health Letter. Updated monthly. Dialog.

**CorpTech**, Corporate Technology Information Service (Current). Comprehensive source of company information on over 35,000 U.S. manufacturers and developers of high-tech products. Updated quarterly. Orbit.

**Corrosion**, Maxwell Online (Current). Contains more than 2400 records on the effects of over 600 agents on the most widely used metals, plastics, nonmetallics, and rubbers over a temperature range of 40 – 560 degrees fahrenheit. Updated periodically. Orbit.

**Cuadra Directory of Databases**, Cuadra/Elsevier (Current). Provides comprehensive and timely information about online databases. Lists over 4700 online databases offered through more than 650 online services. Over 1500 databases on CD-ROM, diskette, and magnetic tape are included. Updated quarterly. Orbit.

**Current Contents Search**, Institute for Scientific Information (Current). AGRI (6-month rolling file) is a full-text database describing agriculture, biology, and environmental sciences. ENGI (most current 6 months) is a full-text database describing Engineering, technical and applied sciences. PHYS (most current 6 months) describes physical, chemical, and earth sciences. CCON (most current 6 months) is a multi-disciplinary database corresponding to Current Contents print editions: Physical, Chemical & Earth Sciences;

Engineering, Technology & Applied Sciences; and Agriculture, Biology & Environmental Sciences. Updated weekly. BRS, Dialog.

**Current Biotechnology Abstracts**, The Royal Society of Chemistry (1983 +). Covers all aspects of biotechnology including genetic manipulation, monoclonal antibodies, immobilized cells and enzymes, single-cell proteins, and fermentation technology. Updated monthly. Dialog, KI.

**Current Patents Evaluations & Current Patents Fast Alert**, Current Patents Ltd. (Current). Provides rapid, weekly access to pharmaceutical, biotechnology, and agrochemical patent information. Updated monthly. Orbit.

**Current Technology Index**, The Library Association, London, U.K. (1981 +). Indexes current periodicals from all fields of modern technology, and all journals indexed are published in the United Kingdom. Updated monthly. Dialog.

**Database Index**, Orbit (Current). Master index to Orbit Search Service Databases. Used as selection tool to obtain a list of appropriate databases on a given subject. Databases are printed in ranked order by number of occurrences for a chosen search term. Updated periodically. Orbit.

**DialIndex**, Dialog (Current). The online information directory to most of Dialog's databases. By entering a basic search statement (up to 240 characters), you can determine which databases are likely to contain the most information on your topic. Updated periodically. Dialog.

**Directory of American Research and Technology**, Bowker Electronic Publishing (Current). Contains the research and development capabilities of approximately 12,000 industrial organizations in the United States. Updated annually. Orbit.

**Dissertation Abstracts Online**, University Microfilms International (1861 +). Online access to citations on virtually every doctoral dissertation accepted at North American universities since 1861. Updated monthly. BRS, CompuServe, Dialog, EPIC, KI.

**DMS/FI Contract Awards**, Jane's Information Group (1981 +). Comprehensive file of all nonclassified U.S. Government prime contract actions of $25,000 or more. Updated quarterly. Dialog.

**DOE Energy**. See *Energy Science & Technology*.

**Dow Jones News**, Dow Jones & Company (Current). Price quotes on stock, performance of over 3200 stocks, projected earnings per share for 2400 companies, etc. Real-time updates. Dow Jones.

**Dow Jones Text Search Service**, Dow Jones & Company (1984 +). Full text of Wall Street Journal, Barron's, and Dow Jones News Service. Dow Jones.

**D&B. Dun's Electronic Business Directory**, Dun's Marketing Service (Current). Information for over 8.2 million businesses and professionals in U.S. Listings include address, phone numbers, SIC Codes and descriptions, and number of employees. Covers both public and private U.S. companies of all sizes and types. Quarterly reloads. Dialog.

**EAASY SABRE**, American Airlines (Current). Low cost reservation system maintained by American Airlines. Allows you to make airline reservations on nearly 300 airlines, check the schedules of over 600 more airlines, book rooms at more than 20,000 hotel or condominium properties worldwide, and reserve rental cars from 50 companies. Tickets can be picked up at a choice of locations or be mailed to you. Update varies. CompuServe, DELPHI, GEnie, PC-Link, Prodigy.

**Electric Power Database**, Electric Power Research Institute (EPRI) (1972 +). Summaries of research and development projects conducted in Canada, Mexico, Japan, and electric utilities and other research organizations involved in electric power. Updated monthly. Dialog.

**Electric Power Industry Abstracts**, Edison Electric Institute (1975 – 1983). Provides access to literature on electric power plants and related facilities. Closed file. Orbit.

**Electronic Materials Information**, INSPEC—Institute of Electrical Engineers, U.K.(Current). Full-text database on the properties of substances used in microelectronics. Provides a rolling state-of-the-art of key materials and concise numeric data on the properties of electronic materials. Updated monthly. BRS.

**Electronic Publishing Abstracts**. Merged into Paper, Printing and Publishing, Packaging, & Nonwovens Abstracts (PIRA).

**Embase**, Elsevier Science Publishers (1974 +). Covers the entire field of human medicine and related topics. Updated weekly. BRS, Dialog, KI.

**Encyclopedia of Associations**, Gale Research Co. (Current). Detailed information on over 90,000 active nonprofit organizations, including professional, labor, fraternal, patriotic and hobbyists. U.S. and worldwide coverage. Includes addresses and descriptions of professional societies, trade associations, labor unions, cultural and religious organizations. Includes the following major categories:
National Organizations of the U.S., which covers more than 22,600 American organizations of national scope.
International Organizations, which covers nearly 10,000 multi-national, binational, and foreign national associations.
Regional, State, and Local Organizations, which covers more than 60,000 U.S. associations with interstate, state, intrastate, city, or local scope or membership. Reloaded semiannually. Dialog.

**Encyclopedia of Polymer Science and Engineering Energy**. See *Polymer Online*.

**Energy Bibliography**, Texas A & M University Library (1919 +). Worldwide literature on energy. Subjects include but are not limited to production, utilization, and conservation of all types of fuels. Updated periodically. Orbit.

**Energy Library**, Mead (1981 +). Provides industry specific sources and major regulatory decisions. More than 40 full-text sources are offered concentrating on energy-related news and issues, plus decisions from federal and state regulatory agencies and commissions. Updated periodically. Mead.

**EnergyLine**, Bowker A & I Publishing (1971 +). Broad coverage of scientific, engineering, political, and socio-economic aspects of energy policy, resources, conversion, and consumption. Updated monthly. Dialog, Orbit.

**Energy Science and Technology**, U.S. Department of Energy (1983 +). Worldwide references on all aspects of energy and related topics. Updated biweekly. Dialog, STN.

**Engineered Materials Abstracts**, ASM International and the Institute of Metals (1986 +). Covers journal articles, conference papers, reviews, technical reports, books, dissertations, government reports and U.S., British, and European patents in the fields of material engineering and related subjects. Updated monthly. Dialog, Orbit, STN.

**Environline**, Bowker A&I Publishing (1971 +). Provides more than 125,000 records on air environment, environmental health, land environment, resource management, and water environment. Updated monthly. Dialog, Orbit.

**ERIC (Educational Resources Information Center)**, U.S. Department of Education and ERIC Processing and Reference Facility (1966 +). The largest education database in the world. Citations to university research findings, technical reports, speeches, unpublished manuscripts, books and journal articles in the field of education. Updated monthly. BRS, Dialog, EPIC, KI.

**Encyclopedia of Polymer Science and Engineering**. See *Polymer Online*.

**Everyman's Encyclopedia**, J.M. Dent and Sons, Ltd; Learned Information (Current). Corresponds to the 12 volumes of the printed 6th edition of the Everyman's Encyclopedia and contains articles on virtually every topic. Closed file. Dialog, KI.

**Fairbase**, FAIRBASE Database Limited, Germany (Jan 1986. 2010). Comprehensive directory of forthcoming trade fairs, exhibitions and conferences worldwide. Updated monthly. BRS.

**Federal Applied Technology Database**, National Technical Information Service (1981 + ). Access to U.S. Government engineering and R & D activities offering opportunities for commercial or practical applications. Updated monthly. BRS.

**Federal Research in Progress**, NTIS (Current). Information about ongoing federally funded research projects in the fields of physical science, engineering, and life sciences. Updated monthly. Dialog.

**Fluidex**, BHRA Fluid Engineering (1974 +). Comprehensive source of information product by British Hydromechanics Research Association (BHRA) on all aspects of fluid engineering and behavior and applications of fluids. Updated monthly. Dialog.

**Food Science and Technology Abstracts**, International Food Information Service (1969 +). Covers literature on food science and technology published in more than 2000 journals in 40 languages. Updated monthly. Dialog, KI, Orbit, STN.

**General Science Index**, H.W. Wilson (Current). A guide to current information in over 100 English-language science periodicals designed for students and non-specialists. Updated periodically. BRS.

**General Services Index**, Wilsonline (Current). Indexes 111 major English-language periodicals covering a wide variety of popular interest scientific topics. Updated periodically. H.W. Wilson.

**Geoarchive**, GEOSYSTEMS, United Kingdom (1974 +). International coverage of all aspects of geoscience indexing more than 100,000 references each year. Updated monthly. Dialog.

**Geobase**, Geo Abstracts Ltd. Norwich, U.K. (1980 +). Worldwide literature on geography, geology, ecology, and their related disciplines. Updated monthly. Dialog, Orbit.

**Geomechanics Abstracts**, Rock Mechanics Information Service (1977 +). Contains bibliographic data covering published literature on the mechanical performance of geological materials relevant to the extraction of raw materials for mankind from the earth and construction of structures on or in the earth for civil engineering projects or energy generation. Updated bimonthly. Orbit.

**Georef**, American Geological Institute (1785 +). International literature on geology and geosciences from 3000 journals, plus books, conference proceedings, government documents, maps, and theses with more than 5 million records. Updated monthly. Dialog, Orbit, STN.

**GPO Monthly Catalog**, U.S. Government Printing Office (July 1976 +). Indexes the wide variety of public documents produced under the provenance of the U.S. Government. Covers agriculture to health and human services to housing. Updated monthly. BRS, Dialog, EPIC, KI.

**Harvard Business Review**, John Wiley & Sons (1971 +). Full-text. Review articles from 1976 to present and bibliographic citations and extensive abstracts for articles dating from 1971 to 1975. Updated bimonthly. BRS, Dialog, KI.

**HazardLine**, Occupation Health Services, Inc. (Current). Access to safety and regulatory information on hazardous substances. Updated monthly. BRS.

**Health and Safety Executive**, Health and Safety Executive (1977 +). Covers occupational health and safety aspects of the following areas: manufacturing and process industries; agriculture; engineering; mines and quarries; nuclear technology; offshore oil industry; railway transportation; and hazardous substances. Updated monthly. Orbit.

**Heilbron**, Chapman and Hall Ltd. (Current). Source database of chemical identification, physical-chemical properties, use, hazard, and key reference data on the world's most important chemical substances, as selected by a panel of experts. Updated semiannually. Dialog.

**ICONDA. The CIB International Construction Database**, coordinated by ICONDA Agency (1976 +). Contains over 230,000 bibliographic references to articles published worldwide in the area of construction, civil engineering, architecture, and town planning. Updated monthly. Orbit, STN.

**IHS International Standards and Specifications**, Information Handling Services (Current). Contains references to industry standards and military and federal specifications, and standards cover all aspects of engineering and related disciplines. Updated weekly for MILSPECS, bimonthly. Dialog.

**IHS Vendor Information**, Information Handling Services (Current). Information on products available from over 25,000 vendors. Updated monthly. BRS.

**Imaging Abstracts**, The Royal Photographic Society (1977 +). Contains more than 65,000 abstracts and references to the worldwide published literature on all aspects of the science, technology, and applications of imaging. Updated bimonthly. Orbit.

**Index to U.S. Government Periodicals**, Infordata International Inc. (1980 +). Broad-based, covers nearly all fields of interest, indexing 85 titles from more than 100 government agencies by subject and author. Updated monthly. BRS.

**Industry and International Standards**, Information Handling Services (All active for over 400 domestic, foreign or international organizations). Voluntary engineering standards from private sector societies and organizations in the U.S., plus selected foreign national standards and international standards. Updated every two months. BRS.

**Information Science Abstracts**, IFI/Plenum Corp. (1966 +). Covers the literature on information science and related areas. Updated 11 times a year. Dialog.

**INPADOC/INPANEW**, International Patent Documentation Center (1968 +). Covers patent documents issued by more than fifty national and international patent offices. Contains approximately 18 million records. Updated weekly. Dialog, Orbit, STN.

**INSPEC (Physics, Electronics, Computers)**, Institute of Electrical Engineers, London, England (1969 +). Abstracts of international journals articles, conference reports, dissertations, books, and technical literature.
INSPEC has the following subject coverage:

Physics subfile includes Acoustics; Astronomy and Astrophysics; Atomic and Molecular Physics; Biophysics and Medical Physics; Elementary Particle Physics; Energy Research; Environmental Science, Gases; Fluid Dynamics, and Plasmas; Geophysics; Instrumentation and Measurement; Materials Science; Mathematics and Mathematical Physics; Nuclear Physics; Optics (including Lasers); Physical Chemistry; Properties of Matter; Quantum Mechanics; Thermodynamics.

Electrical Engineering & Electronics Subfile includes Circuits and Components; Electricity Generation and Supply; Electromagnetic Fields and Waves; Electronic Devices and Materials; Electronic Instrumentation; Optics and Electro-optics; Power Systems and Applications; Radar and Radionavigation; Telecommunications.

Computers & Control Subfile includes Computational Mathematics; Computer Applications; Computer Hardware; Computer Software; Control Applications; Control Systems; Information Science; Systems and Control Theory.

Information Technology Subfile includes Business and Financial Applications; Communications, Computing and Systems; Engineering and Industry Applications; Management; Office Automation.

Updated twice a month. BRS, Dialog KI, Orbit, and STN.

**Integrated Circuit Parameter Retrieval Database**, Information Handling Services (Current). Integrated circuits identified by functional description, manufacturing technology, original circuit number, package options, maximum temperature, and numeric parameters including speed, frequency, voltage, etc. Updated monthly. BRS.

**Investor's Daily**, Bowker Business Research (1986 +). Bibliographic database with abstracts of Investor's Daily, a financial newspaper. Updated monthly. BRS, Dialog.

**Investext**, Technical Data International (1982 +). Full-text. Industry and company research reports generated by the financial analysts of leading investment banking firms in U.S., Canada, Europe, and Japan. Updated weekly. BRS, CompuServe, Dialog, Dow Jones, Mead, NewsNet.

**IPABASE**, The Institute of Petroleum, London (1985 +). Covers more than 4000 records on petroleum and allied literature concerning oil field exploration and development, petroleum refining and products, and economics. Updated quarterly. Orbit.

**ISMEC**, Cambridge Scientific Abstracts (1973 +). In-depth coverage of world's technical literature in mechanical engineering, production engineering, and engineering management. Updated bimonthly. Dialog.

**ISTP Search**, Institute for Scientific Information (1982 +). Covers the most relevant proceedings literature published internationally in journal issues, journal supplements, serials and monographs. This multidisciplinary file of more than 1 million records covers the following major areas: agriculture, applied sciences, biology, chemical sciences, clinical medicine, engineering, environmental sciences, life sciences, mathematics, physical sciences, technology and more. Updated monthly. Orbit.

**Jane's Defense and Aerospace News/Analysis**, Jane's Information Group (1982 +). Contains the complete text from Jane's, Interavia, and DMS. Updated weekly. Dialog.

**Japan Technology**, Scan C2C, Inc. (1985 +). Covers the business, technology, and science of Japan by providing more than 150,000 English abstracts of Japanese journal articles and special reports. Emphasis is on chemistry, computers, electronics, materials science, and manufacturing. Updated monthly. Dialog, Orbit.

**JAPIO**, Japan Patent Information Organization (1976 +). Most comprehensive source of unexamined Japanese patent applications, with more than 2.8 million records in English covering all technologies. Updated monthly. Orbit.

**Kirk-Othmer Encyclopedia of Chemical Technology**, John Wiley & Sons, Inc. (1978 to 3rd Ed. of *Kirk-Othmer Encyclopedia of Polymer Science*, 1984). Online version of 25-volume *Kirk-Othmer Encyclopedia of Chemical Technology* and includes *Wiley's Encyclopedia of Polymer Science and Engineering*. Updated concurrently with the publication of each new volume. BRS, Dialog, KI.

**Knowledge Industry Publications**, Knowledge Industry Publications, Inc. (Current). Descriptions of databases publicly available online in North America. Worldwide coverage. Updated monthly. BRS.

**Legal Status**, International Patent Documentation Centre (1959 +). Records thousands of different actions which can affect the legal status of a patent document after it is published and after the patent is granted. Updated weekly. Orbit.

**Life Sciences Collection**, Cambridge Scientific Abstracts (1978 +). Abstracts of literature in the fields of animal behavior, biochemistry, ecology, endocrinology, entomology, genetics, immunology, microbiology, oncology, neuroscience, toxicology, and virology. Updated monthly. Dialog, KI.

**Litalert**, Rapid Patent Service, Research Publications, Inc. (1970 +). Includes more than 15,000 notices of filing and subsequent action for patent and trademark infringement suits filed in the U.S. District Courts and reported to the Commissioner of Patents and Trademarks. Updated weekly. Orbit.

**Magazine ASAP**, Information Access Company (1983 +). Full-text and bibliographic information for articles published in over 80 general interest magazines. Updated weekly. BRS, Dialog, Mead.

**Magazine Index**, Information Access Company (1959−1970, 1973 +). Bibliographic information for articles published in over 400 general interest magazines published in the U.S. and Canada.

Magazine Index database covers the following topics: Current Affairs, National and International; Business and Economics; Education, Cultural Events; Health, Medicine; Consumer Product Evaluations; Social Science; Environmental Issues; Lifestyle, Home and Garden; Performing Arts, Literature, Entertainment; Regional News; Science, Technology, Agriculture; Travel, Sports, Leisure. Updated weekly. BRS, Dialog, KI.

**Management Contents**, (Aug 1984 +) and **Backfile** (1974−July 1984), both from Information Access Company. Current and retrospective materials on a variety of business-related topics to aid management decision-making and forecasting. Updated monthly. BRS, Dialog.

**Marquis Who's Who**, Marquis Who's Who (Current). Contains detailed biographical information on outstanding achievers in a wide variety of professions and virtually every field of endeavor. Contains over 97,000 profiles. Updated quarterly. CompuServe, Dialog, KI.

**Materials Business File**, The Institute of Metals and the American Society for Metals (1985 +). Techno-commercial developments in iron and steel, non-ferrous metals, and engineered materials (ceramics, polymers, composites, plastics). Updated monthly. Orbit, STN.

**MathSci**, American Mathematical Society (1973 +, Statistics 1902 +). Worldwide coverage of research literature of mathematics, computer science, econometrics and applications in physics, engineering, biology, and other fields where mathematics is used. Updated monthly. BRS, Dialog, KI.

**McGraw-Hill Publications Online**, McGraw-Hill (1985 +). Full-text. Covers over 30 magazines and newsletters owned and published by McGraw Hill, ranging from *Avia-*

*tion Week & Space Technology* to *Business Week* to *Coal Week* to *LAN Times*. Updated weekly. Dialog, Dow Jones News/Retrieval, NewsNet, Nexis.

**Merck Index**, Merck and Company (Varies, depending on subject, 1900 +). Interdisciplinary database containing concise descriptions of chemicals, drugs and substances of biological importance. Updated every six months. BRS, Dialog, KI.

**Metadex**, ASM International and the Institute of Metals (1966 +). Provides more than 830,000 records from the international literature on metals and alloys. Updated monthly. Dialog, Orbit, STN.

**Metals Data File**, ASM and the Institute of Metals (1982 +). Provides designation and specification numbers for ferrous and non-ferrous metals and alloys, composition, forms and applications, manufacturers, element concentrations, mechanical and physical properties. Updated monthly. Orbit.

**Meteorological and Geoastrophysics Abstracts**, American Meteorological Society (1972 +). Current citations for the most important meteorological and geoastrophysical research published in worldwide literature sources. Updated irregularly. Dialog.

**Microcomputer Index**, Learned Information, Inc. (1981 +). Abstracts and citations to the literature on the use of microcomputers in business, education, and the home. Updated monthly. Dialog, KI.

**Microcomputer Software Guide**, R.R. Bowker (Current). Directory of business and professional microcomputer software available in the U.S. Reloaded monthly. Dialog, KI.

**Microsearch**, Information, Inc. (1982 +). Product-oriented abstracts of magazine reviews from microcomputer related literature on hardware. Updated monthly. Orbit.

**Military and Federal Specifications and Standards**, Information Handling Services (All unclassified, active, and historical standards or specifications of the DOD and the Federal Government). Most complete source for information on the active and historical standards and specifications of the DOD and federal Government. Updated weekly. BRS.

**Monthly Catalog of U.S. Government Publications**. See *GPO catalog*.

**National Institute for Occupational Safety and Health Technical Information Center**, Technical Information Branch, NIOSH (19th Century to present). Contains more than 164,000 records covering all aspects of occupational safety and health from NIOSH. Updated quarterly. Orbit.

**National Newspaper Index**, Information Access Company (1979 + and 1982 +). Articles published in New York Times, The Wall Street Journal, The Christian Science Monitor, Washington Post, and Los Angeles Times.

National Newspaper Index database covers the following topics: Current Affairs, National and International; Business, Finance, and Economics; Education, Cultural Events; Health, Medicine; Consumer Product Evaluation; Society and the Individual; Environmental Issues; House and Home Activities; Performing Arts, Literature; Regional

News; Science, Technology, Agriculture; Travel, Sports, Leisure. Updated monthly. BRS, Dialog, KI.

**National Union Catalog Codes**, Maxwell Online (Current). Contains the names, complete addresses, and National Union Catalog codes for libraries cited in the CASSI (Chemical Abstracts Service Source Index) database. Updated periodically. Orbit.

**Newsearch**, Information Access Company (Current month only). Bibliographic file containing daily updates of five databases: Magazine Index, National Newspaper Index, Legal Resource Index, Management Contents, and Computer database. Newsearch database covers the following topics: Arts and Entertainment; Business and Economics; Companies; Computers, Electronics, and Telecommunications; Consumer Product Information; Current Affairs; Education and Literature; Environmental Issues; Finance; Health, Medicine, and Science; Law; Management; National and International News; Products; Regional News; Reviews; Sports, Leisure Activities, and Travel. Updated daily. BRS, Dialog, KI.

**NewsNet**, NewsNet, Inc. (1981 +). Full text of over 170 newsletters in 34 business categories. Newsletters related to biosciences and medicine include Health Benefit Cost Containment, Diack Newsletter, Prescription Drug Update, Micro MD Newsletter, and Medical Abstracts Newsletter. Updated periodically. NewsNet.

**Nexis**, Mead (1975 +). Full text of selected newspapers, magazines, U.S. and foreign news services. Transcripts of the MacNeil/Lehrer NewsHour. Newspapers include the L.A. Times, The Washington Post, American and Times of London. Updated periodically. Mead.

**Nonferrous Metals Abstracts**, BNF Metals Technology Centre, England (1961 – 1983). Covers international literature on the nonferrous metals industry and the production, properties, fabrication, and use of nonferrous metals. Closed file. Dialog.

**NTIS**, National Technical Information Service (1964 +). Abstracts of U.S. government-sponsored research reports and studies in the physical sciences, medical and health sciences, as well as agriculture and social science.

NTIS has the following subject coverage: Administration and Management; Aeronautics and Aerodynamics; Agriculture and Food; Astronomy and Astrophysics; Atmospheric Sciences; Behavior and Society; Biomedical Technology and Engineering; Building Industry Technology; Business and Economics; Chemistry; Civil Engineering; Communication; Computers, Control, and Information Theory; Electrotechnology; Energy; Environmental Pollution and Control; Health Planning; Industrial and Mechanical Engineering; Library and Information Sciences; Materials Sciences; Mathematical Sciences; Medicine and Biology; Military Sciences; Missile Technology; Natural Resources and Earth Sciences; Navigation, Guidance, and Control; Nuclear Science and Technology; Ocean Technology and Engineering; Photography and Recording Devices; Physics; Propulsion and Fuels; Space Technology; Transportation; Urban and Regional Technology. Updated biweekly. BRS, Dialog, KI, Orbit, STN.

**OAG Electronic Edition**, Official Airline Guides, Inc. (Current). Full text of the Official Airline Guide, offering flight and scheduling information for passenger and freight cargo service for more than 600 airlines operating nationally and overseas. Hotel and motel information is also available on the database. Fares are updated daily, schedule changes appear weekly. Tickets can be delivered to your office, picked up at a Thomas Cook Agency, the airport, or mailed to you. Updated weekly for schedules, real-time for seat and fare availability. CompuServe, DELPHI, Dialog, Dow Jones, EPIC, KI, NewsNet.

**Online Microcomputer Software Guide and Directory**, Online, Inc. (Currently available microcomputer software). Current microcomputer software product description, plus related information. Critical review, also includes a short abstract. Updated monthly. BRS.

**Orbchem/Orbpat**, Maxwell Online (Current). Designed to assist crossfile searching of chemical and patents databases. Updated periodically. Orbit.

**Orbit**, Maxwell Online (Current). Database automatically entered when the user accesses Orbit. Provides helpful information about the Orbit databases. Updated periodically. Orbit.

**PaperChem**, The Institute of Paper Science and Technology (1967 +). Covers international patent and journal literature related to pulp and paper technology. Updated monthly. Dialog.

**Patdata**, U.S. Patent and Trademark Office (1975 +). Detailed information and informative abstracts for all utility patents issued by the U.S. Patent and Trademark Office since 1971 and all reissue patents issued since July 1, 1975. Updated weekly. BRS.

**Patent Status File**, Rapid Patent Status Service, Research Publications, Inc. (1973 +). Comprehensive alert to over 20 types of post-issue actions affecting U.S. patents. Updated monthly. Orbit.

**Peterson's College Database**, Peterson's Guides, Inc. (Current year). Comprehensive file of degree granting, post-secondary colleges and universities in the U.S. and Canada. Includes general information, admission requirements, costs, housing, sports, and majors. Updated annually. CompuServe, Dialog, Dow Jones, KI.

**P/E News (Petroleum/Energy Business News Index)**. See *APIBIZ*.

**Petroleum Exploration & Production**, Petroleum Abstracts (1981 +). Bibliographic references to scientific articles, patents, meeting papers, and government reports of interest to geologists, geophysicists, petroleum engineers, and other technical professionals and managers in the oil and gas exploration and production industry. Updated monthly. Dialog.

**Pira. Paper, Printing, and Publishing, Packaging, and Nonwovens Abstracts**, Pira International (1975 +). Coverage of the world's literature on all aspects of paper, pulp, nonwovens, printing, publishing, and packaging. Updated biweekly. Orbit.

**PNI (Pharmaceutical News Index)**, UMI/Data Courier (1974 +). Provides current and retrospective news about pharmaceuticals, cosmetics, medical devices, and related health care industries. Updated weekly. Dialog, EPIC, Orbit.

**Pollution Abstracts**, Cambridge Information Group (1970 +). International technical literature of environmental science and technology. Updated every two months. BRS, Dialog, KI.

**Polymer Online**, John Wiley and Sons (1974 +). Online version of the Second Edition of the Encyclopedia of Polymer Science and Engineering, including supplemental Volume 18. Updated irregularly. BRS, Dialog.

**Popular Magazine Review Online**, Ebsco Industries, Inc. (1984 +). Weekly reference service provides access to the latest popular U.S periodical literature. Updated weekly. BRS.

**Power**, Energy Library, U.S. Department of Energy (1950 +). Consists of more than 30,000 catalog records for books, monographs, proceedings, journals, and other materials in the collections of the Energy Library, U.S. Department of Energy. Updated quarterly. Orbit.

**PTS Aerospace/Defense Markets & Technology**, Predicasts (1982 +). Fact-filled abstracts and full-text articles from more than 90 key journals covering worldwide aerospace and defense activities. Updated daily. Dialog.

**PTS PROMT**, Predicasts (1972 +). Multi-industry database that provides broad, international coverage of companies, products, markets, and applied technologies for all industries. Updated daily. BRS, Dialog.

**Rapra Abstracts**, Rapra Technology, Ltd. (1972 +). Coverage of the world's primary database on technical and commercial aspects of the rubber, plastics, and polymer composited industries. Updated biweekly. Orbit.

**Rapra Trade Names**, Rapra Technology, Ltd. (1976 +). Contains more than 30,000 tradenames and trademarks used in the rubber and polymer industries around the world. Updated biweekly. Orbit.

**Religion Index**, American Theological Library Association (ATLA) (1975 +). Current and retrospective scholarly material on religion, theology, and scriptural and ministerial studies. Updated monthly. BRS, Dialog.

**Research Centers and Services Directories**, Gale Research (Current year's printed edition). Comprehensive source of information on over 26,000 organizations conducting research worldwide. Covers medical and health sciences and biological and environmental sciences. Reloaded semiannually. Dialog.

**SAE Global Mobility Database**, Society of Automotive Engineers (1906 varies +). Provides access to technical papers presented at the SAE meetings and conferences. Topics include safety, design, materials, manufacturing, testing, marketing, and fuels. Updated quarterly. Orbit.

**Safety Science Abstracts**, Cambridge Scientific Abstracts (1981 +). Covers the broad interdisciplinary science of safety-identifying, evaluating and eliminating or controlling hazards. Updated monthly. Orbit.

**Scisearch (Science Citation Index)**, Institute for Scientific Information (1974 +).

An international interdisciplinary index to the literature of science, technology, biomedicine, and related disciplines.

Scisearch database covers the following topics: Agriculture and Food Technology; Astronomy and Astrophysics; Behavioral Sciences; Biochemistry; Biology; Biomedical Sciences; Chemistry; Computer Applications and Cybernetics; Earth Sciences; Electronics; Engineering; Environmental Science; Genetics; Instrumentation; Materials Science; Mathematics; Medicine; Meteorology; Microbiology; Nuclear Science; Pharmacology; Physics; Psychiatry and Psychology; Veterinary Medicine; Zoology. Current files updated weekly. Dialog, Orbit.

**Scientific and Technical Books and Serials in Print**, Bowker Electronic Publishing (Current). Comprehensive subject selection of books and serials in scientific and technical fields. All aspects of physical and biological sciences and their applications are included as well as engineering and what can generally be called technology. Updated monthly. Orbit.

**Semiconductor Parameter Retrieval**, Information Handling Services (Current). Data to identify semiconductor devices by specific functional, technological, and numerical parameters. Updated every 4 months. BRS.

**Soft:Online Microcomputer Software Guide and Directory**, Online, Inc. (Currently available microcomputer software). Current microcomputer software product description, plus related information. Critical review, also includes a short abstract. Updated monthly. BRS, Dialog.

**Soviet Science and Technology**, IFI/Plenum Data Company (1975 +). Scientific and technical information published in Soviet Bloc countries. Updated monthly. Dialog.

**SPIN (Searchable Physics Information Notices)**, American Institute of Physics (1975 +). Covers all major areas of physics research. Updated monthly, Dialog.

**Sport**, Sport Information Resource Centre (1949 +). Bibliographic records, many with abstracts, of serial and monographic literature in sport recreation, exercise physiology, sports medicine, coaching, physical fitness, etc. Updated monthly. BRS, Dialog, KI.

**Sport and Fitness Thesaurus**, Sport Information Centre (Current). Contains all descriptor terminology and hierarchical relationships that are included in the published version of the SPORT Thesaurus. Updated semiannually. BRS.

**Standard and Poor's Register—Biographical**, Standard & Poor's (Current). Extensive personal and professional data on key executives affiliated with public and private, U.S. and non-U.S. companies with sales of one million dollars and over. Reloaded semiannually. Dialog, Orbit.

**Standards and Specifications**, National Standards Association (Current). Government and industry standards, specifications, and related documents. Updated monthly. Dialog.

**Standards Files Concatenated, MLSS AND STDS**, Information Handling Services (Some 1920, some 1930). Combination of STDS and MLSS, includes voluntary engineering standards and codes, domestic and international, as well as military and federal specifications, standards and qualified product lists, and military standard drawings. Updated periodically. BRS.

**Supertech**, R. R. Bowker (1973 +, 1984 +). Covers the fields of biotechnology, artificial intelligence, computer-aided design and computer-aided manufacturing (CAD/CAM), robotics and telecommunications. Biotechnology Applications include medical and pharmaceutical fields. Updated monthly. Dialog, Orbit.

**Textile Technology Digest**, Textile Technology Institute (1978 +). International coverage of the literature of textiles and related subjects. Updated monthly. Dialog.

**Trade and Industry ASAP III**, Information Access Company (1983 +). Full-text and bibliographic information for articles published in over 80 trade and business periodicals. Updated monthly. BRS, Dialog, Mead.

**Transportation Library**, Mead (1989 +). Combines respected industry publications with major federal regulatory decisions and information. Updated periodically. Mead.

**Transportation Research Information Service (TRIS)**, Transportation Research Board (Current). Most general of transportation databases, has short abstracts of ongoing or recently completed transportation projects. Updated monthly. Dialog.

**Tulsa (Petroleum Abstracts)**, Petroleum Abstracts at the University of Tulsa (1965 +). More than 450,000 references and abstracts to worldwide literature and patents related to oil and natural gas exploration, development, and production. Updated weekly. Orbit.

**Ulrich's International Periodical Directory**. See *Bowker's International Serials Database*.

**UMI Article Clearinghouse**, UMI Article Clearinghouse (Core collection 1978+; many titles have pre-1978 availability). Records for more than 9000 periodicals and conference proceedings. Photocopies of articles available from UMI Article Clearinghouse under direct-licensing agreement with the publishers. Updated monthly. BRS.

**US Classification**, Derwent, Inc. (1790 +). Contains all U.S. Classifications, Cross-Reference Classifications, and Unofficial classifications for all patents issued from 1790 to date. Updated biannually. Orbit.

**US Patents**, Derwent, Inc. (1970 +). Provides complete patent information, including complete front-page information, plus all claims of all U.S. patents issued since 1971. Updated weekly. Orbit.

**Wasteinfo**, Waste Management Information Bureau, Harwell Laboratory (1973 +). Contains bibliographic references on all aspects of non-radioactive waste management. Updated monthly. Orbit.

**Weldasearch**, TWI (1967 +). Contains over 113,000 citations with abstracts covering international literature such as journal articles, research reports, books, conference papers, standards, patents, theses, and special publications in the areas of joining metals and plastics, metal spraying and thermal cutting. Updated monthly. Orbit.

**Who's Who in Technology**, Gale (Current). Lists over 37,000 leading technological experts in more than 46 fields ranging from engineering, to robotics, to biomedical science. Searches can be made by name and title, employer, career history, education, honors and awards, publications and patents, areas of expertise, and organizational membership. Updated biennially. BRS, Orbit.

**World Aluminum Abstracts**, ASM International (1968 +). Coverage of the world's technical literature on aluminum, ranging from ore processing (exclusive of mining) through end use. Updated monthly. Dialog.

**World Ceramics Abstracts**, Rapra Technology, Ltd. (1978 +). Provides coverage of world's literature on all aspects of ceramics. Updated biweekly. Orbit.

**World Patents Index**, Derwent Publications, Ltd. (1963 +). Comprehensive and authoritative file of data relating to patent specifications issued by the patent offices of 31 major industrial countries. Some updated monthly, some weekly. Dialog, Orbit.

**World Surface Coatings Abstracts**, Paint Research Association (1976 +). World's primary database, with more than 142,000 records, on all aspects of paints and surface coatings. Updated monthly. Orbit.

**World Textiles**, Shirley Institute, United Kingdom (1970 +). All aspects of textiles and related fields, including industrial and medical applications, chemistry of fibers, and the economics of textiles. No abstracts. Updated monthly. Dialog.

**WPIA/WPILA**, Derwent Publications, Ltd. and the American Petroleum Institute, Central Abstracting & Indexing Service (1963 +). Contains records for more than 5.2 million patents covering petroleum processes, fuels, lubricants, petrochemicals, pipelines, and related topics. Some updated weekly, some monthly. Orbit.

**Zoological Record**, BIOSIS (1978 +). Extensive coverage of the world's zoological literature. Covers biochemistry, disease, immunology, and physiology. Updated monthly. BRS, Dialog.

# Appendix C
# Database abbreviations

A huge amount of "alphabet soup" still exists in Online Systems. This probably resulted from the early days of computerizing records when memory was expensive and abbreviations conserved memory. Here are some of the abbreviations you may encounter in your searches or reading.

This list does not include database commands nor codes for searching.

| | |
|---|---|
| AACR2 | Anglo-American Cataloging Rules. 2nd Edition |
| ACS | American Chemical Society |
| AGRICOLA | AGRICultural On-Line Access (database)EMA |
| ALA | American Library Association |
| APILIT | American Petroleum Institute Literature (database) |
| APIPAT | American Petroleum Institute Patent (database) |
| ARIST | Annual Review of Information Science and Technology |
| ARPA | Advanced Research Projects Agency |
| ASCII | American Standard Code for Information Interchange |
| BALLOTS | Bibliographic Automation of Large Library Operations Using a Time-sharing System |
| BIBCITE | Bibliographic Citation |
| BIOSIS | BioSciences Information Service (database) |
| BKS | Books file in RLIN |
| BLAISE | British Library Automated Information Service |
| BPS | Bits per second |
| BRS | Bibliographic Retrieval Services |
| BT | Broader term |
| BULL | BRS/Bulletin (database) |
| CA | Chemical Abstracts |
| CAB | Commonwealth Agricultural Bureau (database) |
| CAIN | CAtaloging and INdexing System of the National Agricultural Library (database) |
| CALS | Computer-Assisted Literature Searching |

| | |
|---|---|
| CBPI | Canadian Business Periodicals Index (database) |
| CDI | Comprehensive Dissertation Index (database)-now Dissertation Abstracts Online |
| CHEMNAME | CA Chemical Name Dictionary (database) |
| CHEMSIS | CHEMical Singly Indexed Substances (database) |
| CIJE | Current Index to Journals in Education |
| CIN | Chemical Industry Notes (database) |
| CROS | BRS/CROS (database) |
| CNI | Canadian Newspaper Index (database) |
| COHD | Copyright Office History Document |
| COHM | Copyright Office History Monograph |
| CPS | Characters per second |
| CR | Carriage Return |
| CRDS | Chemical Reactions Documentation Service (database) |
| CRT | Cathode-Ray Tube |
| D&B | Dun & Bradstreet |
| DBI | DataBase Index (database) |
| DIMDI | Deutsches Institut fer Medizinische Dokumentation and Information |
| DOE | Department of Energy |
| EDP | Electronic data processing |
| EMA | Engineered Materials Abstracts (database) |
| ERIC | Educational Resources Information Center (database) |
| ESA | European Space Agency |
| GEnie | General Electric Network for Information Exchange |
| GPO | Government Printing Office |
| IAC | Information Access Company |
| IBM | International Business Machines |
| ICONDA | Information Center for Regional Planning and Building Construction |
| ID | Identification |
| INKA | Information System Karlaruche |
| INSP | INSPEC (database). See below. |
| INSPEC | INFormation Service in Physics, Electrotechnology and Control (database) |
| IRCS | International Research Communication Service |
| IRS | Information Retrieval Services |
| ISBN | International Standard Book Number |
| ISI | Institute for Scientific Information |
| ISO | International Organization for Standardization |
| ISSN | International Standard Serial Number |
| JN | Journal |
| KI | Knowledge Index |
| LCS | Library of Congress System |
| LRI | Legal Resource Index (database) |

| | |
|---|---|
| MARC | MAchine Readable Catalogue Project |
| MDC | Mead Data Central |
| METADEX | Metals Abstracts and Alloy Index (database) |
| METRO | Metropolitan Reference and Research Agency |
| MI | Magazine Index (database) |
| MRDF | Machine-Readable Data Files |
| NAARS | National Automated Accounting Research System (database) |
| NASA | National Aeronautics and Space Administration |
| NLM | National Library of Medicine |
| NNI | National Newspaper Index (database) |
| NT | Narrower Term |
| NTIS | National Technical Information Service (database) |
| NUC | National Union Catalog |
| NYTIS | The New York Times Information Service |
| OBAR | Ohio Bar |
| OCLC | Online Computer Library Center |
| ONTAP | ONline Training And Practice |
| ORBIT | On-Line Retrieval of Bibliographic Information Timeshared |
| PAIS | Public Affairs Information Service (database) |
| PLASPEC | Plastics Technology Materials Selection (database) |
| PNI | Pharmaceutical News Index |
| PTS | Predicasts Terminal System |
| RAM | Random Access Memory |
| RASD | Reference and Adult Service Division |
| RECON | REmote CONsole |
| RIE | Resources in Education |
| RLIN | Research Libraries Information Network |
| RT | Related Term |
| SCORPIO | Subject-Content-Oriented Retriever for Processing Information On-Line |
| SDC | System Development Corporation |
| SDI | Selective Dissemination of Information |
| SN | Scope Note |
| SRIF | School Practices Information File (database) |
| SSCI | Social Sciences Citation Index (database) |
| STAIRS | STorage And Information Retrieval System |
| STN | Scientific & Technical Information Network |
| TI | Trade and Industry Index (database) |
| TWX | Teletypewriter Exchange Service |
| UF | Used for |
| UNISIST | United Nations Information System in Science and Technology |
| USPSD | United States Political Science Documents (database) |
| VDT | Video Display Terminal |
| WPI/WPIL | World Patents Index / World Patents Index latest (database) |

# Glossary

**abort**  The procedure for terminating a program when a malfunction or error occurs.

**abstract**  Brief summary of an article, book, report, etc. Lists author, title, publisher, and date of publishing.

**aliasing**  The "stair-step" effect on lines and edges of a computer graphic.

**alphanumeric characters**  Character set containing letters, numbers and other special symbols, e.g., punctuation marks.

**ampersand**  &. Symbol for the·word "and."

**AND**  A boolean operator. A AND B provides an output only if both A and B are present.

**ANSI**  A display mode that gives the IBM compatibles the ability to display color, reverse, and flashing text on your screen, plus some graphics.

**anti-aliasing**  A technique used to blur the image to minimize the stair-step look of computer generated graphics.

**ASCII**  American Standard Code for Information Interchange, used for all communication to represent letters, numbers, and symbols as bit patterns. ASCII files can be read by practically all software.

**application program**  Program written enabling a computer to perform useful work, such as a word processing program.

**aspect ratio**  The ratio of the height-to-width on a display screen or other device.

**asynchronous**  Not synchronous. A method of transmitting signals, one data bit at a time, with an indeterminate amount of time between characters. The beginning and end of a character are indicated by special start and stop bits.

**autoanswer**  A mode in which the modem answers incoming calls automatically, without your intervention.

**autodial**  Modem feature enabling a computer to automatically dial a prerecorded phone number for connection to a host computer.

**backing up**  Making copies of files for use in case the original data is lost or damaged.

**bandwidth**  A range of band frequencies within which a device can operate with specified performance characteristics.

**batch file**  A file that stores an often used software routine.

**Baud** The rate at which data is transmitted over telecommunications lines. 1200 baud is approximately equal to 120 characters per second.

**Bell 103J** A set of specifications provided by Bell Systems for asynchronous, full-duplex modem transmission at up to 300 bps.

**Bell 212A** A set of specifications provided by Bell Systems for asynchronous, full-duplex modem transmission at 1200 bps.

**bibliography** A list of documents relating to a specific subject or author.

**binary** A numbering system based on 2. Two numbers, 1 and 0, represent all possible mathematical values.

**Bit** Contraction of binary digit, the smallest bit of data in a data transmission. Seven or eight bits equal a byte, which is roughly equal to one character.

**bit map** An image of a document or graphic composed of black and white dots, much like a TV picture.

**bits per second** See *bps*.

**block** In word processing, a specific set of text that is to be manipulated (e.g., copied, moved, or erased). In file transfers or other error-checking communications, a block is a group of characters sent together, along with some type of error-checking information. Common block sizes are 128 bytes and 1024 bytes.

**Boolean algebra** Math that expresses logical relationships between inputs and uses AND, OR, and NOT logical operators.

**boot** The process by which a computer turns itself on, literally pulling itself by its own bootstraps.

**bps (bits per second)** The rate of transmission of data. Standard speeds are 300, 1200, and 2400 bps, with speeds up to 9600 used by a small but rapidly growing subgroup.

**buffer** Computer memory set aside to temporarily store information until it can be acted upon.

**BBS (Bulletin Board System)** A computer with a modem dedicated to other computerized callers who can leave, read, and retrieve electronic messages.

**byte** Smallest addressable unit of storage, usually eight bits long.

**CCIT** Consultative Committee for International Telegraphy and Telephony, a body operating under the United Nations' International Telecommunications Union, advising on standards in this area.

**CGA** Color Graphics Adapter. A low/medium resolution color graphics system for PCs.

**checksum** Used in error-checking protocols. Different protocols base the checksum on different aspects of the data. The receiving system compares its own checksum with the one received from the sending system.

**COM port** Communications port. An interface on the computer used for transferring information to another piece of equipment, such as a printer or modem.

**command mode** A search mode in which commands are used in lieu of menus to navigate and search inside a database.

**Connect Time** The amount of time connected to another system.

**CRC** Cyclic Redundancy Checking. An advanced method of error checking using a 2-byte-packet comparison value.

**CRT** Cathode Ray Tube. The picture tube for your monitor or TV set.

**cursor** A short line or other symbol (usually flashing) on your monitor that indicates where the next character will be input.

**daisy wheel printer**   A printer with a removable, flat disk containing characters to be printed by impacting on the paper.

**database**   A collection of interrelated data that can be accessed by computer.

**database vendor**   A company or organization that markets online databases.

**data bit**   One of the seven (or eight) bits making up the code for an alphanumeric or non-printing character.

**data compression**   A process that uses an algorithm to encode the pattern of frequently repeated letters, words or pixels to compress data to occupy less space.

**data link**   Comprised of two modems, each receiving and/or sending data from an attached computer, using a telephone link to send and/or receive data from each other.

**DB25C connector**   A standard connector with 25 pins arranged in two rows that is used for an RS-232C serial interface.

**debug**   In computing, the search for and correction of a mistake in a computer program.

**default**   The value that is entered by a computer program instead of by a user.

**digitize**   To convert a drawing, photograph, or other continuous image into a digital form.

**directory**   An index, a list of filenames and locations of files on a disk.

**DIP switches**   DIP is an acronym for Digital Inline Package. DIP switches are small switches in a printed circuit board that allow setting certain hardware options.

**Disk density**   Density indicates how closely magnetic information can be stored on a disk. The most common disk types are double- and high-density disks. Double-density disks store 360K (5.25″ disk) or 720K (3.5″ disk) of data, while high-density disks store up to 1.2M (5.25″) or 1.44M (3.5″) of information.

**DOS**   Disk Operating System. A specialized, disk-oriented program that provides an easy-to-use link between the user and the computer's disk drive.

**dot matrix printer**   A printer in which each character is represented by a pattern of dots and imprinted on paper.

**downloading**   The process of loading information into a computer from a remote computer, by using a telephone line.

**DSSD**   Double-sided single density disks.

**DSDD**   Double-sided double density disks.

**duplex**   A communications system capable of transmitting in both directions.

**echo**   Online systems can send a caller's characters back to the caller's screen so the caller's system does not need to send or echo outgoing characters to its own screen.

**EGA**   Enhanced Color Graphics Adapter. A medium resolution color system for PCs.

**electronic mail**   E-Mail. A service that permits sending messages to other users on the same on-line system.

**electronified**   Information that can be accessed by electronic means.

**error checking protocol**   A data communications protocol for exchanging files that checks for errors in a preset segment (block) of the field being sent, then retransmits any segment where transmission errors were found.

**field**   Within a database, a field is one specific part of a record (e.g., name).

**file**   A collection of related records treated as a basic unit of storage.

**floppy disk**   Thin, flexible, magnetic disk for storing digital data.

**front-end software**   Software that automates much of the logging on and search functions of a database.

**font**  A complete alphabet of any one typeface in a given point size—uppercase, lowercase, numerals, punctuation marks, etc.

**full duplex**  Simultaneous and independent transmission of data in both directions on the same line.

**gateway**  An *ad hoc* connection between two online services.

**handshake**  For communication with modems, the exchange of signals after the modem being called is online, an acknowledgement that data was received.

**hard disk**  A rigid storage disk that stores much more data than floppies and which can be accessed in much less time.

**hardware**  The physical components or equipment that make up a computer system.

**hertz (Hz)**  Frequency in cycles per second.

**half duplex**  The transmission of data in only one direction at a time on the same line.

**hard copy**  A printed copy of writing.

**Hayes compatible**  Modems that use commands originated by Hayes Microcomputer Products. Although not an absolute requirement, Hayes compatibility is a *de facto* industry standard.

**Hits**  The number of documents in a database search that contain one or more of the specified search terms.

**host computer**  A computer that primarily provides services such as database access.

**ink jet printer**  An output device that prints by spraying a thin stream of ink onto the paper.

**interface**  The point at which two systems interact. It can be a physical interface involving a connector or a communications protocol that allows one device to communicate with another.

**K**  Abbreviation for Kilo or 1000 in decimal notation (e.g., 100K means 100,000).

**KERMIT**  Communications protocol common to mini- and main-frame computers with 7-bit communications environment, used in many academic institutions.

**keyword**  A significant and informative word in a title or document that partially describes the content of the document.

**LAN**  Local Area Network. A communication system that connects several computers together so they may communicate with each other and share data and resources (such as a laser printer and a hard disk).

**landscape format**  A printing format in which the width dimension is larger than the height dimension. For example, a landscape format of a standard A-size is 11″ wide by 8.5″ high.

**laser printer**  A high speed, non-impact, high-quality printer in which a laser beam "writes" on a drum and prints alphanumerics, graphics, and special fonts.

**logoff**  The process of terminating communication between a computer and a user.

**logon**  The process of establishing and verifying the authority to communicate between a user and a computer.

**MacBinary**  A file-transfer protocol used to transfer Macintosh documents and applications over phone lines.

**macro**  A special preprogrammed series of instructions initiated by activating specific key combinations to automate often used functions.

**meg**  Abbreviation for a million. A 20M memory has a memory capacity of 20,000,000 bits.

**menu**  A display listing available functions for selection by an operator.

**menu mode**  A program that is activated by making menu selections instead of by using commands.

**MNP2,3,4**  Created and sold by Microcom, Inc., proprietary, licensed error-control protocols. The numbers indicate specific versions or classes.

**MNP5**  Microcom's proprietary, licensed data-compression protocol, usually results in a 2 to 1 compression.

**modem**  A contraction of Modulator/Demodulator. A modem is the interface box or card that converts a signal into two different frequencies so that it may be transmitted over telephone lines and that also performs the reverse function, converting the signal on the phone lines to 1s and 0s that can be handled by a computer. The modem converts the computer's 1s and 0s into two musical tones that whistle down the telephone line and are turned back into 1s and 0s at the receiving end.

**monochrome monitor**  A monitor that displays information in only one color. Monochrome monitors generally have black backgrounds with white, amber, or green letters.

**mouse**  A type of pointer used to select options from a list or menu presented on a screen or to sketch graphics in a graphics program.

**NLQ**  Near Letter Quality. Pertains to output of some dot matrix printers where the quality is nearly equal to the quality of a daisy wheel or laser printer.

**Network**  An electrical hookup consisting of two or more PCs or computer equipment that allows the equipment to communicate with each other.

**NOR**  A Boolean operator that indicates that an output will occur only when both of the inputs are absent. A NOR B means that no output will result unless both A and B are absent.

**offline**  The modem state when it is not connected to another modem.

**online**  The state in which a computer is connected via a modem to another computer, often located at a remote location.

**online database**  A computer system that a user can dial through the public telephone network with or without first paying a fee.

**OR**  A logical operator that indicates that the presence of either one or both terms provides an output. A OR B means that either or both A or B will provide an output. Also called "Inclusive OR." However, an "exclusive OR" gives an output only if A OR B (but not both) is present.

**parity**  A setting for an error-checking bit (parity bit) during transmission of data, parity can be odd or even.

**password**  A special word or code that must be presented to a computer system to gain access to its resources.

**pixel**  The smallest dot on a video screen, a contraction of "picture element." On a color monitor screen, each pixel is made up of one or more triads.

**portrait format**  A format where the width dimension is less than the height dimension. For an A-size format, the width is 8.5″ and the height is 11″.

**prompt**  A symbol that appears on the video screen asking you to enter information; typically > or ] is used.

**protocol**  A set of rules for transmitting data between computers to detect and correct errors that occur during transmission.

**pulse dialing**  Phone dialing in which numbers are entered by depressing individual buttons.

**RAM**  Random Access Memory. Storage in which data can be input and read out, independent of its location in memory, that is it can be randomly accessed. RAM is normally "volatile;" that is, it loses its memory when power is turned off.

**record**  A unit of data.

**resolution**  A measurement, usually in dots per inch, of the sharpness of an image generated by a monitor or printer.

**RS 232C**  The standard established by the Electronics Industries Association for serial transmission of data for telecommunications.

**ROM**  Read Only Memory. Static memory that cannot be changed by conventional procedures. Retains memory contents with power on or off.

**serial transmission**  A method of transmission where the bits carrying the information are sent one at a time, in a single row, on a channel such as a telephone line.

**shareware**  A method of marketing software where the customer purchases a copy of the program to test, and then is requested to send in a registration fee if he or she decides to keep using the program.

**SIG**  Acronym for Special Interest Group

**software**  Non-hardware component of computers, the "intellect" that activates the computer's muscle.

**soft copy**  A copy of textual and/or graphical material that is stored in digital form on a diskette or other storage media. A printer converts soft copy to hard copy.

**SSSD**  Single-sided single density disk.

**SSDD**  Single-sided double density disk.

**start bit and stop bit**  A start bit alerts the receiving computer that data will follow and a stop bit signals the end of a character, word, or the entire transmission. Start and stop bits may be 1 or 2.

**synchronous**  A system of transmission where data is sent in blocks and the receiver and sender must be in synchronism.

**telecomm**  Telecommunications. Communications over a distance.

**template**  The format or guide for a file that has previously been laid out where the user fills in the data or text fields.

**terminal**  A device that can send and receive information from a computer.

**terminal emulation**  When your terminal is online to another system, your computer is in a terminal mode that emulates a specific terminal type (e.g., VT 100).

**UART**  Universal Asynchronous Receiver/Transmitter. An integrated circuit that converts parallel data from a computer into serial data for a serial device.

**USART**  Universal Synchronous Asynchronous Receiver Transmitter. An integrated circuit that converts parallel data from the computer into serial data for a serial device.

**uploading**  Transmitting local information and storing it at a remote location.

**VDU**  Visual display unit. Monitor or TV display.

**vendor**  A company or organization that markets online databases.

**VGA**  Video Graphics Adapter. A high-resolution color system for PCs.

**V.21**  CCIT standard for modem communication at 300 bps.

**V.22**  CCIT standard for modem communication at 1200 bps.

**V.22bis**  CCIT transmission protocol for 2400 bps.

**V.32** CCIT's standard for communications at 9600 bps.

**V.32bis** CCIT transmission protocol for speeds of 14,400, 12,000, and 7200 bps.

**V.42bis** CCIT's data compression protocol, more efficient than MNP5 from Microcom, offering up to a 4:1 compression.

**XMODEM** An asynchronous communications protocol that uses one-byte control sequences and a simple check-sum for error checking.

**XMODEM** An asynchronous communications protocol that uses one byte control sequences and a simple check-sum for error checking.

**XON/XOFF** An asynchronous communications protocol that ensures that the receiving computer is in synchronization with the sending device. The receiving device communicates with the sender by transmitting an XOFF signal when the buffer is full and an XON signal when it is ready to receive more data.

**X.PC** A subset of the X.25 error-checking protocol used in wide area networks.

**YMODEM** An extension to the XMODEM protocol; uses CRC error checking, 1024-byte blocks, and an extra block at the beginning of the transfer that contains the filename, actual size, and date.

**ZMODEM** Speeds up operation by sending off blocks of data without first waiting for acknowledgement from the host computer. Previous blocks of data can be retransmitted at the host's request.

# Bibliography

Curtis, Carolyn & Majhor, Daniel L. *Modern Communications Bible*. Indianapolis, IN: Howard W. Sams, 1985.

Dvorak, John C., and Anis, Nick. *Dvorak's Guide to PC Telecommunications*. Berkeley, CA: Osborne McGraw-Hill, 1990.

Ferrarini, Elizabeth. *Infomania*. Boston, MA: Houghton Mifflin, 1985.

Glossbrenner, Alfred. *How to Look it up Online*. New York, NY: St. Martins Press, 1987.

_____ *Personal Computer Communications*. New York, NY: St. Martins Press, 1990.

_____ *The Complete Handbook of Personal Computer Communications*. New York, NY: St. Martins Press, 1990.

_____ *Master Guide to CompuServe*. Prentice Hall Press, 1987.

Helliwell, John. *Inside Information*. New York, NY: New American Library, 1986.

Honig David A., and Hoover, Kenton A. *Desktop Communications*. New York, NY: John Wiley and Sons, 1990.

Li, Tze-chung. *An Introduction to Online Searching*. Westport, CT: Greenwood Press, 1985.

Nelson, Stephen. *Using Prodigy*. Carmel, IN: Que Corporation, 1990.

## Periodicals

*CompuServe Magazine*, published monthly by
CompuServe Incorporated
5000 Arlington Centre Blvd.
Columbus, OH 43220

*GEnie*, published every two months by
GEnie Livewire
P.O. Box 6403
Rockville, MD 20850

*Link-Up*, published every two months by
Learned Information, Inc.
143 Old Marlton Pike
Medford, NJ 08055-8750
$25 per year

*Online Access*, published quarterly by
Chicago Fine Print, Inc.
2271 North Lincoln Avenue
Chicago, IL 60614
$4.95 per issue or $19.80 per year, usually available at computer stores or bookstore
newstands

*Prodigy Star*, published by
Prodigy Services Company
445 Hamilton Avenue
White Plains, NY 10601

# Index

DataTimes, 122-123
  basic facts, 122-123
  services, 123
DELPHI, 88-89
Dialog, 109-115
  basic facts, 109-110
  command mode, 139-141
  engineering/scientific databases, 110-113
  Knowledge Index (KI), 113-115, 141-147
  menus, 134-139
  searching for information, 134-147
  using, 133-147
disk drives, 18
dot matrix printers, 24
Dow Jones, 123-125
  basic facts, 123
  DowQuest, 124
  News/Retrieval after hours, 124-125
  searching for information, 154-155
  services, 123-124
  using, 153-155
downloading, 33-34, 59, 81

**E**
E-Mail, 60-61
  advantages, 60-61
EasyNet, 105-108
  basic facts, 105
  commands, 129-130
  menus, 106-107, 130
  searching for information, 108, 131-133
  submenus, 107-109
  using, 129-133
education, continuing, 3
electronic mail (*see* E-Mail)
enhanced graphics adapter (EGA), 19
EPIC Service, 125-126
  basic facts, 125
  commands, 155
  searching for information, 156-157
  using, 155-157
EXPAND function, 54-55
external facsimle, 25-26
external modem, 20

**F**
facsimile, 25-26
  types of, 25-26

facsimile/modem board, 26
forums, 59-60

**G**
GEnie, 85-87
  basic facts, 85
  menus, 85-87, 100
  searching for information, 101-103
  using, 99-103
glossary, 199-205
graphics cards, 19

**H**
hardware, 11-28
Hayes compatible, 38
Hercules card, 19

**I**
IBM PCs, 15-16
  software (*see* software)
  speaking with Macintosh PCs, 41-42
  vs. Apple, 14
inkjet printers, 24
internal facsimile, 25
internal modem, 20-21
internal speaker, 18
International Consultative Committee on
    Telephone and Telegraph (CCITT), 38

**K**
keywords, categories of, 49-50

**L**
laser printers, 25
local access numbers, 69
local area network (LAN), 26-27
  software, 42

**M**
Macintosh PCs, 14-15
  software (*see* software)
  speaking with IBM PCs, 41-42
MCI Mail, 89
Mead Data Central Inc., 118-119
  basic facts, 118
  databases, 119
  searching for information, 159-160
  services, 118-119

**210**    *Index*